Media Strategies for Public Relations and Marketing

About the Book

The Mass Manipulative Model of the Media proposed by academics such as Stuart Hall cites "structured ideological biases" as significant influences on the selection and presentation of news by the media. At a practical level, there have been numerous studies showing osmosis and hegemony - passed down attitudes and practices within the culture of media organisations - exerting a major influence on media reporting. Increasingly in the past few decades, public relations has been cited as a major influence on modern mass media, but journalists reject such suggestions too and cling to an ideologically-based notion of independence and objectivity. This book examines the relationship between the media and public relations (PR), and is timely given worldwide growth of the PR 'industry', a number of recent controversies involving the media and PR, and conflicting claims over the role and impact of public relations.

About the Author

Dr. Kamaljeet Kaur is at present working as Associate Professor in University Institute of Media Studies, Chandigarh University, Gharuan. She has 11 years of teaching experience. She was awarded with Post Doctoral Fellowship in 2011 by University Grants Commission. She has got her Doctorate in 2008 from Punjabi University Patiala. She has done MJMC,M.A.(Religious studies, Philosophy, Punjabi, Education), M.Sc. (I.T.), PGDJMC, PGDCA,PGDIT and D.Lib. She has authored 3 books and 20 research papers in her credit. She is the member of the editorial board of International Journal in Commerce, IT and social sciences, International Journal in Management and social sciences and Euro Asia (Research and Development Association).

Media Strategies for Public Relations and Marketing

Dr. Kamaljeet Kaur

AMIGA PRESS INC.
DELHI (INDIA)

AMIGA PRESS INC.
H.O.: 28-A, Indra Park,
Chander Nagar, Delhi-110051 (India)
Tel.: 011-22504028, +91-98736-57000
E-mail: amigapress@gmail.com
amigaeditorial@gmail.com
amigapub@gmail.com
info@amigapress.co.in
Website : www.amigapress.co.in

This edition is published by Amiga Press Inc.

ISBN: 978-93-87295-29-2

First Published 2019

Printed and bound by Amiga Press Inc.

Preface

Media have been recognized as powerful instruments to mould public opinion. Therefore, various interests have tried to control them. The clash of interests always leads to tremendous pressure on the media and the media men. Besides the possibility of government pressure on media, often there is a clash of interest between media owners and media practitioners, advertisers and public relations men. Interests of media consumers may also clash with the interest of media owners and practitioners. This has led to the establishment of some statutory bodies and formation of several associations and councils to regulate, study, record and pursue interests of professionals of various categories. Yet there has been an extensively documented history of bias in commercial media because of their ownership structure.

The Mass Manipulative Model of the Media proposed by academics such as Stuart Hall cites "structured ideological biases" as significant influences on the selection and presentation of news by the media. At a practical level, there have been numerous studies showing osmosis and hegemony - passed down attitudes and practices within the culture of media organisations - exerting a major influence on media reporting. Increasingly in the past few decades, public relations has been cited as a major influence on modern mass media, but journalists reject such suggestions too and cling to an ideologically-based notion of independence and objectivity. This book examines the relationship between the media and public relations (PR), and is timely given worldwide growth of the PR 'industry', a number of recent controversies involving the media and PR, and conflicting claims over the role and impact of public relations.

–Author

Contents

Chapter - 1

Presenting Media & Culture

Over the last thirty years much has been written about mass society, mass culture, and the mass media. One is the composition of the group of contributors. There are some of the expected names: Gilbert Seldes who, in 1927, with his book The Seven Lively Arts, put the mass media on the agenda of intellectual discussion and has contributed to it ever since; Bernard Berelson, one of the empirical research specialists who, over the last two or three decades, has made mass communication one of the best documented aspects of the American scene.

In the world of today, media has become almost as necessary as food and clothing. It is true that media is playing an outstanding role in strengthening the society, it's a mirror of the society. Its duty is to inform, educate and entertain the people.

They help us to know whats going on around the world. They put their lives in danger during attacks or a natural disasters, just to inform us of the situation. It is partly because of them that awareness is spreading in the society. It is the media who shape our lives. Our lives would be incomplete without the media. Media is the watch dog of the political democracy.

If it plays its role honestly, it will be a great force in building the nation but now a days, media has become a commersialised sector eying only for news that is hot and sells. Instead of giving important information and educative programmes, all that one gets on television is sensational depiction of all news stories, their only goal being gaining television rating points (TRPs). Every issue is hyped for a day or two, so much so that you switch to any channel, they all will be flashing the same story but then when the heat is over there is no following of the case.

The news then jostles for space with other stories that are carrying the heat then. Inspite we all cannot think of a world without television sets, media has become so much a part of us that to recognise its impact, we need to step back and consciously think about how they shape our lives and what they are saying.

The media affects people's perspective not only through television, but also through radio and newspapers. In this way, even many messages, with which we cannot agree, inevitably coming to us from diverse constellations of media.. They can even be turned to our benefit by whetting our understanding and articulation of what we believe, today news channels and even some newspapers are mouthpiece of some political parties.

Their work then, limits only to spread the ideology of the party rather than give correct news. People have to judge on their own by looking and listening to different channels for the same news and then form a conclusion.

Media is an integral part of our society, but that's also a fact that its too much intervention in everything is a matter of concern.

Sometimes, just for making money, an insignificant news is given so much priority that the real news is not even brought into notice. Yes, it does also entertain but again it's a debatable issue because by 'entertainment' we mean healthy entertainment and not those nonsense TV serials.

So at last, like science it is a tool, which we have to use by our judgement to provide maximum satisfaction side by side without harming ourselves. Sometimes, some channels also broadcast and publish the messages in such situation that the real messages are left beyond our hands.

The other disadvantage is that some times they also publish or broadcast some vulgar news, and sometimes unessential activities are served as very important news and broadcasted again and again. This does not broaden the reach of media.

In spite of being sensational and biased, the significant of media can not be ignored, especially in an age, in which globalisation and liberalisation have become the order of the day. In this globalised world, task and duties of media are increasing day by day. There is still a lot to be done by the media for the betterment of the society.

The mass media themselves are mainly represented through spokesmen who have had serious research backgrounds: Frank Stanton, who has done some of the pioneering work in radio research and who is now president of the Columbia Broadcasting System; Leo Rosten who, with his Washington Correspondent, made one of the early contributions to the study of the "communicator," and who is now an influential policy adviser for Look Magazine.

Three other types of participants are not usually represented in this kind of symposium. We find professional historians of prominence in their own fields. Then, there are three well-known philosophers: Ernest Nagel and Charles Frankel from Columbia, and Sidney Hook from New York University. Most unusual, however, is the participation of artists.

This is the first time people who write about culture and those who create it have confronted each other. Among the participants are: Randall Jarrell, the poet; James Baldwin, the novelist; and Arthur Berger, the composer.

The second interesting feature of this volume is a very careful record of the discussion which followed the original presentation; it gives an additional element of depth to what is offered in the formal papers. Many discussants made important contributions but wrote no papers. Some of those whose prepared statements are included in this volume often said more personal, and therefore more important, things in the discussion.

MASS SOCIETY AND MASS CULTURE

It is important, however, to distinguish two strands in it. Shils gives a coherent presentation of almost all the issues, but at many points he also adds his own observations of the situation. The reader might do well to separate these two aspects and to consider first the formal structure of Shils' contribution.

He begins with a brief description of what he considers the essence of mass society. One should not worry too much about the definition. We all know from direct experience that tremendous growth of the population, the complexity of urban life, the mechanization of the productive system, and a changed political structure have engendered in many countries a way of life quite different from the one existing, say, a hundred years ago.

We have to add the rapidly rising standard of living and the development of a large entertainment industry. What the essential features of this new type of society are and how they affect human existence is, as we shall see, one of the major topics of this symposium. The main facts are known to everyone and only the term "mass society" might be new to some. Shils describes the culture of this mass society; he distinguishes three levels of culture which in colloquial terms are often called highbrow, middlebrow, and lowbrow culture.

The classification, although vague, is useful and perhaps inevitable. When we talk of highbrow culture we think of enduring works of art and the contemporary efforts of avantgardists who deserve respect because of the seriousness of their intentions. We think of the average movie, the family magazine, or the respectable television programme when we use the term middlebrow. By lowbrow we mean such things as comics, detective stories, and vaudeville. It is no coincidence that the examples are cultural products offered to people rather than activities in which they themselves engage.

Little was said at the symposium about lowbrow culture. But a distinction between the first two levels is crucial. For in a nutshell one can say that everyone is concerned with two main problems: What happens to highbrow culture in mass society? And what does the great increase in middlebrow culture do to people? The focal point at which both these problems can be unravelled appeared to Shils to be the mass media.

All through the symposium this emphasis on the mass media is hardly ever questioned, and yet I shall try to show that this is not a completely obvious point of view. Shils also deals with the consumers and the producers of the various forms of cultural products. He briefly summarizes what is known of the social stratification of "audiences." It is useful to learn that a simple classification of the population by education or by some index of social economic status permits reasonably safe predictions of what people will select on their television sets or do with their free time.

But Shils adds an observation which has rarely been made. The cultural activities of young people at least in this country are much less related to their social status. Here he implies an interesting problem indeed: Will these young people twenty years hence, recreate the stratified pattern of their parents or should we expect greater homogeneity of cultural interests in the future?

There is the question of historical comparisons. Certainly many more people participate in "culture" today than took part, say, one hundred years ago, and that has necessarily made for lowering the level of the average supply. But if we were to look at strata comparable to the upper class and aristocracy of the nineteenth century, would the same be true? The tendency towards and the difficulty of seeing historical trends are very marked in such discussions.

Handlin's paper in this volume provides a characteristic example.

He sees a great difference between the folk art of the past and today's mass culture. But a careful reading of his contribution shows that what he means by folk art could have played only an occasional role in people's lives. What did they do on long winter evenings?

Were they desperately bored? Or is boredom itself an experience which has developed in industrial society? From Handlin's personal remarks one gathers that historians know very little about how people used to spend their time, so comparisons become speculations. But Shils correctly raises a second question: Is there an inherent threat to highbrow culture in mass society? Where does this threat come from? Are commercial interests corrupting the public? Or is it that a mediocre audience, which can afford to pay for entertainment, is distracting valuable talent from more worthy pursuits?

Is there a withering away of elites who are a necessary breeding ground for cultural innovations? The keynote paper also introduces a notion of "mediocre intelligentsia." These are the men and women who, while highly trained themselves, produce the middlebrow culture. We shall later see that they are a special problem for the creative artist.

Shils is optimistic on most of the points and it was this strongly expressed optimism which obscured for many participants the merits of his general formulations. Both Van den Haag and Arendt more or less explicitly stressed that Shils had omitted one important category.

Their argument was that Shils had omitted one look at the nature and content of the cultural supply; one should be much more concerned with the way it is received. Van den Haag argues that people in mass society have lost the ability to take cultural issues seriously. The whole idea is symbolized in a statement by T. W. Adorno: "Radio has made of Beethoven's Fifth Symphony a hit tune which is easy to whistle."

The theme of Miss Arendt's contribution is related; she says popular culture has made of the classics something to be consumed rather than understood. In a way, Handlin's paper belongs in the same group. When he compares the folk culture of an earlier period with the mass culture of the industrial age, he finds a change in function. Folk art was not necessarily better but it was much closer to people's daily lives and their social traditions; "it dealt with the complete world intensely familiar to its audience and permitted a direct rapport between those who created and those who consumed this culture."

Nathan Glazer suggested that from a combination of the content level of the cultural product and the way it is received, one should derive four types of situations. In an oversimplified form, these are:

- Serious work seriously received;
- Serious work denatured by the attitude of the "consumer" — looking at the reproduction of a great painting inserted in a picture weekly, listening to a Mozart aria preceded and followed by some popular bit in the frame of a television set;
- Mediocre works received in a serious mood as exemplified by a woman who listens to a day-time drama in order to understand her family problems better or the Book-of-the Month Club subscriber who honestly wants to improve himself;
- Finally, there is bad stuff consumed to fill empty time, this being the enemy of the people.

Each of these situations might have been discussed in its own terms, but it would take a long time to explore them systematically. In retrospect, I can only urge the readers of this volume to penetrate in their own way and as best they can this notion of functional variation in reception which is the common theme of Handlin, Arendt, and Van den Haag.

Attention should be drawn to characteristic differences between various contributions. The social scientist Van den Haag e.g., in the last part of his contribution, gives a list of properly numbered indictments of the deterioration of human relations in mass society: we have lost the taste for privacy and contemplation, have replaced sincere personal contacts with an empty gregariousness, and so on.

Randall Jarrell, the poet, in the first part of his paper, uses—purposely, he says—a stream of metaphors and impressive aphorisms which he feels communicate more. One other comparison should not be missed.

Shils characterizes mass society in terms which show his basic optimism: Social participation has increased, the rights of each individual are more respected, rationality is more widespread. Van den Haag, in the second part of his paper, takes up all these points and so to say reverses their sign: Social participation is uninformed and vulnerable to slogans, individualism has broken all human bonds, rationality comes about at the expense of deep and sincere experiences.

The interchange might give some readers the feeling which Hughes at one point expressed only half facetiously: that whomever he listens to he has to agree with. Perhaps the fact that positive and negative elements are so interwoven in the contemporary scene is one of its most characteristic features.

MASS CULTURE AND MASS MEDIA

The first papers in the symposium, while supposed to deal with mass culture in general, devote much space to the mass media. As the sequences progress, the mass media increasingly become the centre of attention, with television receiving the major share.

By the end of the volume, one can tell that they have become the main topic of the programme. In some ways this should not cause surprise. Since, the participants are mostly people who make their living from writing, problems of communication are nearest to their hearts. Still this bias deserves some further comment. I have for a long time noticed the intensity with which topics related to broadcasting and to a lesser degree movies and the printed media are discussed in the United States.

"Twenty or thirty years ago liberal organizations were concerned almost exclusively with questions of social betterment—child labour, woman suffrage, economic insecurity, the exploitation of workers, and so on. These same liberal organizations are today almost as exclusively concerned with the danger of radio, the danger of newspapers, and the bad effects of motion pictures.

Broadcasters think of themselves as honest, hard-working, and decent people; why is it then, that doctors and preachers and teachers dislike them? The liberals of today feel terribly gypped. For decades they and their intellectual ancestors fought to attain certain basic goals—more leisure time, more education, higher wages. They were motivated by the idealistic hope that when these goals were reached, the "masses" would develop into fine human beings. But what happened?

After the liberals had won their victories, the people spent their newly acquired time and money on movies, radio, magazines. Instead of listening to Beethoven, they listen to Johnny Mercer, instead of going to Columbia University, they go to the Columbia Broadcasting System. The situation of the liberals is much like that of the high school boy who, after weeks of saving, accumulates enough money to buy a bracelet for a girl, and who then learns that the girl has gone out with another boy to show off her nice new trinket."

It seems that this interpretation is still valid today. And the position of the spokesmen for the mass media has also remained unchanged. Rosten and Stanton stress that they make considerable contributions to adult education. Of course they are first of all responsible to their stockholders but they plow much of their profits back into public service features.

The manager of and advisers to the mass media feel that their economic success is proof that they do "what the people want"—and that in addition they provide cultural leadership. Interestingly enough, a similar attitude is reported as characteristic of the attitude of businessman even if their own profits are not involved.

One contributor to this volume, Mr. Sweeney, at the time Director of the Museum of Modern Art, blames the board members of many museums for resorting to mass appeal when it is not economically necessary. Museums have the double function of serving the trained mind and being educational agents for a broader public. it is regrettable that no expert in adult education was included in the symposium. His opinion would have helped to develop further Mr. Sweeney's interesting observations.

The emphasis on the mass media is characteristic of the American scene and obscures certain other aspects of mass culture. This can be somewhat remedied by a short digression into the way similar discussions are conducted in another country, France. In one respect the French and the American situations are like one another.

The social scientist and the man of letters in both countries are likely to be politically left of centre. But in France, because they have as a frame of reference strong labour parties, they debate cultural values more in their relations to political militancy. The central theme in discussion of mass culture is usually the use of leisure time. Mass media only play a marginal role.

The great symbol of the first labour government under Leon Blum in 1936 was the enactment of laws guaranteeing paid vacations and regulating details of week-end arrangements. Equally characteristic are a number of government supported activities like the popular theatre and the youth sport movement. The issue hidden behind the intensive theoretical discussions about leisure time is whether it will lead to an independent labour class culture or whether it will end in assimilation of all workers into a middle-class pattern.

One gets a good picture of this climate of thinking through an issue of the magazine Esprit which appeared in June, 1959, simultaneously with the symposium, which led to the present volume. The issue is devoted to "Le Loisir." The theoretical papers are primarily concerned with the relation between leisure time and participation in social movements.

Empirical studies analyse bow the legally guaranteed vacation period is utilized by various groups of employees. Data on mass media exposure are used to bring out the sociological meaning of various types of work. Thus, for instance, one study compares two groups of white collar people who have about the same income but differ according to the degree their work is mechanized.

The group with more interesting work shows a normal distribution of activities like movie attendance or listening to the radio. Those who have monotonous work show bimodal behaviour, they either engage in an excessive amount of mass media activities or they retreat into an isolation, which takes them either to the saloon or leads to an impoverished family life. It is this retreatism which is considered the main cultural danger by many authors. One has the impression that mass media exposure is looked on as a hopeful sign of incipient concern with the larger world.

Quite a number of other aspects are often crowded out from discussions of mass culture among American intellectuals. Only Hazard in this symposium points out that the objects of daily use have an aesthetic aspect which is definitely part of the surrounding culture. He seems to feel, for instance, that by and large the design of home equipment achieves quite high standards.

The social scientist might make a distinction between objects which have high social visibility and lend themselves to social competition and which are often in bad taste—some types of cars would be a good example.

Other objects like refrigerators and dictating equipment are more easily left to the control of the professional designer, and do indeed often display considerable taste. In poorer countries, alcoholism is usually an important topic in mass culture discussions.

THE VOICE OF THE ARTIST

While the scope of this symposium is restricted in one direction, it is enlarged in another. Included in the present volume are the statements of three creative artists and the record of the discussion includes the comments of some others. I have tried to extract from all this a statement of their position. They all agree that the goal and task of the artist is to interpret human experience. There is some disagreement as to whether he does so mainly by describing other people's lives or by being especially articulate about himself. But they have no doubt that life for everyone would be much harder if art didn't help to make sense out of it.

Some idea of a division of labour is implied. Not every human being can, by himself, add this kind of depth to what happens to him. Only the artist is in a position to perform this task because he lends all his efforts to it; but throughout history he has done this at a great sacrifice.

Because the artist's social function is intangible and its importance not easily appreciated, he is usually economically insecure and the contact with his audience, if it exists, is precarious and frustrating. Today additional difficulties are added because of the nature of mass society, the role of the mass media, and in the United States also because of some consequences of its economic system.

On the first point the main complaint is that the mass man is unreceptive to contemplation; that a complete separation has come about between artistic production on the one hand and occupational and community life on the other; that it has become less and less clear for whom the creative artist is working; and that he is often restricted to addressing himself to just a small group of experts.

The mass media complicate the matter in a variety of ways. By providing endless diversion, they corrode people's willingness to pay attention to serious thought. The mass media emphasize the fleeting events of the moment and weaken people's connection with the past, as it is expressed in myths and the kind of symbolism which epics or the Bible provide. This has grievous consequences for the artist, for his creativeness consists essentially in providing new variations on pervasive themes.

The record is most explicit on two dreaded features of the American scene. The one could be called institutional temptation. It is true that artists are not likely to starve as they did a century ago; there are fellowships, foundation grants, and teaching positions at the universities. But they all require the artist to do a great many things that are not essential to him. He is rarely paid for performing his mostcreative function.

The objection was made that nothing keeps him from starving as his ancestors did and working on what the spirit moves him to. But I think there was real understanding that in an overpowering institutional setting such individual solutions are hardly possible.

The second target of the artist's complaints—and also pointed out at length by Miss Arendt—is the role of the popularizers. The existence of a large audience wanting some easy information and eager to pay for it creates a new group of technicians who take the original and make it palatable, be it fashioning a movie out of a drama or a magazine article out of a serious piece of analysis.

This again increases the sense of despair for the serious artist. In terms of fame land material success, he finds himself pushed into the background as compared to the mass communicator; compared with the past, he suffers less absolute and increasing relative deprivation.

This point lends additional complexity to the debate with the defenders of the mass media. Rosten in his paper points out how hard he and his colleagues try to popularize important subject matters. However, the artist can more easily condone the ineptness of a bad writer than the slickness of a popularizer. The grievance, incidentally, does not seem to be restricted to the artist. The physicist Holton mentioned in the discussion that he and his colleagues resent the image of the scientist portrayed by the mass media.

It was surprisingly difficult to get artists to talk in terms of their own experience. Notice, for instance, how Mr. Jarrell's paper clearly falls into two parts. In the first he describes mass society mainly in the same detached way as any social scientist would—but his style is different from Van den Haag's.

Only in the second part of his paper does he write about his own experiences. And the most personal and revealing remarks of Mr. Baldwin are found in the record of the discussion and not in his paper. Perhaps in such a symposium the artists resent playing the role of guinea pigs. In this sense then the presence of the creative writers was a noble experiment but not a complete success.

The partial failure shows, however, how important it would be to pursue the effort further. What is needed are men and women who are willing to talk to us social scientists about themselves as artists in the world of mass culture, rather than about the nature of art.

Interestingly enough, it is the musician Arthur Berger who is most specific and articulate. Perhaps it is reading and explanation of musical scores which gave him analytical training. He makes many interesting points. Among these is the idea that one should not be overjoyed by the extensive performance of classical music over radio, because the unanticipated effect might be a freezing of musical taste.

The trend in artistic style has always been towards increasing complexity, and it usually takes a new generation of laymen to accept what was considered revolutionary and unharmonious in their parents' day. Such acceptance might now take much longer because broadcasting puts all its weight behind works which people are accustomed to bearing.

Berger singles out quite a number of other impediments which are built into the technology and social structure of the mass media.

New works, e.g., are difficult to play and require a great deal of rehearsal. But because of union rules and other traditions developed in broadcasting, lengthy rehearsals become almost prohibitive today. Incidentally, magazines too develop a style of their own, and television has producers who are believed to know what the medium requires. All this means that in many areas professional techniques interpose themselves between the artist and the public. Whatever the need for or the justification of this trend, the artists do not seem to take it kindly.

Berger suggests concretely that broadcasters should make unconditional grants to modern writers and composers. Their contribution should not be linked to the suitability of a work for television or radio. It should rather be looked on as an additional tax, because a broadcasting license turns over a public property—the airwave—for the benefit of a private businessman.

While he did not put it quite this way, the remarks of A. W. Brown went in the same direction. A former president of the Metropolitan Educational Television Association (which provides educational television stations with programme material), he pointed out that, because of lack of funds, only about 50 education channels have been put in operation out of 250 available channels.

More such stations would give artists a larger number of outlets. If one adheres to the formula that commercial broadcasters should make somewhat less money than their franchises permit in the free market, it is easy to conclude that they should give active financial support to educational television.

I might be permitted to add one remark which is personal in the sense that it concerns only my own professional specialty. The artists in the symposium request effort and respect for difficult modern art. At the same time they are impatient when they are confronted with the corresponding problem in the social sciences. Mr. Jarrell said at one point that he loved anthropologists but hated sociologists.

The context made it quite clear that what he dislikes are statistical tables difficult to read and what he is pleased by are essays on cultural subjects more akin to poetry. Two men who took pessimistic positions in the discussion have a similar record. The Reporter, of which Mr. Kristol was the Managing Editor, and Commentary, of which Mr. Glazer is a frequent contributor on social sciences, have been consistently hostile to all modern trends in the social sciences. As Mr. Hazard put it in an aside, empirical social research might be the counterpart of atonal music. It seems to create the same hostility among modern artists which their work creates among the general public.

And yet there is one type of research which might help on some of the problems which the artists brought up. I mentioned above that the way people receive or "consume" cultural products is of con siderable concern to some of the participants. Seldes, for instance, comments on the passivity of modern audiences; Hook, on the other hand, insists that he does not understand what is meant by this frequently used term.

Now it so happens that mass communication research has developed sophisticated interviewing techniques which bring out what people feel while they watch a movie or television programme, at what points they are involved, where they misunderstand the content, and so on.

Such analysis of the listening experience has been used mainly for the purpose of improving the effectiveness of propaganda, commercial or otherwise. There is no reason, however, why it should not be used for more objective ends.

As a matter of fact, such an effort was made once by I. A. Richards, who was one of the pioneers of the "New Criticism" which started in England after the First World War. His Cambridge group was mainly interested in substituting for the romantic approach to the personality of the author a structural analysis of the work of art itself. Richards wanted, in addition, to look at the other side of the coin and to study the structure of the readers' experience. He developed a procedure which seems to be little known and to which more attention should be given.

Richards asked a number of his students to read carefully and repeatedly an array of poems ranging from serious pieces to conventional trash. He then requested them to describe in detail all the reactions, associations and opinions they had. These reports he analysed and classified carefully. The main product is a detailed description of what today we would call the audience experience. The purpose of Richards' experiment as well as the organization of his book is best described in his own formulation of his three aims:

"First, to introduce a new kind of documentation to those who are interested in the contemporary state of culture whether as critics, as philosophers, as teachers, as psychologists or mainly as curious persons. Secondly, to provide a new technique for those who wish to discover for themselves what they think and feel about poetry (and cognate matters) and why they should like or dislike it. Thirdly, to prepare the way for educational methods more efficient than those we use now in developing discrimination and the power to understand what we hear and read." [Emphasis supplied]

Perhaps it falls in a no-man's land between psychologists and students of literature. Perhaps Richards' rather primitive techniques seem disappointing. But as the studies quoted above show, we now know that one can give a very good picture of how a specific type of person understands a work of art, how he is affected by it, and how it fits into the stream of his personal experiences.

A convergence of these research techniques with serious artistic concerns be more widely tried. Obviously, the goal is not the custom tailor creative production to the wishes of the man in the street. But a great many interesting and mostly unpredictable outcomes can result from a systematic confrontation of the artist with his actual and potential audiences. To say the least, the type of controversies which the present symposium exemplifies could be referred to a firmer body of facts.

DILEMMAS OF REFORM

Stuart Hughes takes the position that one cannot have political without cultural democracy; we are paying for our freedom of opinion by letting the people have the freedom of choice in cultural matters. Phillips in the discussion objects: he does not see any necessary connection. A somewhat different formulation might make the issue more concrete.

The expression "paying for" is indeed somewhat vague and perhaps fatalistic. What actually happens is that, in the mass media field, we are confronted with a set of basic values which we hold equally dear but which cannot be all fully realized. Schlesinger, for instance, argues for a stronger role of the government in broadcasting policies. Even if television is accepted as a business, the idea of free enterprise does not preclude some government regulation.

He correctly points out that at many points in our economic system we have laws on wages and hours and similar business decisions. In the communications field, however, we run into a conflict with the First Amendment which specifically precludes government interference in the realm of ideas.

Even if this difficulty could be resolved by stating that television, like the movies, conveys mainly entertainment and, therefore, doesn't fall under the First Amendment, a realistic problem remains. American broadcasting is really quite free so far as political controversy goes. It is questionable whether the opposition party would have a fair chance in a government controlled system. One would, therefore, have to look for a form of regulation which affected cultural matters only.

Once this is conceded, another question comes up. In a democracy, is there any justification for imposing elite standards on the whole country? In this connection a distinction which is often overlooked must be made. The realistic issue is not whether the majority should accept what the intellectual minority prefers.

The problem is whether within the realm of what was referred to mudlebrow culture standards could be developed and should be maintained. The Federal Communications Commission, for instance, receives many complaints about the abundance of violence in television dramas. The question then arises whether one does not find less violence there than, for instance, in Hamlet. Everyone has an uneasy feeling that this is a specious argument, but it would be difficult to articulate clearly under what conditions an overbundance of violence is regrettable.

While there is no answer on this specific problem, there are similar issues on which communication research can provide answers. Everyone is familiar with the programmes called "soap operas." They are about families which get into trouble, solve a predicament somehow, only to start a new episode of difficulties. It is certainly not high art, but it is sometimes entertaining and listeners should not be deprived of this kind of relaxation.

However, even if one accepts the basic formula, one can point to some specific deficiencies. Arnheim has analysed a score of such plots and has shown that the troubles in which the families find themselves are usually created by men while the happy solution is provided by women. It is not difficult to understand the purpose of this tradition: it makes the soap opera more attractive to women, and this is the audience in which the advertisers are primarily interested. But the same type of entertainment could be provided without such elements of bias and this would be an intrinsic improvement.

What I am trying to say is that even if we accept the legitimacy of middlebrow culture, it is still possible to develop standards which make for improvement on its own terms. The role of the elite then would not be that of dictators but of advisers. Concretely this role can take a variety of forms. Hyman's contribution to this symposium describes what he as a college teacher does to influence the standards of his students.

On another occasion Robert Hutchins stressed the importance of periodic reviews. One of the proposals of his Commission on the Freedom of the Press was that the content of mass media be sampled under appropriate categories so they could be subjected to the limelight of public opinion. This is supposed to make for improvement without specific regulation. The success of such a scheme depends very much of course on the introduction of creative descriptive ideas like the ones exemplified by Arnheim's study.

A third dilemma which deserves attention is due to a special piece of broadcasting legislation. The Federal Communications Act provides that, in order to avoid collusion on the setting of advertising rates, the anti-trust laws should apply to broadcasting. On this it proved ineffectual. But in present application it also precludes concerted action on programme content. Stanton in his paper points with justified pride to the many fine programmes one finds in an average week on CBS.

Competing networks could make the same claim. But what would be overlooked is the fact that for competitive reasons all of these programmes are usually heard at the same time. The value of the existing programme supply could be greatly enhanced by a very simple procedure. Now the networks pit against each other programmes with mass appeal at one time and programmes with elite appeal at another time.

Nothing but legal traditionalism prevents an arrangement by which on some days one network has a large audience and another network has a smaller number of connoisseurs: on other evenings the situation would be reversed by agreement.

It is not so much the commercial nature of broadcasting but a narrow interpretation of commercial competition which accounts for some of these difficulties.

Since, this symposium was held, interest in the problematics of the mass media has extended, at least temporarily, to broader public groups.

It is rather characteristic that this interest was not aroused by the cultural critics but by moral indignation over cheating on a television, show. This raises the question whether discussions like the one published in this book have any practical utility at all.

And here we can once more turn to the teachings of history. The contribution of Leo Lowenthal shows that every technological innovation the field of communication was experienced by some people as a cultural danger: the less expensive book, the lending library, the magazine and so on. It is really startling how timely the discussions which Lowenthal reports from the 17th and 18th century sound today.

Stimulated by his material, I went back to the first recorded discussion of mass communication: Plato Phaedros, the dialogue concerned with the skills and the social implications of the public orator. Socrates, of course, takes the position which the pessimistic critics in this volume take and he, too, goes back to history. He feels that the misery started with the discovery of writing.

"For this discovery will create forgetfulness in the learners' souls, because they will not use their memories; they will trust to the external written characters and not remember of themselves.

They will appear to be omniscient, and will generally know nothing; they will be tiresome company, having the show of wisdom without the reality."

In spite of this dire foreboding, writing, orating, printing and now broadcasting have spread, and society still survives. Matters often look bad, but somehow they always stop short of being disastrous. True, as in other fields, especially in social legislation, it was often an accidental event which triggered an improvement. But this would not have happened if a continuous stream of criticism had not kept us prepared to take advantage of such opportunities. It is the tragic story of the cultural crusader in a mass society that he cannot win, but that we would be lost without him.

❐

Chapter - 2

Media in Public Disengagement

The current political system is plagued by dramatically declining political participation, civic engagement, and political trust. Some scholars argue that this cynicism and alienation from civil society may correspond with the emergence of television as a leisure activity, replacing collective with individual interests, while others contend that this process results from specific attention to news genres.

Alternatively, communication technologies and messages may not be directly promoting or constraining participation, but instead facilitating such engagement for groups with access to social, political, and economic resources. This study begins by examining the connections between political participation and social capital, manifest through civic engagement and political trust.

These relationships are then explored in terms of television viewing and news genres. This work builds on sociological discussions of participation and social capital, and communication scholarship on the role of media in political socialization.

POLITICAL PARTICIPATION AND SOCIAL CAPITAL

Political participation, civic engagement, and political trust have declined. These trends are evident in observing proportionately fewer people voting in elections in the last thirty years, while proportionately more people report distrust of the government. Analyses demonstrate that distrust grew from less than one-third in 1975 to 75 per cent in 1992.

While citizens appear to be less engaged with their political community, they are also less likely to be involved in community networks. Over time memberships in support groups and secondary associations (such as

AARP and NOW), where people do not know each other personally, have been increasing, whereas community association memberships have been decreasing.

The nature of the relationship between people who belong to these tertiary associations, united through sharing certain symbols, values, and identities, is assumed to be qualitatively different from the type of bond enacted between people who work together directly in local organizations. Schudson offers a valuable critique of this argument by reconceptualizing "civic participation."

Measuring participation in "conventional forms" misses critical factors, such as level of involvement, as opposed to number of organizational memberships, or even participation in other types of groups, such as commercial, professional, or advocacy organizations. Further, Schudson suggests that, instead of characterizing this trend as a "decline," perhaps it represents a return to "normalcy".

According to other observers, the noted decline in political participation is directly related to eroding social capital. This view assumes that a democratic system requires a strong and active civil society, through which members build social connections. These social connections, facilitating social networks, norms, and trust, constitute social capital.

Social capital serves as an important resource, used by participants to pursue political and economic gain. Sources of social capital, based in structures of social relations and internalization of community norms, (lifter from social capital itself, indicating the benefits accrued through memberships in social structures and other networks, and from potential consequences of social capital (such as social control and support).

Focusing on social capital recognizes the importance of social context, in addition to economic and human resources, in understanding human behaviour. According to Bellah, some indices of social capital may include membership in community organizations and trust in public institutions.

Although political distrust may be described in terms of cynical attitudes towards government representatives and agencies, it is important not to conflate distrust with apathy or cynicism with skepticism. While conceptually linked with political alienation, apathy, indicated through low involvement in political processes, and distrust hold different relationships with voting intentions; Austin and Pinkleton demonstrate that distrust can motivate people to vote under certain conditions.

Capella and Jamieson suggest that cynicism, as an all-knowing critical stance, be differentiated from skepticism, as a critical mode of asking questions. This nuance is critically important in understanding political attitudes, though perhaps difficult to capture in many measures of political distrust.

The initial set of assumptions to be tested address this relationship between political participation and social capital, conceived as civic engagement and political trust. Before attempting to address connections with media technologies and genres, these initial dynamics need to be established.

THE ROLE OF MEDIA IN POLITICAL SOCIALIZATION

While some scholars are concerned with the role of television viewing in general, others focus on the contributions of television news, newspapers, and computers to the political socialization process. Although media may provide news, persuasive information, socialization, and entertainment, some researchers emphasize the entertainment function of television when they contend that television viewing may explain the decline of democratic processes and of social capital, by creating more superficial community experiences.

Television, according to this argument, facilitates the privatization and individualization of leisure time, which then inhibits possibilities for civic engagement. This position assumes that television erodes social capital by displacing time spent on community activities with private, individual behaviors, and by negatively influencing viewers' attitudes and actions.

Although this sense of civic and political engagement seems to favour interpersonal connections, Schudson counters that it is not interpersonal conversation that constitutes democratic life, but rather media that contribute to public memory.

As multidimensional forces in our social and political worlds, media do more than provide sources of information, but also serve to legitimate and perpetuate political and social communities.

Other scholars differentiate genres and channels in explaining the extent of political participation. For example, some blame the nature of news coverage, emphasizing political scandal, for emerging cynicism. Distrust of political institutions appears to correspond with distrust of the media, which tends to be associated with membership in civic and professional associations.

Attempting to distinguish differences in political socialization according to channel use, research generally confirms that reading newspapers and watching television news tend to be associated with political knowledge, though the relationship between media use and political participation is less clear.

Pinkleton and Austin propose a more nuanced approach, acknowledging the potentially positive benefits of media use, by providing information and inspiring interest, which may reduce cynicism and increase participation, as well as the potentially negative consequences, when media sources frustrate viewers who want information, thereby increasing cynicism and lowering participation.

Recent literature on political communities has suggested the importance of emerging computer technologies, as a link between the government and the public, and as a bridge across constituents. Kellner contends that new technologies, such as computers, may promote democratic debate and participation.

Even though these scholars admit that access to this channel is restricted to an elite, they believe that computer technologies have the capacity to foster social capital and citizenship, as an interactive technology that may serve as an alternative to dominant media systems. One key factor that may differentiate this medium is its potential for interactivity, thus blurring traditional boundaries between mediated and interpersonal communication.

In order to address concerns with the role of media in political socialization, this study explores a variety of media uses in relation to political participation, civic engagement, and political trust. In this study, media use is analysed in terms of general television viewing, television news viewing, newspaper reading, and using computers to seek political information.

CONDITIONING FACTORS

Situating political participation within a broader structure, some individuals have greater access to social capital than others, and are thus afforded more political and economic opportunities. Studies of voting demonstrate clear differences across gender, socio-economic status, and other demographic variables.

Similarly, civic engagement appears to be a luxury activity among those with higher incomes, serving as a way to reduce the government's responsibility for problematic social conditions. Another important factor to consider is level of education.

Putnam and others demonstrate the importance of education in explaining political and civic engagement, assuming that those with more education are more likely to participate in formal political processes due to their closer access to powerful social networks.

This research accounts for the structural positions of individuals as potential conditioning factors in attempting to understand political participation, civic engagement, and political trust. Given that dominant values in the United States privilege white, male, and upper-class constituents, the intersections across gender, race, ethnicity, and education constitute potential degrees of power among select groups.

Media contribute to the political socialization of community members, legitimizing political and economic systems, and promoting ideological values that serve the interests of dominant groups in society. With these concerns in mind, background variables are meant to represent potential conditions of marginality, which themselves may tend to correspond with lower levels of social capital and political participation.

RESEARCH QUESTIONS AND HYPOTHESES

The first set of research questions explores the relationship between political participation and social capital, operationalized as civic engagement and political trust. It is speculated that increased indices of social capital may be associated with increased levels of political participation.

Specifically, those who are more active in civic affairs may be more likely to engage in formal electoral processes, while those who are more distrustful may be less likely to do so. The next set of research questions addresses the role of media use in explaining political participation and social capital.

It is hypothesized that higher levels of television viewing may be associated with lower levels of political participation and indices of social capital, but that specific attention to news genres (television news, newspapers, and computers) may correspond with higher levels of civic and political engagement, and of political distrust.

Finally, it is hypothesized that participating in political rituals and holding social capital may be conditioned by participants' relative social conditions (including level of education, identification as White and as not Hispanic). Although gender was included in initial models, these results are not presented here because findings were consistently not significant.

METHOD

In order to explore relationships across political participation, social capital, and media use, survey research was conducted in November 1996, following the national election.

This work was supported by a Special Research Grant from the University of Texas at Austin, coordinated by the Office of Survey Research of the University, and conducted for class credit by students in a research methods course. Random digit dialing, based on proportions of known prefixes, was used to approach a random sample of adult residents of Texas (N=257), achieving a response rate of approximately 41 per cent. Interviewers telephoned 848 randomly constructed telephone numbers.

Based on other polls conducted through this organization in Texas, we estimate that approximately 29 per cent of an RDD sample is not eligible for household survey research, being businesses, fax machines, or numbers not in use. Given this estimate, approximately 641 of the original list were believed to be appropriate for this survey, with 13 per cent not reached after three separate attempts and the remaining refused.

Other polls in this state, using these techniques, have typically achieved a 43 per cent completion rate. Appropriate respondents included only those household residents who identified themselves as U.S., citizens and were at least 18 years old, in order to focus the sample on eligible voters.

Hypotheses were tested through bivariate analyses, and through analyses of variance as a multivariate approach to assess the relative effects of individual factors on degree of political participation and levels of social capital.

In different analyses, political participation, civic engagement, and political trust served as dependent variables, with media variables as independent factors and background variables as covariate factors. In some bivariate analyses, gamma was used as an appropriate statistic for ordinal-level variables, when cases did not tend to fall in one row or column.

Scales were created to measure political participation, civic engagement, and political trust, while separate variables were selected to indicate media use and background factors. Many of these measures were recoded in standardized form in order to conduct multivariate analyses. Political participation was measured with an original scale characterizing formal participation in electoral politics.

The scale of political participation includes belonging to a political party (39%), being registered to vote (83%), voting in the recent national election (79%), and voting in an earlier local election (76%). The scale has moderate reliability.

The emphasis on formal characteristics of electoral political participation corresponds with a narrow conceptualization grounded in the literature reviewed above, lending face validity to this scale. The scale is recoded into low (0-2 points), medium (3 points), and high (4 points) categories. Most respondents claim to have acted in three of these four ways (median=3), while about one-third report conducting all four of these activities.

Social capital is operationalized, as suggested by Bellah, as involvement in community activities, membership in community organizations, and trust in political institutions. About two-thirds (68%) report being actively involved in their communities in a five-point Likert scale, while almost half (43%) of the studied sample report belonging to some type of community organization, separate from their membership in a religious organization.

These two variables are combined into a scale of local community involvement (r=.31, p [is less than].01): 25 per cent are categorized as having low, 38 per cent as medium, and 37 per cent as high involvement. A separate scale to assess level of political distrust was created by combining answers to three five-point Likert items, including whether people report trusting the government to enforce laws (52%), trusting the current President (39%), and having confidence in the political system (54%).

These items are included in a scale of political trust (alpha=.59; Eigenvalue of first factor =1.65, explaining 55% of the variance) and then recoded in dichotomous form for subsequent analyses. About half (51%) are categorized as having trust in the political system. The alpha value for this scale is slightly below a more desirable.60 to establish reliability. Results from factor analyses, however, lend some justification that these three factors work together towards a unidimensional variable.

Several media variables are included in this model. First, respondents were asked how many hours of television they had watched the day prior to the interview (mean = 2.7 hours) in order to assess; extent of television viewing; this variable was recoded in subsequent multivariate analyses to distinguish less frequent (0-1) from more frequent (2+) viewers.

Then, respondents were asked specifically whether they had watched television news (65%) or read a newspaper (58 per cent) the day prior to the interview. In order to understand whether computers were used as a channel for seeking political information, respondents were also asked whether or not they had used a computer to learn about the recent political campaign (7% reported using this technology at some time during the campaign season).

Several background factors are used to assess structural position of respondents. These include level of education (11 per cent have less than high school education, 54% have a high school degree, and 35% have a college degree), self identification as a member of the Hispanic community (20%), and self identification as non-White (28%).

SOCIAL CAPITAL AND POLITICAL PARTICIPATION

The first set of analyses concerns the basic premise that indices of social capital may be associated with political participation. Multivariate analyses use political participation as a dependent variable, with civic engagement, political trust, and media variables as main independent factors and background variables as covariate factors.

Civic engagement and political distrust appear to be among the stronger predictors of political participation. First, findings confirm the first hypothesis that people who perceive themselves to be actively involved in their communities and in community organizations, as one indication of social capital, are more likely to participate in electoral politics than those who do not.

Only about one-fifth (22%) of people with low community involvement engage in a high level of political participation, compared to one-third (34%) of people with moderate levels and almost one-half (44%) of people with high levels (F=5.57, p [is less than].05, eta squared=.247).

However, the second hypothesis, that people with political trust would be more likely to engage in political participation, is not supported by these results. While civic engagement appears to be associated with political participation in a positive direction, political trust appears to work in a negative direction: people who voice their distrust of the President, government, and political system are more likely to engage in electoral politics (40%) than people who are more trusting (29%; F=4.14, p [is less than].05, eta squared=.215).

Given the different directions of these relationships, confidence in political institutions, and figures serves as a different factor than involvement in local civic activities and organizations. Confirming this conceptual distinction, these two constructs, civic engagement and political trust, bear no statistical association. Consequently, these variables are analysed separately rather than as integrated components of social capital.

THE ROLE OF MEDIA

Analyses explore how experiences with television, television news, newspapers, and computers might be related to political participation, civic engagement, and political trust. In this section, political participation is first explored as a dependent variable with indices of social capital and media use as main independent variables and background factors as covariates; next, civic engagement and political trust are each used as dependent variables in separate analyses.

Multivariate analyses demonstrate that media factors do not appear to mitigate the associations between civic engagement and political participation, or between political distrust and political participation. However, two media variables appear to hold their significance in this model predicting political participation: watching television news and reading the newspaper.

These findings confirm hypotheses that people who attend to television news or newspapers are more likely to participate in electoral politics than those who do not. For example, about twice as many people who watch television news participate fully (41%) compared with those who do not watch television news (21%).

Contrary to some scholars' expectations, the extent of television watching bears no relationship with tendency to participate in the political system. Thus, hypotheses suggesting that people who watch more television will be less likely to engage in political participation, or that people who use computers to seek political information will be more likely to engage in political participation, are not confirmed.

When focusing on civic engagement or political distrust, none of the media variables appear to be statistically significant when controlling for other factors. Thus, hypotheses concerning media use and social capital are not supported. It is worth noting that in bivariate analyses, however, people who report using a computer to learn more about recent elections are about half as likely to have political trust (26%) than those who do not; however, multivariate analyses establish this dynamic to be in part a product of educational status.

CONDITIONING FACTORS

It was hypothesized that people in relatively more marginal conditions might be less likely to engage in civic or political participation, or to hold political trust. Bivariate analyses confirm assumptions that people with higher levels of education, who identify themselves as White and not Hispanic, are more likely to participate in civic life and in electoral politics than their counterparts. However, multivariate analyses suggest that education appears to be the most critical factor when controlling for other conditions, while race and ethnicity appear to be less consistently significant; the exception here is the relationship between race and trust, described below.

More than half (52%) of the respondents with college degrees engage in civic activities compared to about one-third (30%) of those with high school degrees, and one-fifth (18%) of those with less formal education. Participating in electoral politics holds a similar trend.

Although the educated class appears to be more likely to join formal community organizations and to participate in the electoral system, this group does not trust the current political system or its leaders. Rather, this elite group appears more likely to be skeptical about the government than those in relatively more marginal conditions.

Less than half (39%) of people with college degrees report political trust, compared to 55 per cent of people with high school degrees, and 70 per cent of people with less formal education. In addition, those who identify themselves as not White are more likely to hold political trust (68%) compared with others who identify themselves as White, contrary to expectations.

DISCUSSION

This study confirms an initial premise that political participation is associated with civic engagement. People who are more involved in local community affairs are more likely to be engaged in the political process as well. Thus, civic engagement may reinforce political participation, particularly among people with human capital.

Conceptualizing social capital as civic engagement demonstrates clear relationships with political participation, but not when conceived as political trust. It was posited that a lack of social integration would be associated with lack of trust in public institutions, and that this distrust would contribute to a lack of political participation.

However, political distrust is more likely to lead to political participation, rather than to discourage it. Instead of viewing distrust as a problem within a system that requires consensus, distrust may be a valuable part of a political process. Distrust may indicate a reasonable frustration with the political system, as well as a belief in one's self-efficacy.

A model of democratic participation that builds on conflict may place more value on the role of skepticism among participants. Given that distrustful constituents are more likely to vote than people who are more complacent, perhaps another tactic to improve political engagement might be to educate people towards having a critical perspective.

These results suggest that people with higher levels of education and those who identify themselves as White, despite having greater access to social and political networks, are more likely to be distrustful, as well as involved in civic activities and the political process. One might see education as part of a socialization process that encourages civic and political participation.

As a form of human capital, education facilitates social position through networking, or access to social capital. The educated classes may participate because they have more opportunity to do so, and with more to gain. However, if political participation has decreased over time among the educated class, this may imply that the network of power has become even more exclusive.

Despite current theoretical interest in the role of computer technologies in our political processes, this remains an exclusive information source for the elite. Moreover, blaming television for public disengagement from political life appears to be too simplistic.

Television exposure, in general, does not appear to be related to political participation or social capital. Instead, watching television news and reading the newspaper are more likely to be associated with political participation than watching television in general. These two channels need to be considered separately. First, it is less clear what content a newspaper reader may focus on than a television news viewer. Second, while reading the newspaper is highly associated with level of education, watching television news appears to transcend educational distinctions. Newspapers may then perpetuate the interpretations and practices of an elite, while television news may be an appropriate vehicle to encourage political participation among diverse groups.

As for further research, longitudinal analyses of political participation, civic engagement, political trust, and media use, based on a nationally representative sample with a higher response rate, would contribute more solid evidence of these relationships.

Future research may also need to reconceptualize conventional theoretical assumptions regarding the nature of media use, social capital, and political participation. Assumed relationships between trust and participation, as well as media use and engagement need to be reconsidered. Conceiving of social capital as political trust may be unfounded.

Shifting frameworks of social capital from a micro-level to a macro-level analysis would allow us to envision potentially negative consequences, such as the exclusion of some groups and the reinforcement of others. The changing nature of political participation may be situated within the rise of individualism in our ideological values and in our political practices. The survival of the democratic process may be contingent upon understanding the value of political action based on skeptical thinking.

❐

Chapter - 3

Fundamentals for Establishing Media Relation

Since, passage of the Superfund Amendment Reauthorization Act of 1986 (SARA), Title III, Section 313 of which required companies to inform the public about chemical emissions, much has been written about the role of "risk communication" in a relatively new field, "risk management." Scholarly and professional research has been undertaken, seminars and workshops presented, and articles written about how to explain environmental risk.

Academics have offered thoughts on what "models" of communications should be used, and even how to design communications for "risk-takers"— those willing, even eager, to take chances. A cottage industry in environmental risk communication consulting has taken root in less than half a decade, giving prominence to research-oriented major players and number of others. The literature continues to grow exponentially and risk communication seem assured of a pre-eminent role in industry and government public information and risk management programmes for many years to come.

Therefore, it would behoove public relations professional with risk communication responsibilities to become intimately familiar with current literature in the field, as well as understand past failures and success in communicating environmental and other forms of risk. To that end, following the chapter below, a selected bibliography and list of references id offered, which might be a good starting place for those wanting to immerse themselves in easily-available literature. While the following draws upon research in risk communication, it is not purely theoretical, nor is it merely a "laundry list" of how to deal with the news media (although some "basics: of good news media relations will be inherent).

Utilizing a number of studies and proven concepts, this chapter looks at and analyses to some degree the media relations aspect of risk communication strategies, how journalists tend to treat the subject of "risk," and offers suggestions to help improve communication with and through the news media. Because reporters act as "filters" for your messages, the media are the crucial link in disseminating risk messages to key publics.

While risk communication can be thought of as reporting on the hazards of everyday life, organizations face their own "hazards of communication." Among them are: not fully understanding how to present the facts to the news media; the problem of making journalists understand or care about your particular risks; and, perhaps most important, understanding journalists' limitations and what to do about them.

It has been written that risk communication shouldn't be left solely to public relations "technicians." Instead, goes this thinking, it should be an integral part of risk management and thus the responsibility of plant managers and environmental officials. In reality, though, risk communication is a public relations function; and it's especially true in media relations, clearly the purview of the communications professional (although other managers should be schooled in such concepts).

We are becoming ever more wary and fearful of risks involving real or imagined safety and health hazards. We can almost play "Risk of the Day' as we watch television (especially during "Sweeps Week"), read local or national periodicals, listen to state and federal governmental agencies and watchdog and environmental groups and others who regularly bring us the latest in bad tidings about threats to our health and well-being—from the disappearing ozone layer to the latest tainted food product.

MEDIA'S ROLE MUST BE UNDERSTOOD

Who tells us about these hazards? Most often it's the news media, usually staffed by underpaid, overworked journalists, one of whom may have been covering city council meetings prior to being put on the "toxicology beat" the day before calling you about the latest perceived hazard your organization presents to the city's health.

And, expect this journalist to display a certain ingrained skepticism and adversarial outlook that must be understood and dealt with if your message or response is to be accurately conveyed by the news media to your publics. Before your organization has a chance to be deemed "a menace to the public health"—whether by the news media, activist group, government agency, or a combination of all three—anticipatory, skillful, frequent and truthful communication can often mitigate such charges.

Understanding what journalists need to get the story right the first time is a key to successful risk communication through the news media. For whatever reasons, if your communications efforts with the media have been non-existent, lax, or less than truthful, you run the risk of suddenly being on the defensive and put in the position of:

- Saying nothing and explaining that your lawyers are looking at the charges; or
- Offering hastily-contrived explanations which could be misconstrued to mean you believe profits and jobs come ahead of safety and health issues.

While your management may even endorse such responses, they can damage credibility with the news media and lead to unwanted headlines, such as: "Menace to Public Health Not Denied," or "Profits Above Safety at Local Plant." This is not to say similar headlines and stories won't result with even the best-managed risk communication, but why take the chance?

HAZARDS OF RISK COMMUNICATION

The following media relations "don'ts" may seem self-evident, but it's amazing how often they've become staples of unsuccessful attempts at risk communication. To employ these methods is to ensure media enmity:

- Disseminating self-serving data
- Making irrelevant comparisons/downplaying risk potential
- Using technical jargon
- Employing non-credible or incompetent sources
- Taking an adversarial posture
- Stonewalling or inaccessibility
- Ignoring public concerns

As mentioned earlier, not making such mistakes won't ensure accuracy by the news media, but could go a long way towards building a solid and "symmetrical" media relationship. Writing in The New York Times, Peter Passell noted that "To make sensible choices between greater safety and the alternatives...need more and better information, presented in ways that stimulate a sense of perspective."

It follows, then, that we must communicate essential facts from which the public can make these choices, such as how much risk to balance against benefits—economic or otherwise. It also follows that journalists have a measure of responsibility to interpret and convey such communication, while keeping their traditional posture of "unbiased observer," skeptic and "friendly adversary."

"HAZARDS GET HEADLINES"

The above axiom is found in scholarly research as well as anecdote-based reports on risk communication. While seemingly obvious, the concept is an integral part of understanding how the news media is likely to respond (or not) to your communication efforts. If we anticipate how and why journalists might react to risk issues, we may be able to anticipate and/or mitigate damage caused by inaccurate or incompetent reporting.

A good starting place would be to understand that "risk" isn't a news story, while "hazard" is. Once a hazard has been established, the risk becomes news, and the media's job becomes one of reporting, not education about some potential or future risk. In short, the news media are best at reporting "risks" that become "hazards"-and, eventually, "crises".

Along with a tendency to ignore risk and report on hazards and their negative consequences, journalists generally emphasize those hazards that are both serious and relatively rare. And, there seems to be a "lack of congruence between the size of the risk and amount of media attention." Thus, in dealing with the news media, risk communicators should be aware of and anticipate three "maxims" often governing perceived newsworthiness:

- Rare hazards are more newsworthy than common ones (e.g., "toxic shock syndrome" affected just.01% of menstruating women).
- New hazards are more newsworthy than old ones (e.g., the Alar controversy).
- Dramatic hazards (sudden and/or mysterious) are more newsworthy than long-familiar ones (e.g., Legionnaire's Disease; the radon controversy).

INFORMED PRESS = INFORMED CITIZENRY

One could just as well place a question mark after the above heading, inasmuch as communications research often indicates such an equation is at best only wishful thinking on the part of communicators. Nonetheless, educating the news media about risk and your organization's efforts in risk management is at least a solid starting point in keeping your publics informed.

The more we try to understand journalists—their idiosyncracies, their biases (What? But the media are supposed to be unbiased...), their likes and dislikes—the more success we're likely to have in risk communication. Or, at the very least, we'll have fewer surprises.

Drawing from research and more than 25 years working with the news media, I offer the following observations about journalists and their modus operandi when it comes to reporting on risk. Along with each observation are potential solutions to these dilemmas facing risk communicators.

The news media will generally ignore your organization's experts in favour of government or activist sources, especially people they already know. A number of studies have shown industry spokespeople are used far less frequently than "outsiders" to respond to risk-related questions.

This adds still another potential "filter" to messages you're trying to get to your publics. One Solution: Establish outside credible sources, imbued with knowledge about your organization and its risk management programmes. Get them with "beat" journalists early and often. (Be aware, however, that no matter how solid the credentials of your "outside sources" may be, there's still the chance the news media will treat them as "tools" of your organization.)

Journalists often lack knowledge of anything past "who, what, when, where, why and how," as opposed to understanding risk assessment fundamentals or environmental science as a whole. This often makes them susceptible to "pro" and "anti" arguments, with no shades of grey or room for interpretation.

According to the Foundation for American Communications (FACS), journalists desperately need increased education in science-related areas, especially risk assessment. Increasingly "event-centered," the news media must develop analytical skills about the beats they cover. And, as noted above, yesterday's court reporter may well need to be today's epidemiology expert.

Therefore, FACS produces educational seminars and research materials for journalists—something their publishers often don't have the time, inclination or funding to do—such as its new "Toxicology Study Guide." One Solution: Develop credible, objective and simplified background materials for the news media, especially that new "beat" reporter; and support independent organizations such as FACS and The Media Institute in their efforts to improve journalism education.

Journalists tend to "personalize" risk-related stories. This drives your experts and technical sources crazy, but in media parlance, it makes for a "good read," or "good TV." Editors ask reporters to "bring dead issues to life; to focus on real people facing real decisions." So live with it. The story will be covered; you just might disagree with format and focus. One Solution: Be prepared with answers; try to do your own "personalizing" of the situation (if management and/or your lawyers will allow it; even something as hokey as drinking a glass of allegedly "tainted" beverage, or other dramatization of the risk situation in question).

Eschew jargon; offer metaphors and good, solid, meaningful comparisons. (NOTE: Be careful here, and use only "like" comparisons-not voluntary vs. involuntary risks. Don't be perceived as trivializing risk potential: And don't get caught with comparisons such as: "It's much safer working in our mines than being at home;" the miner's spouse might disagree.)

SEVEN STEPS TO HEAVEN: YOU'RE OPPORTUNITIES FOR SUCCESS

Despite the potential pitfalls in dealing with news media "filtration" of your risk communication activities, there are some things you can do to prepare yourself and your management.

Here are seven steps to consider when planning your risk communication programme:

- Recognize risk communication as part of a larger risk management programme and understand the whole is based on politics, power and controversial issues, which encompasses more than just "open and honest" communication.
- Get your management in the "communications loop," and help train them to deal effectively with the news media; especially those tapped as "official spokespersons."
- Develop credible outside experts to act as "news sources" for journalists. Train them, also.
- Know your stuff; become an expert in your area of risk to instill a measure of credibility into your relations with journalists covering your organization.
- Go to local, regional or national news media with solid facts and figures before they have to come to you. Make certain your data:
  - Has statistical significance;
  - Can be successfully duplicated by other research;
  - Is specific as to what "conditions" it causes or problems it presents;
  - describes potential research weaknesses; and
  - Is understandable and easily translatable into newspaper or broadcast copy.
- Research perceptions of your organization by the media and other publics to gauge credibility and help determine if your messages will be believable. It's generally understood that the credibility of the message-sender is crucial to communications effectiveness, so why not see where your organization stands and be prepared to adjust accordingly.

- Understand your target audiences and how the news media can help you effectively communicate. For example, is there an unusual preponderance of "risk-takers" in your target population? What kind of messages/media and frequency will it take to reach them?

Regardless of your understanding of the news process or the likes and dislikes of journalists, it' wise to keep in mind that effective risk communication generally will come from perception of your organization's actions. Put another way, in the long run it's not so much words as deeds that count in communicating risk.

On March 1, 1995, Vladislav Listyev, a prominent Russian journalist was gunned down outside of his apartment in Moscow. What had transpired to make a journalist the target of such an act in a country where the mass media has traditionally been subordinate to the state? On the whole, specific journalists have not been singled out. The role of the media is changing.

In Russia and Poland since, the fall of communism, there is hesitancy to place the mass media in their former position as a mouthpiece for the government, but, on the other hand, there may be even greater hesitancy to give them the liberal freedom dictated by an increasingly democratic orientation.

What has the role of the mass media been in these transitions from authoritarian rule? What will it be in the future? The government institutions and leaders who have been placed in power have not reacted to the mass media consistently. These relationships have ranged from attempts at near complete, communist-like control to indifference and attempts to court the mass media for their own "public relations" purposes.

This chapter presents the results of a comparative study of Poland, from the fall of the communist government in 1990, and Russia, from the election of Boris Yeltsin in 1991, to the present. Utilizing research on media effects in society combined with the general theoretical framework suggested by transition theorists, discuss the role of the media in forming governmental institutions, though not necessarily democratic ones.

After a brief historical overview, I will examine some of the obstacles which the media will face in the future, such as economic problems, the pluralization and fragmentation of society, the rising emphasis on democratic- oriented journalism. Finally, I will propose possible roles (based on Harold Lasswell's classic work describing the social functions of communication), which media systems could adopt in the future. The research will show that the media systems will not be able to choose these roles independently for there are numerous other factors which affect their function and even their existence.

The mass media, as well as other institutions and systems within these countries, are in a definitional period. As the institutions within the political, economic and social systems in these nations become more concrete, the mass media find a role within those systems. The opposite is also true. The mass media will take an active, dynamic role in shaping these institutions in order to find a place within them.

There is never a complete consensus of the mass media's role because of the high degree of political, ideological and social differentiation in these countries. Yet the mainstream, elite mass media will begin to follow a general path which is acceptable (not necessarily in action, but in role) to themselves and the institutions around them.

Because of their past and probable future global importance, as well as their current instability, questions concerning Russia and Poland are crucial items on the international agenda. As the core of a former power in a bipolar system, Russia will, in the next few decades, attempt to regain its position economically and politically. The Cold War mind-set has not entirely faded and "Russia-watching" will continue.

Poland also will assert itself as an example of how free market and democratic reforms might be beneficial to itself and the region. The mass media systems in both countries have the potential to help and hinder these processes, often simultaneously.

This study will be limited to the print media in the form of newspapers and magazines. Using sources of the media and current events, such as Editor and Publisher, Current Digest of the Post-Soviet Press, Radio Free Europe/ radio Liberty daily bulletins (now the Open Media Research Institute), and The New York Times, among others, this research focuses on the media as a connecting - and often catalytic - factor between the political, economic and social institutions currently in the process of finding a place in Russian and Polish society.

Electronic media are equally important, especially because of their wide exposure and the immediacy of their coverage. In fact, there is significant desire and action on the part of the Russian and Polish governments to retain control of television and radio. But, because of the different dynamics between the electronic and print media or press, and the durability and accessibility of the written word, anything other than general references to radio and television will be left for a later analysis.

TRANSITIONS AND THE MASS MEDIA

To understand the relationship between the media and the political institutions during a transitional period, it is useful to look at the theories behind transitions. This places the overall events of the last few years in

Eastern and Central Europe into a more generalizable context of social change (specifically transition research on Latin America and Southern Europe).

Literature along these lines tends to fall into two broad categories which are separated by their ends: (1) transitions to democracy and (2) transitions from authoritarian regimes. Both are open-ended theories, but one is open at the beginning (i.e., the genesis of democracy) and the other is open on the outcome (i.e., the end result of transitions from an authoritarian regime).

TRANSITIONS TO DEMOCRACY AND THE MASS MEDIA

First, the literature on transition theory that leads to democracy focuses on the conditions which are necessary for a democratic end. Francis Fukuyama claims all roads eventually lead to liberal democracy because the world and the individuals in it will want it so, Robert Dahl addresses the global conditions which are necessary for democracy, including civic participation, equal representation and appropriate institutionalization.

The role of the media in this type of transition has been the subject of thousands of pages, most noticeably from scholars in democratic societies.

Since, the acceptance of the role of the printed word in the French and American revolutions, the mass media, and especially the print media, have been utilized as a forum for democratic thought and a mechanism for the transfer of democratic ideals.

This is often associated with Western, and particularly American, mass media. Russia and Poland have become a new proving ground for Western journalists seeking to promote the democratic ideals of speech and press freedom. U.S., journalists and academics have been instrumental in media assistance programmes and financial aid for the former Soviet bloc. It does not necessarily follow that implementing democratic press reforms will lead to a democratic form of government, though it has seemed to help.

Journalist Walter Lippman believed the purpose of newspapers is not to mirror the world, just signalize events. They cannot "perform the functions of public enlightenment that democratic theory requires." As will be seen, Lippman was right to a certain extent. The mass media can contribute to democratic political systems, but there are other factors which also contribute to the transition process, for which the mass media are an underlying connector. By itself, the press is less powerful.

TRANSITIONS FROM AUTHORITARIAN REGIMES AND MASS COMMUNICATIONS

The second type of transition theory, transitions from authoritarian societies, is much more apropos to our geographical area of focus. Both types attempt to explain transitions in political, social and economic structures, but the first is much more normative. The second group does not claim democracy as the only possible outcome.

"What [was] overthrown [in the former Soviet bloc countries] is much clearer than the answer to question of what will have to replace the obsolete and outmoded structures. Or...'transition from what?' is quite clear, whereas 'transition to what?' will for some time remain an open-ended issue." This lack of predictive capability with, the authoritarian transition literature has been accepted.

The most serious impediment to the accumulation of scientific knowledge about social reality is the prospect that different causes could produce the same effect. In other words, there are different roads in the process of political and economic transition that might lead to the same outcome and, conversely, there are similar roads which might result in different outcomes.

I have attempted to synthesize the literature on transitions from authoritarian regimes into themes. First, there are many ways to pass through this transitory period. In 1986, a collection of authors discussed these various roads through the time of transition. At the time, these transitions were occurring primarily in Southern Europe and Latin America and each of these cases had diverse characteristics which affected the transition.

Some of these ideas can also apply to the cases in Eastern Europe. Second, there are various conditions which led to the transitory period. Adam Przeworski focuses on the factors leading to the breakdown of authoritarian regimes and the causes of their liberalization. Third, typologies of transitions exist, but they are never all inclusive. Situations may overlap with others, have unique characteristics or both.

Schmitter and Karl recently attempted to include the Eastern European countries in the general authoritarian transition literature. They proposed a matrix of Weberian "ideal-type" transitions, with space in the centre for the overlapping situations.

Finally, transitions take time. it is difficult to analyse effectively a situation as it is happening. it is much easier in retrospect. Yet, there are ways to measure aspects of the transition.

A key issue in the establishment of a new type of government after one has fallen is the speed and strength of the institutionalization process. If democratic institutions are established more quickly, there seems to be a greater chance that some form of democracy will ensue. It is the same with more socialistic institutions. Karl and Schmitter believe the arrangements crafted by key political actors during a regime transition establish new rules, roles and behavioural patterns which may (or may not) represent an important rupture with the past.

These, in turn, become the institutions shaping the prospects for regime consolidation in the future. In short, looking at institutionalization, as well as specific roles and actors can be an indicator of the transitional process and, sometimes, the direction. The mass media institutions are part of the communications processes existing and operating in and around these factors leading to transition.

In the same way the mass media has been studied as a facilitator of democracy, the role of the mass media in these transitions from authoritarian regimes (as well as research on the media and social change more generally) is important to consider. Research on this subject has not been as completely covered as other types of institutionalization during transition.

For purposes of this study, the most relevant writings can be described by the general category of communications systems (including interpersonal, as well as media and technology) and social change. The subject of social change is so broad that its relationship to communications systems is difficult to define in concise terms.

Yet, intuitively, there can be a correlation between the expansion and reach of the mass media and types of social change, though the strength and causal links of that correlation can only be speculated. Theories can clarify these relationships. Denis McQuail has categorized communications and social change theories into five groups:

- Theories of mass society which "suggest that the mass media encourage and make viable a rootless, alienated, form of social organization in which we are increasingly within the control of powerful and distant institutions";
- Marxist theory which presents the "mass media as a powerful ideological weapon for holding the mass of people in voluntary submission to capitalism";
- Theories which describe communications as a force for both integration and for dispersion and individualization within society;

- Theories demonstrating the effects of mass media and their capacity to take over the cultivation of images, ideas and consciousness in an industrial society and, by so doing, forming new bases for collective thought and action; and
- The "Global Village" of Marshall McLuhan in which a worldwide community, which supersedes existing boundaries, is established through direct and common experience from primarily television.

From these theories, Joseph Klapper proposed some generalizations about the effects of mass communication on social change which can apply to Russia and Poland. Mass communication does not usually serve as a necessary and sufficient cause of something, but rather functions with other factors and influences.

This is important to our study as mass communications alone seems to have little or no effect. These other factors and influences use mass communication in the process of change. For example, institutions, such as Solidarity and the Catholic Church in Poland, are willing to utilize the power of mass communication.

On the occasions that mass communication is used in the service of change, one of two conditions are likely to occur:

- The other factors and influences are likely to be inoperative and the media effect will be direct or
- The other factors and influences, which normally reinforce the status quo, will be found to favour change.

The second option seems much more likely in these cases. There are always situations in which mass communication will produce direct effects or serve psychophysical functions. There are some things which mass communication can do that other factors cannot do, such as the continued presence of printed material in an individual's home.

The effects of mass communication on change are affected by the nature of the media and communications themselves (i.e., aspects of textual organization, the source and medium, public opinion).

One common thread running through these theories and generalizations is that what we experience is increasingly indirect and mediated and that, whether by chance or design, more and more people are receiving a similar version of the world through similar types of mass media. The differences come in the "versions" of reality proposed by the various media and theories. It is:

> very clear that the mass media do have important consequences for individuals, for institutions and for society and culture. That we cannot trace very precise causal connection or make reliable predictions about the future does not nullify this conclusion.... All that remains is to discover not whether the media have power and how it works, but who has access to the use of this power.

Generally this means asking questions about ownership and other forms of control, whether political, legal or economic. The question, then, is one of power. How effective are the mass media? If they are effective, who should control them or should they be controlled at all? Does the entity which has control over the mass media control other parts of society?

This question of power is key in Russia and Poland during their political, economic and social transitions. The conflict arises as the mass media assert their own power and the political institutions attempt to arrest that power in their own manner. The media do not want to be controlled, but the political structure must harness and use their power for its own benefit if it is to succeed and survive.

Contemporary literature which looks both at the mass media and its effects in Russia and Poland is scarce. These two nations, which have begun to liberalize their political systems, have used and reacted to their respective mass media in different ways. Poland had an extensive samizdat press which was highly influential during the 1980s.

Since, the official collapse of the ruling communist party in 1990, the media has been decreasing in its social relevance, cohesiveness and power. The Polish mass media are in need of direction and definition in regards to ownership, role and power. In Russia, the Soviet press was the epitome of the Marxist propaganda arm. Its liberalization process has been quite slow.

Though it is still economically dependent on the state, the Soviet press also is now in a "limbo," but coming from a different direction than the Polish press, it is gaining social relevance, cohesiveness and power while at the same time searching for some identity and role.

There has been very little written about the role of the press in these types of societies. Many questions have been left unanswered, but the issue continues to persist. Russian journalists George Vachnadze and Elena Androunas have recounted the more recent experiences of the Russian press as it has attempted to liberalize itself.

But these are more narratives and anecdotes and have not placed present experiences into the broader theoretical context. An edited volume by Sarah Sanderson King and Donald Cushman and Slavko Splichal's work have begun to look at communications systems at the transitional level, but have not specifically linked the use of the mass media in transitional countries to social and economic change. Instead, they have focused on the media and political stability.

Before looking at the contemporary relations between the government and media, it is useful to examine the history of such relations in each area. The history of communications systems within Poland and Russia has a strong relationship to the communist press systems which were imposed on their societies, but the reactions were different.

The Soviet press was able to maintain its monopoly on mass media-disseminated information whereas the Polish press succeeded in creating underground communications networks for the dissemination of more credible information. Because the present identity crisis in the media is linked to those communist systems, the historical overview will focus principally on the point at which these authoritarian systems were implemented.

RUSSIA

The communist press system had its origins in Lenin's implementation of communism as the ideological foundation of the Soviet single political party system. As described by Schramm et. al, the communications system in communism, like every other system and institution in a Soviet state, existed to do only what it is specifically assigned to do by the leaders of the state. In communist states the leaders seek to ensure their power through control of key organizations: trade unions that discipline the workers, collective farms that organize the peasantry, and writers' unions that keep intellectuals in line.

Schramm says this idea is at the root of the communist press theory. It stems from general ideologies of control in Karl Marx's writings, then it was adapted by Lenin and Stalin, stating that the media can be a useful tool in fomenting revolution. Even today, the theory has been interpreted differently than Lenin applied it seventy years ago.

"But the key to the whole system is control of the media through which the negative sanctions wielded by mass organizations are positively reinforced by the propagation of communist ideology and policies."

The media, in a communist system, can be crucial to the ruling elite in times of crisis. Lenin understood the central role of the press in 1901 when he offered his now famous dictum that "a newspaper is not only a collective propagandist and a collective agitator, but also a collective organizer."

Stalin declared twenty-one years later: "The press is the most powerful instrument with which the party daily, hourly, speaks with the laboring class in its own vital language. There exists... no other such flexible apparatus."

Brezhnev in 1967 reiterated that the mass media were "... a powerful means of rearing the people and propagandizing the party's ideas."

This attitude about the role of the media led to a contradiction. If the purpose of the press was to agitate people towards revolution as Lenin had proposed, what was its purpose after the revolution? They would respond that its new purpose would be to motivate revolutionary change in other parts of the world.

They subsequently embrace an authoritarian approach to the press for their own countries and use the media to reinforce and maintain the status quo. Some countries began to see the paradoxical decisions and began to utilize the media as a weapon to fight the existing structure.

During the period from 1917 to 1985, the communists were able to maintain effective control over the media. Journalistic alternatives were scarce. "For decades up to 1991, the role of the opposition press in the USSR was played by the foreign mass media. Bauer discusses the importance of secondary channels of information (of which Western media are a part), often found in societies based on Soviet ideology, which substantiate or refute known information.

A wide variety of sources attest to the importance and pervasiveness of informal, unofficial communications in the Soviet Union [and its satellites].... The regime itself tacitly acknowledges the importance of such [unofficial] media not only in its propaganda against rumor mongering but, and more directly, in its use of informers, arrests for "alien" ideas, and intellectual "delousing" of Soviet citizens and soldiers to the West.... More important, however, is the fact that so many of them [informants] go on to report that much of what they knew of day-to-day events and policies in diverse areas of Soviet life came to them via the unofficial, word-of- mouth channel.

These unofficial channels of communication were in the form of mass media in many instances as well as word-of-mouth communication as with the academic and some religious publications. The Russian people found that the literary form of the written word was another effective tool for the circulation of "truthful" information.

Authors and playwrights banned by the Soviets - such as Pastemak, Solzhenitsyn and Medvedev - told the truths of Russian history or, through metaphor and allegory, parodied the Soviet system. "There is a world of difference in Soviet and Russian culture between the writer (pisatyel) and the journalist (zhurnalist).

The former has a social and political influence with no exact parallel in contemporary Western societies." Copies of literary works and other types of print media found their way through the country. Millions of copies of the outlawed Bible and Koran managed to work their way into Russia.

Then the mass media found a chance to break away from the control. Mikhail Gorbachev was made party secretary and began to actively promote the ideas of glasnost and perestroika.

Irena Maryniak believes this "glasnost brought a breath of air into Soviet public life, it released the Soviet people from a fear entrenched for three generations. It acted, too, as a form of collective therapy to help heal nearly 70 years of state-induced amnesia." She believes that journalists facilitated this therapy with the publication of generally known, but suppressed, truths.

For example, the liberal magazine Ogonyok (Flame) printed documentation "about the fate and work of repressed writers from the archives of the KGB." From 1985 until 1991, open opposition in the print media to political institutions increased. In fact, "the Soviet press... is leading the processes of perestroika." Then, in 1991, the fall of Communist Party paved the road to more liberal media systems.

POLAND

Over the years, the Polish media has been at the forefront of political and social movements in the country. This does not happen in every country, but the tradition of the pre-world War II Polish media was "a good heritage of a pluralistic media system."

When the communists took over they attempted to destroy this legacy, but it kept rising against all obstacles again and again to oppose and finally aid in overthrowing the regime that was repressing it.

Since, the 1950s, the Polish press system has been a communist press system as described earlier. Yet it has also been as much a product of its history and the shifting demands that have been placed upon it, as it has been a product of the Soviet model of the ideal Marxist-Leninist press.

The Marxist charge for the press was to serve as a collective organizer, agitator and propagandist for the masses, raising them up through education and images of correct behaviour. For the most part, the traditional Polish press was focused on a limited intellectual audience.

Historically, there was little local capital for an extensive and permanent mass press, and there was a high level of illiteracy in Poland, as elsewhere in Eastern Europe, until after World War II. The Polish system during the past 40 years, in both its structure and emphasis, has reflected all of this. It has focused on discussion, analysis, and culture — addressed primarily to the intelligentsia and only secondarily to the desires of the mass population.

Furthermore, whenever possible, press names and images hearken back to their non-communist, prewar predecessors. Even the writing award of the Association of Polish Journalists (a communist organization) is named after a leading Polish publicist of the early 1900s because he was one of the only heroes the Polish journalists felt they could emulate.

But, in the late 1940s and early 1950s, because of the then-unknown communist way of thinking, the Polish press was different. It was directed to be written primarily for and by workers and peasants. The prewar journals of non-communist political groups, religious organizations, and intellectual or professional associations were closed down as power was secured by the communists.

During the 1980s, it was this unbending Soviet control that led the Poles to turn to other places for more credible sources of information. The publications by the Committee for Social Resistance (KOR) were some of the nation's most widely circulated documents. Solidarity's publications, from the Tygodnik Solidarnosc to sporadic bulletins describing situations throughout the country, were also widely read and discussed.

But the government-sanctioned press also had a voice. Because it felt it had total control of the Polish information systems, even the ruling communist regime claimed the Poles believed the existing press. In an article in the World Marxist Review, Jerzy Urban, the Government Minister and Press Spokesman for Poland, said the purpose of the press is to tell the public the truth about what the government is doing. In the best sense of the phrase, it is a "public relations" arm of the government.

According to Urban, in May of 1989, the state was conducting five public opinion polls a week to determine changing attitudes towards government policy. During 1988, the government had discovered that people did not believe the government's claim that wages grew faster than prices during the previous year. Yet, "when we expose past mistakes and criticize our own record, the public believes us absolutely," Urban said.

There is evidence to place this assertion in doubt. The Poles turned to other sources of information. This led to the rise of the samizdat or underground press, which was born in the mid-1970s as Solidarity began to take root. Samizdat literally means "self-publishing."

The striking feature about these samizdat publications was "their sheer quantity, their variety, the length of the individual publications, [and] the openness with which the editors and contributors to those publishing enterprises carried out their activities."

The role of the underground press in eroding communist power in Poland over the last 15 years is often overlooked in the West. "Ninety per cent of those interned during the martial-law crackdown of 1981 were not union or political activists, but those responsible for writing, printing and distributing opposition pamphlets." It can be safely asserted that the cause of the 1989 break up of the communist monopoly was not singular, but the role of the media was great.

To be sure the new media were an agent of the several revolutions, but at the same time it was disillusionment both with the old media and the regimes they represented that fueled support for change.... The samizdat press was the thread that wove together the [revolution's] disparate social elements.

These uncensored publications were only a part, but the most important part, of a general self-defence of society against the totalitarian apparatus of a state whose goal was the control of all human activity, whether political, cultural or economic. The result... was the breaking of the communist state monopoly of information.

These underground newspapers had another audience, sympathizers in Western nations. "It was, I think, the role of things like the East European Reporter and the links that were made between the Czech dissidents, the Hungarian dissidents and the Polish dissidents" that made the West sits and up and take notice.

Newspapers were not the only type of media to make a mark. Literary magazines, such as Kultura, loudly voiced opposition and dissidence throughout the decades. Kultura editors describe risks taken by many who read Kultura at night, the "chain of readers all eagerly awaiting their turn" (because the publication has a print run of only 7,000 copies) and the disappearance and reappearance of copies of Kultura in places that caused alarm to the Polish authorities. "Kultura was so feared by Polish authorities that it became the target of fierce press attacks and was used as evidence in trials."

Solidarity's national newspaper Tygodnik Solidarnosc, which appeared in the spring of 1981, had 500,000 copies printed in its first edition, but "it was read by far more people." This was the case for much of the print media during this time. This expansion of print media continued through the delegitimation of communism in the late 1980s and early 1990s. Then, as society became more pluralized, the print media followed.

CURRENT SITUATION OF THE RUSSIAN AND POLISH PRESS

Now the media have reached a similar point in both countries: a need to define their role in relation to the political, economic and social institutions which are being created in the wake of communism's delegitimation.

As Russia and Poland form the institutions needed to stabilize their political infrastructure; create the institutions necessary for a more liberal economy; and mobilize into institutions such as political parties to solidify the social strata, the media seem to be reforming, creating and mobilizing as well.

There are several obstacles which the mass media in Poland and Russia will have to surmount in order to define a role that works for them as well as for those who read, fund and criticize them.

First, they will confront the economic problems stemming from the path taken towards a freer market economy.

Second, they will have to deal with the pluralization and fragmentation that is taking place within their own structure and within society itself.

Third, they will need to recognize the democratic ideals about communication which conflict with those they have become accustomed to over the past decades.

And fourth, they will need to find the role(s) which suit them ideologically and economically.

ECONOMIC PROBLEMS

First, with the trend towards a more liberal free market economy, the print media are plagued by economic problems. The tradition of being subsidized by the government has created a false sense of security. In a freer world, the Russian and Polish press want to change their image as puppets of an authoritarian regime to one of greater autonomy and control.

But, they are discovering that independence also means a greater difficulty in obtaining the funding necessary for continued printing. Founded in 1917 as the official mouthpiece of the Soviet legislature, Izvestia (News) is an example of the economic hardships which threaten the Russian print media. In 1991, Izvestia announced its independence from its editor in chief and the Supreme Soviet for which it had disseminated information for 74 years. "Reporters paraded their liberation from party and state sponsorship in pieces that openly criticized even the highest Soviet and republic leaders and bodies."

The result was increased circulation and a ban from the authorities. Enforcement of such governmental action was becoming more and more difficult in the open society, so the government turned to another form of coercion. Izvestia discovered that independence came with a heavy price — loss of funding and preferential treatment from the communist party and the state.... [It] had long been insulated from the practical problems of supply, production and distribution... [and], to make matters worse, nearly all of the essential publication services remained under governmental monopoly.

Results of this situation were disheartening, and Izvestia was not the only publication affected. The combined effects of economic price liberalization and the monopoly on publications services nearly led to a collapse of large print media in Russia. For example, the financial director of Moscow News said that "the government-monopolized printing plants charge prices equal to about 30 per cent of a newspaper's cover price, whether the press run is 2,000 or 2 million — a basic contradiction of the tenets of economy of scale."

Because of this, the Moscow News has had to cut its press run nearly in half. There is a similar set percentage in the distribution system. If the paper decides to raise its price, its printing and distribution costs are automatically increased. In February 1992, Boris Yeltsin proclaimed a "Decree on Additional Measures of Legal and Economic Protection for the Periodical Press and State Book Publishing." By so doing he provided some relief, but the loss of circulation and the cost of printing will continue to be a factor in newspaper size and content.

In the euphoria of the transformation of 1989, Polish media proliferated, despite the fact that the communications industry was "reeling" from both increases in printing costs and plummeting sales because of increased cover prices. "Before, it was clear — the censor, the party, those were our enemies.

Today it's the price of newsprint, distribution, all those things that our Western colleagues know all about, but we are just beginning to discover." The Russian newspapers and public felt these price increases as well. O'Clery believes it is a conscious process on the part of the government to retain control of the print media.

The Russian government has raised "the price of paper, printing, and delivery. This has forced newspapers to increase the price they charge readers, and they are losing circulation.... Since, Ogonyok raised its charge from forty kopeks to one ruble, its circulation has fallen to 1.5 million, a drop of 35 per cent."

The Russian and Polish print media are dealing with these economic challenges in various ways. Moskovsky Komsomolets (The Moscow Young Communist) is selling advertising space and other newspapers are publishing classified ads. Reporter's salaries are slim, but there are perks, such as dividing up "five or six free trips abroad... each month, in return for giving a tourist agency free advertising space."

Some publications have pursued relationships outside their borders. The Polish government daily Rzeczpospolita (circulation 250,000) has reached an investment agreement with the French publishing group Hersant. Gazeta Bankowa, a financial weekly, has established a joint venture with French, U.S., and Spanish publishers.

PLURALIZATION OF SOCIETY

Despite these economic obstacles, the number of publications in both countries has increased. The increase has reflected a second obstacle to the print media: a pluralization of purpose, scope and ideology. In an open society there is more acceptance of comment, criticism and feedback and, therefore, there will be more avenues for those activities. The Russian government has budgeted 30 billion rubles to help 400 publications.

"The top priorities are children's, scientific, cultural and other special journals that are ill-equipped to survive in a market economy." In Poland during the first year after the fall of communism, the number of journals and newspapers increased by 600 in five months. More than just creating new publications, the Poles also began to provide avenues for publishing.

New publishing companies were formed to replace the Robotnicza Spoldzielnia Wydawnicza (RSW, the Workers Cooperative Publishing House), the organization that had control 80 per cent of Polish publications for 40 years. "So we form new publishing companies. We expect within a year more than 500 new small local newspapers to be in print," said Stefan Bratkowski, director of the newly legalized Polish Journalists Association.

This pluralization is also reflected in the social and political realms of Russia and Poland. In both countries, the number of political parties, representing thought across the political spectrum, and grass-roots movements has mushroomed.

As mentioned earlier, Klapper explains that one of the characteristics of mass communications and social change is they will not usually serve as a necessary and sufficient cause of something, but rather function with other factors and influences. There is a connection between the print media and these disparate groups and ideas.

Vladimir Orlov, a journalist from Moskovsky Novosti, said that Yeltsin fears the media because he knows that there is always the possibility that "strong opposition newspapers can mobilize marginal groups" and that is not a pleasant prospect.

In 1991, 60 new Russian journals were launched and "45 of them have flourished to become even more outspoken critics of the president and the Party." The political leadership has dealt with this attitude in the mass media in two different ways: following the democratic process of regulation through legislation and falling back on the old authoritarian habit of total control of the mass media.

For example, in February 1994, the Duma (Russian Parliament) passed an act which would dictate the media's responsibilities in the coverage of its activities. This was to ensure what the Duma believed should be more positive coverage of Russia's political processes. Poland has also enacted legislation to control the actions and ownership of the mass media.

An example of the second type of reaction came in October 1993. In response to a coup attempt, Boris Yeltsin declared a "state of emergency" and imposed censorship on 13 newspapers and the television show "600 Seconds," which he felt would foment the opposition. "Publications and broadcasts carried by these newspapers have to a great extent promoted the destabilization of the situation during mass disorders in Moscow and the end of September and early in October, and the organization of the revolt," the Russian Press and Information Ministry is quoted as saying. The reaction was unprecedentedly explosive and Yeltsin repealed the order after only two days.

Regarding the event, Orlov said that "the old system of censorship couldn't work" in this new society. Sevoydna (Today) wrote that there was no logical cause for the censorship because there was the belief among the print media that "under the present circumstances, only guaranteed freedom of speech can save the regime from degeneration and tyranny."

DEMOCRATIC AND AUTHORITARIAN IDEALS

This leads to the third area of challenge for the future, the implementation of more liberal press freedoms in nations which have become habituated to authoritarian systems and thinking. The concept of the freedoms of speech and the press for society, journalists and the government is different in Poland and Russia than it is in the West.

As stated earlier, the West (especially the United States) has been at the forefront in providing programmes to Russian and Polish journalists which emphasize the importance of a free press in the newly-emerging political systems. In fact, freedom of the press has often been the battle-cry for movement and the outcry against attempts at control. Foster believes that the justifications for the freedom of the press were strikingly similar to those in the United States.

Proponents argued that an independent Fourth Estate would expose and check potential abuses and mistakes by executive, legislative and judicial branches; provide the citizenry with the full and objective information essential for democratic self-governance; assist in the spiritual liberation of the population from the shackles of socialism; offer a forum for introduction, comparison, and debate of reform proposals; and consolidate Russian citizens in support of their embattled government during a time of most difficult sociopolitical changes and economic trials. [That] reality has diverged markedly from these high-sounding phrases.

It seems that the post-soviet era has been characterized by continued clashes between the governments of Poland and Russia and the mass media, both electronic and print.

Both the journalists and the government are learning to relate to each other on a new level. The superficial declarations of speech and press freedom will have no effect unless the principles implicit therein are adhered to. Lidiya Kalinina, writer at the magazine Domostroi, has said, "We have no censorship now, but the main body of people working in the media are conformists whose views will change with the prevailing wind."

There are exceptions with publications such as Moskovy Novosti and Moskovsky Komsomolets, which are outspokenly critical of Russian politics and are increasing their circulations as well. But, many mainstream journalists are afraid for their jobs. As previously discussed, the government is fearful of a powerful mass media and is hesitant to deal with them on the level of a democratic, free press.

When newspaper analyst John Morton attended a conference in Russia entitled Free Economy and the Mass Media" he was concerned to hear numerous complaints from journalists that "the government, despite its announced devotion to a free press, is subtly distinguishing in dispensing newsprint and official information between `pure' media operations (those friendly towards the government) and `impure' ones (those that are critical)."

One of the principal obstacles in the improvement of this relationship is the history of censorship within communist societies. This form of control has become associated with communistic media theories since, Lenin's time. In Russia, the Bolsheviks took control of the media as a necessary source of propaganda.

Censorship naturally accompanied this type of mass media use. Censorship was introduced in Poland by temporary decree in 1946 and lasted unchanged until Solidarity's uprisings in 1981. "In July 1981 the Polish Parliament finally passed legislation that invalidated the 1946 decree and substantially liberalized censorship.... On December 13, however, martial law was introduced and the law was suspended."

Actions involving what more liberal mass media analysts would call censorship or prior restraint of news, are a part of the flow of information in both Russia and Poland. "Vladimir Solodin, who had had the job of defending freedom of the press in the Yeltsin government, switched to be the chief of censorship [during the October 1991 coup attempt] without a visible qualm."

Some of the confusion in the relationships between the mass media and political institutions can be explained with the idea of enemy imaging. In the late 1950s and early 1960s, both Kenneth Boulding and Ole Holsti introduced research on the subject, principally emphasizing the relationship between the United States and the then Soviet Union. In a paper regarding his now famous research on John Foster Dulles, Holsti writes, "The relationship of national images to international conflict is clear: decision-makers act upon their definition of the situation and their images of states - others as well as their own."

He continues by saying that these images must coincide with "commonly- perceived reality" in order to be supported. There is great value in enemy imaging.

By classifying something as an enemy, "one's own values are enhanced, the cohesion of the group is strengthened, [and] the indistinct inner fear can be projected out onto some specific cause."

This is what happened to the media in Poland, especially during the 1980s when it was linked to the Catholic Church and the Solidarity movement.

For the communist press, the enemy was capitalism and inside the Soviet Union, the government itself was the enemy of the literary movement.

As the new political systems learn to relate to the new mass media, they, too, must find new enemies. With the collapse of the communist ideology, the enemy is no longer the world. It must be something within the society such as crime, social and economic progress or the environment.

These governments are discovering that the mass media can play an integral role in the process of finding and focusing on a new enemy. Unfortunately, the mass media are wary, given the past history of such relations.

FINDING A ROLE

Finally, there will be a need for the print media in each country to define its role. In a classic essay, Harold Lasswell, a political scientist and a pioneer in communications study, identified three social functions of communications:

- Surveillance of the environment,
- Correlation of the different parts of society in responding to the environment, and
- Transmission of social heritage from one generation to the next.

Since, Lasswell, scholars have suggested that entertainment as a social function of communications would be added as a fourth category, but this function is only beginning to be observed in Russia and Poland. These social functions identify the choice (or a combination of choices) of roles which the mass media in Russia and Poland can play: (1) information giver (surveillance of the environment), (2) an agenda setter and mobilizer (correlation of parts of society) and (3) a reinforcer of values transmission of cultural heritage (transmission of social heritage).

The first role is as an information giver seems to be the most talked about. Russian and Polish journalists want to be able to disseminate what they feel is more objective and truthful information. Orlov said this is one of the principal desires of the post-Soviet press. "The role of the press in Russia today is the same as it is the United States: make investigations, do interviews, report what happens, criticize and analyse."

But the content of that news is being examined. Orlov believes that Russians are becoming tired of negative political news. "The public is not so interested anymore in the media as a news source. They want entertainment." According to Lev N. Gushchin, editor of weekly Ogonyok, "In general, the readers are tired of politics, tired and disappointed with the political changes that have not brought about any real changes" and newspapers are responding by turning to entertainment, crime, sports and pop culture.

The feeling in Poland is that journalism is just a by-product of the authoritarian system and journalists will have to relearn news-gathering skills. "We in Poland have forgotten how to take an interest in the rest of world," laments Ernest Skalaski, an editor at Gazeta Wyborcza. Journalists had forgotten how to exchange information. More than that, this generation of journalists had never really learned how to look for stories, cover beats and sniff out news.

The next role of the media could be as an agenda setter or mobilizer. According to George Gerbner, the agenda setting process can be seen in the dominant agencies of communications which produce the message systems that cultivate the dominant image patterns. They structure the public agenda of existence, priorities, values and relations.

People use this agenda to support their ideas and actions in ways that tend to match the general composition and structure of message systems provided that there is other environmental support for these choices and interpretations. In other words, people use the information in the press to justify and motivate their mobilized activities.

In both Russia and Poland this is currently seen in the fragmented political parties and mobilization on a local level (though Zhirinovsky may be an exception). To set the agenda there is one important prerequisite: media access. Most senders are professionals and if journalism remains in the hands of professionals, others tend to be excluded as potential journalists/senders from having access to this media which is the means to reach the rest of the public.

Grassroots discussion among citizens tends to be displaced, in the mass communications situation, by discussion among columnists, public relations practitioners, and other professionals, or among experts or political figures debating one another. Currently the dialogues are taking place on this level. As mentioned before, Orlov feels the general interest, in political dialogue at least, is minimal.

Finally, the media can be a reinforcer of values and ideas and, as McQuail mentioned earlier, can also cultivate images, ideas and consciousness. This is the goal of the marginal right and left wing publications. Again, Zhirinovsky is a good example. His nationalistic movement hopes to cultivate an alternative approach and reinforce those ideas. Yeltsin sees the print media as a forum for his government as well.

On March 4, 1994, he created a new presidential information department with the goal to "provide the public in Russia and abroad with objective information on Russian government policy." Orlov said these new information strategies are part of a larger public relations campaign to improve the Yeltsin government's image with the public and the press.

To a certain extent, the press relies on these organizations for information and reciprocally, the organizations rely on the press for the dissemination of it. In this way, the institutions become more beneficial to each other.

Russia and Poland can provide useful information for studies on the mass media in transitions from authoritarian rule and, should they eventually reach some type of democracy, they will be increasingly valuable as case studies in this area as well. Their history and cultures are different from other countries which have already experienced this transition, but some general trends can be delineated.

First, transitions from authoritarian systems, and especially from hard- line communism as in the case of Russia and Poland, usually result in a period of flux while the mass media acts differently than it did under the authoritarian regime.

For example, the large samizdat press in Poland had to change its focus, and the print media in Russia moved out from under state control. Secondly, this transition period is marked by a fragmentation of society, which is reflected both in the numbers and orientations of the press. Third, political, economic and social institutions are fluid and constantly changing together with the goal of great stability (though how that stability will be attained is in question).

The press is changing with society, attempting find a role that will fit it economically and ideologically or it is actively promoting a certain course of action, as with the Westernization (democratization) of the press or the nationalistic movements.

It can be argued that society is always in a state of change so the above assertions would not be significant. Yet, there are relative levels of stability. The mass media will continue to look for a role in society - in relation to other systems and institutions - where it fits in with other societal institutions.

There is no clear threshold to discern when comfort becomes stability or vice versa, but that is the beauty of comparative politics. Comparing both geographical areas and general trends, can provide indications of stability as the world has come to define it. An additional thought is that stability does not last.

There is a place for opposition, even in societies where institutions feel relatively comfortable. But, if that opposition becomes too strong and is able to mobilize portions of the populace, the political structures will surely attempt to silence it. Then the political structures, if they were more democratic, will be changing as well.

The mass media never seem to lay down and let current political institutions abuse their power, but there are indications that the ebb and flow of the political, economic and social tides of a nation have an impact on them. But the reverse is also true. The mass media will continue to give a voice to the wide spectrum of mainstream and marginal thoughts which are sure to be a part of Poland and Russia during this transition from communist rule.

❐

Chapter - 4

Responsibility of News Media

News media-newspapers, magazines, broadcast journalism, and websites with journalistic content-usually start worrying about ethics only in times of crisis, says French scholar of mass communication Claude-Jean Bertrand. In fact, codes of ethics, ombudsmen, press councils, and journalism reviews have been created during times of great social disaffection and "increasingly angry disillusionment" among the public about the news media, when people have "a growing sense of being baffled and misled," as Walter Lippmann once put it.

For example, the first code of ethics for journalists was created in 1923, shortly after World War I, following criticism about the influence of political propaganda and the advertising industry on news media content.

Ombudsmen, press councils, and local journalism reviews, meanwhile, flourished in the United States during the social upheavals of the late 1960s and early 1970s. They all can be called instruments of media self-regulation because ombudsmen and authors of journalism reviews and of codes of ethics, as well as members of press councils, are generally media professionals who engage in monitoring, investigating, and analyzing developments in journalism and in the media business.

As such, they expose mistakes, point towards potentially harmful developments, and encourage attention to ethics among journalists. Bertrand describes press councils, codes of ethics, journalism reviews, ombudsmen, and some nongovernmental institutions concerned with media issues as "media accountability systems," defined as "any non-State means of making media responsible towards the public." Since, the State should not participate in monitoring the news media, "except by delivering the threats that media often need to start the process of selfregulation,"

Bertrand urges media owners, media professionals, and media consumers to hold the news media accountable.

But then, because media consumers often prove too "apathetic or unorganized," Bertrand emphasizes the importance of self-regulation by media owners and media professionals, who are asked not only to hold politics, business, and other systems of society accountable, but also to inquire if media professionals fulfill their primary responsibility, which is "to provide a good public service."

The goal of media accountability systems is thus to "improve the services of the media to the public; restore the prestige of media in the eyes of the population; diversely protect freedom of speech and press; obtain, for the profession, the autonomy that it needs to play its part in the expansion of democracy and the betterment of the fate of mankind."

To reinforce media accountability by means of media self-regulation, media professionals are limited to "moral pressure." "But their action can be reinforced by the authority of media executives or persisting legal obligations," adds Bertrand.

In addition to the "systems" mentioned before, Bertrand includes "media reporting" and "media criticism" in his list of media accountability systems. He emphasizes that specialized journalists should monitor the news media and write critically about them for a mass audience. Since, the news media "have become one of the nervous systems in the social body, the public needs to be informed about them.

Some journalists must specialize in that field so as to cover its news well and investigate uncompromisingly." But Bertrand says: "With exceptions (usually due to ideological animus or business rivalry), media do not criticize each other: blind eyes are turned on the failings of colleagues.

Self-criticism is almost unknown.... In this profession, as in others, solidarity sometimes verges on collusion." Although written more than fifty years later, his conclusion recalls the 1947 Hutchins Commission's critique, issued after its inquiry into the social responsibility of the media: "We recommend that the members of the press engage in vigorous mutual criticism.

Professional standards are not likely to be achieved as long as the mistakes and errors, the frauds and crimes, committed by units of the press are passed over in silence by other members of the profession."

Bertrand's accusation about a lack of media criticism is no longer valid. Since, the mid-1990s, there has been "an absolute explosion of the genre" of media reporting and media criticism in the United States. Leading newspapers like the New York Times, the Washington Post, and the Boston Globe now regularly report about developments in journalism and the media business, as do magazines like Time and The New Yorker.

Howard Kurtz of the Washington Post, David Shaw of the Los Angeles Times, Felicity Barringer of the New York Times, and Cynthia Cotts of the Village Voice have become well-known for covering the news media. They call their relatively new beat the "media beat" and describe themselves as "media reporters," "media writers," "media critics," or "media columnists," while they speak about their journalistic work as "media reporting" or "media criticism."

Today, media issues are also discussed in the broadcast media like CNN's "Reliable Sources," the National Public Radio's weekly "On the Media," and productions with a regional focus, such as "Beat the Press" in the Boston area. Finally, many online media have been established for such critiques.

Among them are media consumers' sites like Mediachannel.org and Websites for media professionals, such as Jim Romenesko's MediaNews, now part of the Poynter Institute's Web site. In a special edition of the Columbia Journalism Review describing the booming media beat in March 2000, James Boylan concluded: "At the turn of the century, media critics are blossoming like spring."

It could be argued that the impetus for this increase in media reporting and media criticism has again been a growing public discontent with the news media. For example, the excessive reporting about the O.J. Simpson case and about the affair involving former President Bill Clinton and White House intern Monica Lewinsky stirred intense criticism. The news media might have reacted by monitoring each other more intensely; at least, many of the "media scandals" discussed in the late 1990s have been investigated and publicized by the news media themselves.

For example, the Boston Phoenix was involved in exposing Mike Barnicle's and Patricia Smith's plagiarism and invention of quotes in the Boston Globe. When the Los Angeles Times entered a profit-sharing agreement with one of the subjects of its reporting, the sports centre "Staples Arena," the paper was caught by one of its local competitors-and the L.A. Times reacted with the publication of an in-depth, self critical report about its own failure.

Similarly, the Ncii' York Times published long, self-critical pieces recently after reporter Jayson Blair was discovered to have fabricated quotes and interviews. Obviously, not all "mistakes and errors" have been "passed over in silence."

Media economics also helps explain the increase in media reporting. The last decade was marked by numerous big-time media mergers involving, for example, CBS and Viacom, or AOL and Time Warner, and by a boom in the media business due to new media technologies like cable and satellite television and the Internet.

Finally, media professionals themselves have increasingly become a topic in the news media. Jonathan Yardley already laments: "The good intentions... have gone seriously awry. The laudable idea that the press should police itself in the best way it knows how-by covering itself with the same object and thoroughness it tries to bring to all other subjects-has been twisted, and diminished into just another variation on the culture of narcissism, celebrity and gossip." While many more media professionals now write and comment on the media, little research has been done so far on media reporting and media criticism as a media accountability system. The bulk of academic literature available deals with the history of media reporting and media criticism, or with single high-profile media critics. Half a dozen content analyses examine how the news media covered the news media's work with reference to specific events, such as a war or political campaigns.

Merger and acquisition activities have also been studied. Pieper and Hughes found that Time and CNN generally restricted their coverage of the merger of their parent companies to the business aspects of the transaction, i.e., the consequences for the stock market. They left it to competitors like the Washington Post and The Nation to question the consequences of the deal for the independence of the newsrooms at Time and CNN.

Similarly, Turow found allusions to "self-censorship" in the newsroom of Time with regard to the company's business strategies. Robinson's 1983 content analysis of articles on media issues in leading newspapers found that most news media, with the exception of the Washington Post, shied away from criticizing themselves.

Instead, print media emphasized the problems of the broadcast media, while national organizations covered the local media. Northington, having surveyed two dozen journalists on how they reacted to being criticized in trade magazines like the Columbia Journalism Review, found that journalists generally did not change their professional behaviour.

The media reporters and media critics specifically have not been studied so far, but ombudsmen have been surveyed several times. Research indicates that the ombudsmen's interest in remaining on good terms with their peers and the news organization can interfere with their potential as instruments of self-regulation.

Also missing in the context of media reporting and media criticism are studies about media owners and media managers as well as media consumers- if and how they follow the "media beat," and what they make of the information they receive there.

METHOD

This exploratory study of leading media reporters and media critics in the United States involved interviewing media reporters and media critics about three key issues:

- How do these journalists cover peers and employers; are "blind eyes" still turned on the failings of colleagues and bosses?
- Do they address a general audience, an "insider audience" of media professionals, or both?
- To what extent do they regard media reporting and media criticism as a media accountability system?

The total number of media reporters and media critics in the United States is small. A comprehensive list on the web site MediaNews names 32 "media people" (media reporters and media critics) and 37 media critics from "alternative weeklies." For this study, 30 media reporters and media critics were selected.

This sample included: (a) journalists presumed to have widest reach within the peer group, because their papers or magazines are most widely read by other journalists, according to Weaver and Wilhoit; and (b) journalists who have been proven "innovators" in the field of media reporting and media criticism: for example, the media critic from the Village Voice, which was a pioneer in media criticism in the 1970s; Jim Romenesko, whose web site Media News has been ground-breaking in providing online articles on media issues; and one of the editors of the now-defunct Brill's Content, which sought to pioneer as a "media consumers' magazine."

In addition, journalists from the Columbia Journalism Review (CJR) and the American Journalism Review (AJR) were interviewed because, in contrast to the other interviewees, they explicitly address an insider audience with their trade magazines.

From the sample of 30, 21 journalists agreed to be interviewed in person. None of the full-time TV and radio media reporters responded or agreed to participate in the study. The interviews took place in the United States in November and December 1999. The average length of the interviews was 50 to 60 minutes, with the longest one taking about two hours. The tapes were later transcribed by the author.

Nine interviewees described themselves as "media writers" or "media reporters," with the task of objective reporting about the content of the news media and the development of the media industry. They will henceforth be referred to, for the sake of brevity, as "media reporters." For example, Felicity Barringer, of the New York Times, described herself as "a media reporter."

"That involves covering journalism, the business, and lots of other things, but I abhor commenting on my colleagues and my profession. I just describe what they do.... What's happening with corporate earnings and mergers... what's happening in the coverage of a major news event...."

Twelve interviewees emphasized their critical approach by describing themselves as "media critics" or "media columnists." They will be described as "media critics." They said their task was to comment on the content of the news media and the structure of the media industry; they offered "critiques" or "opinions," or provided "checks and balances" on the news media, as the New Yorker's Ken Auletta put it.

However, no clear-cut distinction between the two role models has yet emerged in this nascent beat. For example, at one point media reporter Mark jurkowitz also referred to himself as a "media critic."

All but 2 interviewees covered or criticized the news media full-time. Of the 21 journalists, 17 wrote for leading newspapers, magazines, and online publications, and could therefore potentially reach large audiences. Two interviewees, Mark jurkowitz and Geneva Overholser, reported having worked as ombudsmen for some years, but both had stopped doing that long before the interviews took place.

FINDINGS

Peers and Employers as the Subject of Media Reporting and Media Criticism. As discussed earlier, the work and the decision-making processes of journalists have become a more frequent subject in the U.S., news media in the last decade. Many media professionals react to the public criticism with high sensitivity, according to most interviewees.

For example, Howard Kurtz of the Washington Post said "you inevitably anger and alienate many people in the business who would otherwise be your friends. People are wary around you, even in your own newsroom...." Dan Post said that as the San Francisco Chronicle media critic he would face "a lot of scrutiny" by the fellow journalists who followed his columns. "So you have got to make sure that you got it right."

Establishing a professional distance from peers was described as being difficult by the interviewees, because they already knew many of the people they write about. This was very different from covering a foreign country, for example, or a government agency. "[Y]ou've been through a lot of what they've been through," said Felicity Barringer, the New York Times media reporter.

Dan Kennedy, the Boston Phoenix media critic, stated that it took him "an awful long time really getting comfortable and confident in going after other journalists. I know how difficult the job can be. Sometimes you are going after people who are more accomplished than you are. But then you have to step back and think, gee, if a movie critic just trashes a Stanley Kubrick film, that doesn't mean that the critic thinks he should be a better director than Stanley Kubrick. I have to put myself in the same slot."

Many interviewees indicated that they felt a responsibility for the consequences of their writing. Cynthia Cotts of the Village Voice expressed sympathy for the use of anonymous sources on the media beat because "simply to be suspected of being a source for someone like me could jeopardize that person's job." Likewise, freelance journalists who she criticized had to fear for their livelihood afterwards, which made her more cautious when criticizing their work. Similarly, Mark Jurkowitz was aware of his influence on peers and other media organizations, and was cautious to criticize small publications, for example. On the other hand, Cynthia Cotts described "puff pieces that media journalists do, including me." She explained that writing only critical pieces "diminishes the chance of anyone ever talking to me."

Many interviewees identified strongly with fellow journalists. David Shaw, the Los Angeles Times media reporter, said: "Actions that I might have previously regarded as a result of some carefully calculated decision, or perhaps even a conspiracy,... are very often a product of ignorance and stupidity and inefficiency...." Like most other interviewees, Ken Auletta was convinced that mistakes made by journalists were often a result of the high business pressure in today's media companies, led increasingly by managers unfamiliar with journalism.

Covering one's own employer was likewise described as a challenge, since, "you are certainly aware of your relatives." However, all interviewees stressed their efforts to avoid the impression that "you're trying to further the interest of your own newspaper or company that owns your newspaper." Howard Kurtz always disclosed his affiliations, and said he would make an effort to be tougher on CNN as well as the Post, because of his connection there. David Shaw said that he would sell the Los Angeles Times shares he regularly received as soon as possible.

On the other hand, the interviewees also reported that although they were "inside the building," they were treated no differently by their own employers than any other reporter. Mark Jurkowitz recalled covering the scandals involving his colleagues at the Boston Globe, Mike Barnicle and Patricia Smith: "You are hoping that your own publisher will talk to you, which sometimes he didn't.... I got the same press releases...." Dan Post's experience covering the sale of the San Francisco Chronicle was similar.

Still, these journalists conceded that their employers' business interests might influence the way they covered the problem of media concentration. All regarded media concentration as dangerous for journalism. Nonetheless, journalists from smaller publications who were not part of a large media conglomerate, like the Village Voice, the Boston Phoenix, the former Brill's Content, and the trade magazines AJR and CJR, seemed more eager to tackle the issue of ownership and its consequences.

They also complained about the quality of media reporting in the major news media: "It is always the business implications-what does this mean for stockholders.... It's never, what is this going to do with the diversity of opinion...." Meanwhile, media reporters from large newspapers like the New York Times and the Boston Globe doubted that media concentration would be a number-one topic for their audiences.

Mark Jurkowitz said that since, "the public has never really cared about this issue," writing about the stories that do not get covered was difficult: "You are trying to prove the negative." He added: "My problem with it is, I just don't see how you turn back the clock any more.... Everything's been deregulated."

In sum, the interviews indicate a high degree of peer orientation. The media reporters and media critics considered the implications of their work on fellow journalists arguably more than they might when they covered politicians or businesspeople, with whom they did not share a professional background. This does not necessarily imply that they are softer on media professionals.

The harsh reactions of media professionals to Howard Kurtz, for example, indicate that he is hard-hitting. And the account the interviewees offered about how they strove to cover their own employers as objectively as possible can be taken as proof that they seek to achieve impartiality even under difficult circumstances. On the other hand, only a few interviewees were as frank as Cynthia Cotts, who even admitted to writing "puff pieces."

And many interviewees conceded to producing "too little coverage of the commercial interests of our bosses and the subtle pressures that that imposes on journalism," because these journalists apparently assumed that this would interfere with the business interests of their employers. Additional research will be needed to determine whether journalists apply the same ethical standards to members of the Fourth Estate as they do to representatives of other social groups.

Media Users and Media Professionals as Target Groups of Media Reporting and Media Criticism. Of course, the journalists from AJR and CJR focused on a professional audience. But many interviewees adhered to Bertrand's thesis about a relatively passive general audience.

The majority of both media critics and media reporters doubted the public's interest in media reporting and media criticism, generally because they received little feedback from the popular audience, and a lot of feedback from insiders. Tim Jones, for example, was firmly convinced that the majority of his Chicago Tribune readers were "more interested in complaining about the media than reading about and understanding the media."

Few of the interviewees reported a high degree of feedback from the general audience. One exception was Howard Kurtz: "Those who think that my primary readers are simply other journalists... totally misconstrue how interested the general public is in media coverage and media criticism."

Mark Jurkowitz said he wanted to "train" the media users to skepticism towards the news media by "treating it like a consumer beat in some ways." Slate's Scott Shuger, who also reported considerable feedback from lay users, described his goal: "Readers should ask themselves: Whose interests are being served by this story told in this way and whose are being left out?" The varying degrees of response from the general audience may result from different ways of covering media issues. Several interviewees said they could attract larger audiences among media professionals with insider stories about media celebrities. Sean Elder, former Salon media critic, gave an example: "Tina Brown: Just mentioning her name-always gets hits.... [T]hings that are considered a little more fringe, like... supermarket tabloids... don't get that much interest."

While few interviewees admitted explicitly that they pander to media professionals, quite a few seemed to do it-and a glimpse onto MediaNews confirms that much "media gossip" is published in the news media every day. Mark Jurkowitz commented: "A lot of the media writing is inside baseball. It's about us, it's for us, it's gossip about our industry." He added: "The public is... interested. But if you only talk about your own industry gossip, they are not going to be interested."

Those who exploit their peers' craving for gossip without regard to the interest of the general public usually get away with it, since, media reporters and media critics seldom go after other media reporters and media critics. It could even be assumed that "media gossip" and "insider reporting" is encouraged by some news medi a executives, if one considers Dan Post's account of how his own column was created: "I think that is also part of the idea behind having that type of a column in the paper, to be perfectly candid.... By writing about the media, it is sort of a way to get other media reading your paper. [I]t helps the newspaper's reputation...."

In sum, the majority of the interviewees received more feedback from media professionals. This apparently tempts many media reporters and media critics to pander to their professional audience by providing insider news. Those who strove to choose topics relevant and understandable for a popular audience also reported substantial feedback from average media consumers. It could be argued that media reporters and media critics need to watch each other more closely to make sure that their peer orientation does not result in more and more "inside baseball."

MEDIA REPORTING AND MEDIA CRITICISM AS A MEDIA ACCOUNTABILITY SYSTEM

The central goals of media accountability systems, Bertrand said, are improving the news media's service to the public, restoring the news media's prestige among the public, and preserving its autonomy from state interference. Do the interviewees use "moral pressure" to further these goals? While most interviewees said they had an impact on peers, many said they or the media business in general.

Few interviewees were fully confident that they could help improve the news media's service to the public by holding the media accountable. Those who believed they had influence were the best-known and most respected media reporters and media critics in the United States. For example, The New Yorker's Ken Auletta said he wanted to "educate" corporate leaders to be more sensitive towards ethical matters. The Washington Post's Howard Kurtz stated that the "essence" of his job was "to hold journalists and news organizations accountable."

He added that he had often been described by other editors and reporters as having had "a bit of an impact." "A former editor of Newsweek once wrote a memo to his staff on ethical matters, and included a line, saying: Don't do anything that you wouldn't want to see in Howard Kurtz's column.... I have certainly seen instances where media outlets have changed policies, at least in part, because of something that I have written, apologized for stories that turned out to be wrong, for example."

Meanwhile, many of the younger interviewees-even those who were aware of their immediate impact on peers-considered their influence on the improvement of the news media to be limited, and took an explicitly humble approach. They wanted to be reporters, not "reformers," and could only "sometimes" help serve readers. Sean Elder, from Salon, wanted to keep "people honest," but added that he had "a little more sympathy for the point of view of the editors, who're just trying to keep their jobs and sell something." Eric Alterman, of The Nation, was convinced that "the media is large and so amorphous" that "they can absorb any criticism you make."

He said that there had never been a more important time to be a media critic-but that he would not kid himself that it made a whole lot of difference. Geneva Overholser saw too much media gossip instead of thoughtful media criticism. Therefore, she asked, "[W]hat difference does it make?"

Only the two journalists from the trade magazines emphasized that they also wanted to help restore the media's prestige, at least among colleagues, by trying to "write about examples of things we've done well," as Alicia Shepard from the AJR put it. And Mike Hoyt from the C]R said that "not enough attention is given to the positive side of what journalists do."

Also, David Shaw of the Los Angeles Times, a veteran on the media beat, was the only interviewee to mention the danger of state interference when he said that media reporting and media criticism was "better than nothing. We don't have anything else. I certainly don't want any kind of government regulation." Meanwhile, the professional spectators of the news media interviewed here apparently did not regard media freedom as endangered, since, almost none mentioned the danger of state interference.

In sum, media reporters and media critics disagreed about the purpo of media criticism and media reporting. A minority of journalists considered themselves "advocates" of the public and adopted a "missionary approach" to their work. Among this faction were the few well-known media reporters and media critics, who were confident that they could improve the news media's service to the public by holding journalists accountable.

The two journalists from the trade magazines who saw themselves also as "ambassadors" of their profession were another exception. Many of the younger journalists emphasized that while they wanted to inform readers about the news media and teach them to analyse the media, they did not want, nor did they think themselves able, to change or even improve the news media in general, or restore their prestige.

Many long-time prejudices about a "conspiracy of silence" among media professionals can no longer be considered valid. The journalists on the still- young media beat generally strove to cover the news media, its structure, and even their own employers comprehensively and impartially.

They said that as media reporters and media critics, they could have an impact on their peers who have lost jobs or were confronted with changed newsroom policies, for example, after having been criticized by them. This suggests that media reporters and media critics have a considerable potential as instruments of media self-regulation. This potential, however, is not yet fully exploited.

Many media reporters and media critics still appeared to be more reluctant to go after fellow journalists, as well as media managers and media owners, than after politicians or businesspeople, for example. The apparent reason for their cautiousness is their dependency on other media professionals as sources, colleagues, and employers.

Media professionals are also the most important target group for their writing, since, many media reporters and media critics lamented a lack of feedback from the popular audience. And in fact, the expansion of the media beat went along with an increase in "media gossip" in the news media. Media reporters and media critics might need to be reminded at times that their prime duty should be service to the public, and not their peers.

That said, media reporting and media criticism in the news media have emerged from the media boom of the 1990s as a promising media accountability system in the United States. Once the media beat is even more established in the news media, media reporters and media critics might also become more confident in their "watchdog roles."

Some find tradition like the proverbial bag of salt on the back of the donkey which wanted to cross a river, and some others perceive it as a beauty of the past that is to be treasured forever: for some, tradition is a cataract in the eyes of humanity, while for others it is the eyes themselves.

Some tend to eulogize everything that is traditional, while others are too ready to condemn everything that is traditional. Perhaps the issue here is the relation between the past and the present, between continuity and change and the creative ambiguity inherent in the relationship, because an overcritical attitude is as harmful as blind obeisance.

The object of this chapter is to focus on the dynamic aspect of tradition within the context of nation, community and identity. A preliminary discussion of nation, community and identity provides a backdrop for an analysis of the dynamic aspect of tradition. In the course of this study an attempt is made to delve into the three components of tradition: the emergence of 'invented tradition', the appearance or disappearance of negative tradition and the little and great tradition with specific reference to India.

NATION – COMMUNITY AND IDENTITY

Nation is a modern phenomenon arising out of specific modern conditions providing a possibility for a large participant culture. Nation is neither immemorial nor self-generative but a construct. Nation-building, according to Karl Deutsch, was the result of the twin processes of communication and social mobilization.

The emergence of nation-state is generally attributed to three related processes of centralization: "the emergence of supra-local identities and cultures (`the nation'); the rise of powerful and authoritative institutions within the public domain (`the state), and the development of particular ways of organizing production and consumption (`the economy')".

Setting aside the various disputes1 regarding the nature of the relationship between these three processes, it can safely be remarked that the forging of identity - more specifically in a pluralistic society, simultaneously creates diversity. As it is evident from the break up of the former Soviet Union, the anti-national rebellions in giving birth to new nation states have attained respect and recognition as successful nationalist movements.

In the words of Peter van der Veer, "the centralizing force of nation building itself sprouts centrifugal forces that crystallize around other dreams of nationhood: nationalism creates other nationalisms - religious, ethnic, linguistic, secular - but not common culture."

The differences in pluralistic societies and the consequent attempts towards centralization and homogenization contain also the seeds of heterogenization because of the explosive dimension inherent in the tradition of smaller communities. The explosive nature of their traditions irrupts powerfully when they are pushed to the periphery and when their very existence is under threat.

Smith speaks of two overlapping concepts of nation. The first view - civic or territorial - is very much a western conception. As per this understanding, the following four vital spheres constitute a nation: territory, human populations with claims to a common ancestry, a democratic solidarity, common customs and languages and a common native history.

The features that figure in the latter conception of nation are, according to Smith, precisely those features of community which define ethnicity and ethnic identity. He defines an ethnic community as "a named human population possessing a myth of common descent, common historical memories, elements of shared culture, an association with a particular territory and a sense of solidarity". Smith's view provides a more general perspective.

It accepts the fact that a nation is a modern construct found only in modern conditions, and on the same vein asserts that it is not a wholly modern construct because it requires pre-modern ethnic elements. Hence, nations are formed out of civic and ethnic components.

Obviously Avijit Pathak is right in stating that a nation remains abstract and empty without a living, concrete experience like family, ethnicity, religion and language. The story of the new nations like India, Indonesia and Nigeria manifested the necessity of creating overarching loyalties that would transcend the more primordial ones like ethnic membership, religious affiliation and linguistic identification. But these loyalties are neither blind nor are they easily replaceable. Apter rightly points out, "Race, ethnicity, religion, and language are the means whereby people identify themselves, organize their community, find meaning for their sentiments and express their beliefs. All critical elements of man in society appear to be touched in some important manner by each of these matters". Indeed it is a community that gives its members an identity and thus provides a situs in which to define themselves individually.

Identity is perceived in a dialectical process or experience: how a community sees itself or is seen by others, how it contrasts itself and its character as against each `other,' and how it perceives and selects its history. Thus identity indicates who some one is and also provides one a sense of belongingness while simultaneously setting one apart from various 'others'.

In different words, "Identity is a matter of the outs as well as the ins.... ethnic identification arises out of and within interaction between groups". Jenkins finds significant similarity of perspective in the views of Everett Hughes and Clifford Geertz. For Hughes, an ethnic group is one wherein "people in it and the people out of it know that it is one; because both the ins and the outs talk, feel and act as if it were a separate group".

Geertz's elegant definition of ethnicity reflects the dialectic polarity between ins and outs, and between similarity and difference. Ethnicity is the `world of personal identity collectively ratified and publicly expressed' and `socially ratified personal identity'.

Clifford Geertz calls these 'loyalties' primordial sentiments. He asserts that a state is built on fellow-feeling, which is a feeling of corporate sentiments of oneness. When the members of a state are charged with corporate sentiments of oneness they begin also to experience their belongingness to one another.

This fellow-feeling, or `we-ness' binds together those who have it strongly, overriding all differences arising out of economic conflicts or social gradations and as well severs them from those who are not of their kind. The existence of this fellow-feeling or we-ness, Geertz understands, as the foundation of a stable and democratic state.

Probably, to hold the view that the sense of nation emerges powerfully as a tangible experience when it is confronted with the 'other' is also not far- fetched. For instance Rupert Emerson holds the view that when the chips are down a nation effectively mandates its members' loyalty, setting aside the claims of the smaller communities within it and those ties which cut across it or potentially enfold it within a still greater society.

TRADITION

The term 'tradition' is studded with innumerable interpretations. Without going into different definitions of tradition, it suffices here to say that in the common usage the term tradition means the same as `something from the past'. Durgan and Sinha characterize tradition as the accumulated experience of a community which provides a base as well as guidelines to its members through its beliefs, rituals, attitudes, values, customs and institutions.

Tradition comes into play whenever one refers to any link between the present and the past. Jerzy Szacki, a Polish sociologist, perceives tradition not simply as any type of link between the past and the present, because only that aspect of heritage that is viewed as necessary and relevant can in reality force its way into the present.

In the words of Szacki, "Only that is remembered and preserved which is actually important to the group, and the whole rest is irreparably forgotten".

The subjectivist element in Szacki's conceptual scheme of tradition appears clearly when he stresses the highly malleable nature of tradition and the way each generation can select a certain heritage, evaluate, reform and adjust to its present needs.

According to this perspective, a tradition must be continually reshaped and revalued to meet the changing situation of a group if it is to survive as tradition. Further, when heritage fails to supply convenient items, these may even be invented. The invented ones may be in opposition to the sentiments of the inherited tradition; what is important is that they are attuned to the prevailing psychological climate.

A useful illustration of how a generation selects a certain aspect of its heritage and attempts to adjust it to its present need is the way Lokmanya Tilak, a great nationalist leader, used the feast of Ganesh caturthi during the freedom struggle. Ganesh is the elephant-faced God in Hinduism.

This Ganesh caturthi feast is celebrated in August-September every year. Tilak revived this feast as a means to bring the hindu community together. Although Tilak belonged to Chitpavan community, a priestly class in the hierarchical hindu caste system, he did not choose the Saraswati feast, which has its origin in the great tradition, but instead chose the Ganesh feast which belongs to minor tradition.

He selected it from the cultural heritage of the masses in order to fit the specific needs of his time. Tilak realized the necessity, in the words of Pradhan, "of giving a deep-rooted cultural basis to the political movement by breaking through the routine of the somewhat academical nature of the Congress movement, and he strove to bridge the gulf between the present and the past and to restore continuity to the political life of the nation".

Tradition consists of three components: how a tradition is transmitted, what is being handed over, and the nature of involvement of the participants.

Szacki speaks of these three dimensions of tradition as three complementary concepts of tradition: Social transmission (tradition in the functional sense), Social heritage (tradition in the objective sense) and Tradition (in the subjective sense) respectively. The first focuses on the act of transmitting certain values of a given community from generation to generation.

The way these values are transmitted can take innumerable forms, for instance, orally or through the press, mass media, performing arts and the celebration of festivals. The second dimension of tradition emphasizes the content of tradition. It is the accumulated and accumulating storehouse of a community's systems of beliefs and rituals, values, attitudes, customs and institutions.

The third stresses neither the act nor the object of transmission but the attitude of a given generation to the past and consequently its approval or disapproval of a certain aspect of its heritage.

For instance, the disapproval shown by the British public towards the traditional practice which ruled against hoisting the flag over Buckingham Palace following the death of Diana, the Princess of Wales, was no secret.

The importance of the third dimension of tradition comes from the conviction that it is illusory to believe in the possibility of being into faithful to one's earlier generations, as that would mean living in their socio-cultural world.

Tradition is often taken for granted in common parlance as something which man uses to replace reason, but frequently it happens to be an object of complex intellectual operations. Szacki points out two types of intellectualization. He ascribes one to E. Husserl and the other to Bert F. Hoselitz

The intellectualization of tradition on the strength of the statement that a given pattern would be good even if it were not traditional goes to Husserl's credit, whereas the other type, namely, the intellectualization of tradition qua tradition is attributed to Hoselitz However both these processes of intellectualization take place in the social consciousness.

Szacki points out another process of intellectualization which is unlike the above-mentioned two types. He explains briefly: We have a rational pattern of behaviour, and we try to provide it with a tradition of its own.

Behaviour patterns which for some reasons are accepted as rational must for some other reasons be presented as complying with patterns to be found in the past. It is so because, a community has a tendency to accept something more willingly when it is shown as rooted in the past and this tendency is more prevalent in traditional societies. L. Krzywicki's concept of historical substratum, which Smolicz refers in his article, is here in place.

According to him it is a sum total of passive factors in one's social heritage, which is capable enough to arrest the rise of new social movements by restricting the freedom of the individuals. His understanding of social change seems to be too narrow and in opposition to social change and new innovations.

The dynamic concept of tradition perceives tradition not as a sum total of historical substratum, inevitably bound to be backward looking and conservative, but as a forward-looking activity which seeks its basis in the accumulated experience of earlier generations.

"It is tradition which offers a framework in which to breathe, and an invitation to play our own part.... The very wholeness of tradition in which we live certainly demands much of us".

Tradition as a forward-looking activity in a dynamic continuity with the past is free from suffocation and superfluity.

For, openness without rootedness is superfluous, and rootedness without openness is fanaticism. Therefore tradition is not necessarily to be seen in opposition to social change and innovation. "A tradition can only survive the vicissitudes of time and continue to flourish if it accommodates itself to the present".

A healthy relationship of the past (tradition) with the present is brought into being through three processes: through a reinterpretation or modification of cultural heritage to the contemporary situation, through the influence of other cultures, and through the influence of creative developments and inventions within the given society. When a society is open to these processes its tradition will cease to be a burden of the past.

The relationship between the past and the present should not be viewed as a one-way traffic directed towards modification of the past.

A healthy relationship between the past and the present also implies that the present is confronted and challenged by the past - by the core values of the nation's culture. Thus cultural continuity between the past and the present gives due respect and importance to both the present and the past, allowing the necessary space and freedom for processes that are mutually complementary.

The notion of cultural continuity brings us to the question of the fundamental elements of culture or the core values of a given culture. When one perceives of culture as a static concept, then the core values of a culture appear to be immutable in nature; but when culture is perceived as a continuing accumulation of social heritage then one comes to the conclusion that the core values of a culture also undergo changes in their nature and as well in accordance with the interpretation given to them by successive generations.

Thus, referring to Hinduism, Dalmia and von Stietencron explain tradition as "an entity that is neither a permanent unchanging heritage of the past, nor entirely fictitious, but constantly being selected and modified in response to social change and to visions of the future".

The questions that have to be honestly faced are the following: what are the core values and how important are they for the identity of a given society? How stable or fragile are such core values in the contemporary time? How persistently they are activated or reconstructed?

The subjectivist interpretation of tradition understands the term 'handing down' in a metaphorical sense because of the modification a culture undergoes in the process of social transmission. Each generation makes its own selection of elements from its heritage, making the new elements again and again the basis for valuation, changing approvals into disapprovals and vice versa, or simply becoming indifferent to what used to be key issues.

Consequently, this view admits the possibility of creating tradition that would be not the valued part of the actual heritage, but the valued part of an alleged heritage. There are examples of traditions which are either pure fantasy or which have little agreement with the past.

Eric Hobsbawm and Terence Ranger call this phenomenon "inventing tradition". Inventing tradition is essentially a process of normalization and ritualization characterized by reference to the past.

According to Hobsbawn `invented tradition' includes both traditions that are consciously constructed and formally instituted and traditions that emerge in a less easily traceable manner but which establish themselves with great rapidity. The goal of invented tradition is generally to establish continuity with a suitable historic past, a continuity that is largely fictitious,

The earlier part of this chapter referred to the phenomenon of modern nations as largely artificial constructs, and also pointed to the search for establishing 'overarching loyalties' in the process of such contemporary nation-building.

Consequently the modern nations of the world cannot be adequately understood without paying careful attention to the invention of tradition. The nation-state, national-symbols, histories, and multi-ethnic societies are comparatively recent historical innovations. Hobsbawm points out that plenty of today's political institutions, ideological movements and groups were so unprecedented that even historic continuity had to be invented; entirely new symbols and devices came into existence as part of the attempt to create these modern national movements and states.

On the richness of these emotionally and symbolically charged, invented symbols, Hobsbawm says, "The national flag, the national anthem, the national emblem are the three symbols through which an independent community proclaims its identity and sovereignty, and as such they command instantaneous respect and loyalty.

In themselves they reflect the entire background, thought and culture of a nation". No in-depth study of national phenomena can be achieved without giving due attention to the 'invention of tradition'; the modern 'nation' is a construct which relies heavily on the possession of appropriate symbols.

Another important aspect of the subjective interpretation of tradition is the negative evaluation of tradition. Members in a group never shape their attitudes in a vacuum; while developing their attitudes they also take into consideration the attitudes of other members. George Allan in an autobiographical tone writes, "I live together with other human beings in a community that has distinctive traditions.

Those who comprise my social group share particular conditions and undertake or permit characteristic activities. We believe certain things to be significant, and we act on the assumption that certain things are right or useful or opportune.

Other communities of people arrive at quite different conclusions, accepting beliefs which we reject, legitimating actions which we prohibit".

Different social groups tend to espouse different traditions and if such groups are in an antagonistic relationship to each other, the positive tradition of group A becomes a negative tradition of the members of group B.

Three points must be mentioned with regard to the negative evaluation of tradition:

- In a plural society there is never a shortage of such alternative and competing traditions.
- Changes in these evaluations do not remain constant. They depend on the political, social and economic status of the group. This partly explains why the content of cultural tradition grows continually, so that each social group within a society comes to be particularly influenced by systems of ideas belonging to different periods in its development. Consequently what was greatly esteemed in one period may not enjoy equal favour among all groups in another period.
- Changes in the negative traditions of the various groups in a given society are probably an excellent indicator of inter-group relations and also of the status of a given group within a given society.

In a plural society, minority groups usually manifest a tendency to abandon their traditions in favour of the majority group's tradition.

Szacki calls the minority groups the new recipients of currently respected tradition of a wider community. The process of Sanskritization in the history of social change in India can be cited as an example.

Popper holds the view that this break from one's tradition is in reality not a freeing from the bonds of tradition but only a change from one brand of tradition to another. A particular group's interest in switching its loyalty to another tradition has to be seen within its historical context.

However, one should note that highly complex plural societies with different ethnic strands seem to underplay the value of cultural continuity, precisely because the reconstruction of the past often tends to be incoherent. Therefore competition between different traditions makes any appeal to cultural continuity and to the past unattractive and ineffective. The wider the cultural diversity in a given population, the greater will be the difficulty in attempting to see its past as a monolithic block.

The first of the above-mentioned three observations, namely, 'plural society with alternative and competing traditions' leads us on to consider Robert Redfield's comments on 'little and great traditions'. Redfield asserted that every civilization consists of traditions. That of the elite, of the reflective few who give it formal articulation, he termed 'great tradition'.

That of the unlettered mass of the folk, he christened 'little tradition'. Redfield assumed that all civilizations began with an orthogenetic or primary process of growth and kept on transforming themselves through heterogenetic contacts as they moved towards a more universal form of civilization.

Milton Singer and McKim Marriot applied Redfield's approach to study the social change in India. Milton's statements about cultural change in India can be formulated in the following way:

- He asserts the continuity of India's great tradition with the little tradition because he holds the view that India's primary or indigenous civilization had been fashioned out of pre-existing folk and regional cultures.
- This cultural continuity is an outcome of a common cultural consciousness, which most Indians have in common and which they express in essential similarities of attitudes and ethos.
- He attributes the formation of this common cultural consciousness to the influence of certain shared factors and processes, such as common sacred books and objects, and a shared appreciation of a special group of literati and other agents of cultural transmission.
- In countries like India, cultural continuity with the past plays an enormous role that even modernizing and progressive ideologies had to be traditionalized.

Further, he also concluded that the resilience of the Indian tradition is such that changes take place in it through selective adaptation rather than basic transformation. Dube criticized Singer's dichotomization of traditions as insufficient, stating that traditions in India are organized not in a bipolar but in a multi-polar system.

Dube postulated a six-fold classification of traditions. They are: the classical tradition, the emergent national tradition, the regional tradition, the western tradition, the local and sub-cultural traditions of social groups.

However, Yogendra Singh, a sociologist from Delhi, criticized Dube's classification as unsatisfactory because his classification stands again on an ad hoc and nominalistic principle. Singh remarks further that in substantive realm the emphasis is more on culture than on social structure.

Tradition is a social fact and it has been understood differently. The course of this study has sensivitized to the different dimensions of tradition, highlighting the fact that tradition cannot be regarded as simply any type of link between the past and the present. It also requires an active display of sentiments of acceptance or rejection. The relationship between continuity and change in tradition primarily depends on the key issue of core values of a given society.

The future debates centered around the question, "Was it (tradition) the repetition of earlier patterns, or the recognition that the past is a story of change, accepting the invitation to develop what we inherit in certain ways?" and consequently the discussions on the nature of tradition, its boundaries and viabilities for change and development cannot be conceived without reference to the nature and viability of core values of a given society. Indeed, an understanding of nation, community and identity is more intimately related to the dynamic concept of tradition than one ordinarily perceives it to be.

❐

Chapter - 5

Technology of Advanced Communication

The International Classification of Functioning, Disability and Health of the World Health Organization defines disability as a "condition in which people are temporarily or definitively unable in performing an activity in the correct manner and/or at a level generally considered 'normal' for the human being." According to this definition, disability is considered a specific situation in which a person is not able to fully exploit his or her relationship with everyday contexts rather than a characteristic of the individual.

For these reasons, technological rehabilitative tools have to move from a specific activity-centered approach to a general user-centered one. In particular, the focus of technology should be the improvement of the quality of the life of the individual, through its effective support of his or her activity and interaction.

In this chapter, we consider the role of two emerging technologies-virtual reality (VR) and ambient intelligence (Ami)-in rehabilitative care. These technologies may be capable of enhancing quality of life for a variety of rehabilitation populations because of their ability to enhance the user's feeling of presence, defined as the "feeling of being in a world that exists outside the self".

More specifically, VR and Ami can be used for a new breed of rehabilitative applications focused on a strategy described as "transformation of flow." Debilitating illnesses such as Alzheimer's disease often draw individuals into themselves, and to counteract this tendency VR and Ami technologies are used to evoke a feeling of presence or engagement in the external world. The flow experience is one of feeling highly engaged with the world, a feeling that many diverse groups report as empowering.

VIRTUAL REALITY AND AMBIENT INTELLIGENCE: TWO PRESENCE-ENHANCING TECHNOLOGIES

VR can be considered the leading edge of a general evolution of communication interfaces such as television, computers, and telephones. Unlike historical communication interfaces, VR provides full immersion of the human sensorimotor channels (auditory, visual, and kinesthetic), thereby creating a vivid and global experience. VR is an advanced human-computer interface that has recently been used in rehabilitation to allow people to "interact with and become immersed in a computer-generated environment in a naturalistic fashion". Subjectively speaking, it is the feeling of presence that distinguishes VR from other interface technologies.

These aspects of VR offer two main advantages to rehabilitators. First, patients receive immediate feedback about their performance in a variety of forms and sensory modalities.

This allows for the creation and provision of more ecologically valid assessment and rehabilitation scenarios. Furthermore, it allows the provision of "cuing" stimuli or tailored sensory modality presentations designed to improve availability of assessment and rehabilitation.

In other words, the creator of the VR environment has the capability to build in systematic assessments that provide ongoing feedback regarding improvements over base-rate performance. second, the therapist/ rehabilitator using VR can create and control a dynamic and interactive 3-D scenario within an immersive environment.

Thus, VR allows for complete performance capture and the availability of a more naturalistic/intuitive performance record for review and analysis. Furthermore, it offers the capacity to pause assessment, treatment, and training for discussion and/or integration of other methods.

In a computer-generated environment such as VR, the full range of behaviour-including overt behaviour as well as physiological measures such as heart rate and galvanic skin response-can be captured and correlated with the subjective experience of research participants.

In summary, VR provides a new human-computer interaction paradigm in which users are no longer simply external observers of images on a computer screen but are active participants within a computer-generated 3- D virtual world. In a particular virtual environment created with VR technology, the patient has the possibility of learning to manage a problematic situation related to his or her diagnosis in a more realistic and ecologically valid context than is typically provided in most clinical settings.

The term ambient intelligence refers to a specific vision of the Information Society Technologies Advisory Group (ISTAG) of the European Community according to which humans will be surrounded by intelligent interfaces supported by advanced technologies distributed everywhere and embedded in everyday objects such as furniture, clothes, vehicles, and roads.

Although the term ambient technology may be specific to the ISTAG, its concepts, methods, technologies, and interfaces are shared by different groups all over Ae world. Some examples are the smart medical home concept introduced by the Centre for Future Health, the notion of pervasive human- centered computing proposed by the Oxygen MIT project, and the ubiquitous computing vision detailed by Georgia Tech.

For example, the Smart Medical Home Research Laboratory is a five-room house equipped with infrared sensors, computers, biosensors, and video cameras. The goal is to develop an integrated personal health system where all technologies are integrated seamlessly, allowing people to maintain health, detect the onset of disease, and manage existing diseases. To illustrate, the Centre for Future Health provides a video of an older person asking the system whether or not she can take an aspirin and what may be causing her headaches.

The system asks her questions about her condition, recalls her physician's advice, and notes that headaches may be a symptom of her other medications. On the practical side, Ami may be roughly described as the flip side of VR: VR puts people inside a computer generated world, and Ami puts the computer inside the real world to help us.

If combined with mobile technologies, Ami may enhance the activity of a mobile user by embedding one or more interactive Ami objects (e.g., holograms, videos, images, texts, sounds) in his or her clothes, automobile, or even a bicycle. Through "tangible user interfaces," it is possible to employ physical objects, surfaces, and spaces as specific embodiments of digital information.

For example, one can imagine an Ami interface built into a bicycle that provides information about the grade of upcoming hills, traffic approaching from all directions, and rider fatigue, and makes recommendations to the rider or even occasionally assists with pedaling.

Following this paradigm, we can embed an active interface in any assistive device, helping the user to understand how to use it effectively. In this way, tangible interfaces may transform the ambient environment (e.g., walls, desktops, ceilings, doors, windows) into an active interface between the user and his or her activity.

According to the Ami metaphor, people will live in enriched environments in which the technology is sensitive to their needs, personalized to their requirements, anticipatory of their behaviour, and responsive to their presence.

Considering the Ami-enhanced bicycle described above, such an interface would need not only to sense objective conditions such as hill grade and weather conditions, but also to assess the subjective preferences of individual riders at each particular moment.

Different riders are likely to find different kinds of information useful and be more or less willing to receive help at different times. Presumably, this assessment is made on the basis of a combination of previous experience with specific riders, sensory inputs from the present environment, and judicious questioning of the rider.

Recently, Riva introduced a psychological definition of Ami based on the experience of the user: "Ami is the effective and transparent support to the activity of the subjects through the use of information and communication technologies".

This definition suggests that the role of Ami in rehabilitation is related to its ability to support action. It also identifies effectiveness (defined as attainment of the objective of the activity) and transparency (defined as an absence of breakdowns during the activity) as the main characteristics of any rehabilitative Ami system.

Following this vision, the most important reason for developing Ami assistive tools lies in their potential to compensate or expand the activity of users through new forms of human-computer interaction. For instance, an Ami system may identify the impairment of a blind man and signal him by voice the instructions presented on a wall. Furthermore, Ami assistive tools may use gaze analysis to expand possibilities of interaction in paralyzed subjects.

PRESENCE AND AGENCY

We argue that the key feature of both VR and Ami technologies is that they offer an effective support to the activity of the subject by activating a stronger sense of presence. Presence is usually defined as the "sense of being there" or the "feeling of being in a world that exists outside the self".

A growing group of researchers considers presence as a neuropsychological phenomenon, evolved from the interplay of our biological and cultural inheritance, whose goal is to increase emotional fidelity and perceptual accuracy to produce a strong sense of agency and control.

Some VR researchers consider the subjective sense of presence in VR worlds simply a "perceptual illusion of nonmediation". However, recently some VR researchers have conceptualized presence more broadly to address the question of why people feel a sense of presence in any setting, computer generated or otherwise. In these works, presence is conceptualized as a continuous variable, so that individuals may feel different degrees of presence in different situations depending on the degree of meaning experienced in an environment.

Thus, an inhabitant of the Amazon rainforest, rich in ethnobotanical knowledge, may feel a fuller sense of presence while walking through die forest than might an urban visitor admiring the beauty. Similarly, a computer- literate person may feel a greater sense of presence while surfing the Web than might a computer novice.

From this point of view, presence has a simple but relevant role in our everyday experience: Ë is the control of agency through the unconscious separation of "internal" and "external."

The sense of presence allows the nervous system to differentiate between internal and external states. As infants develop, they learn that some aspects of their perceptual worlds (such as the movements of their arms) are part of the "self" and that other aspects of the environment (such as the movements of a mobile) are not "self." Were it not for the development of the sense of presence, it would be impossible for the nervous system to reference perceptions to an environment beyond our boundaries.

As we will see below, the meaning of "internal" and "external" is related not only to the body but also to the social, emotional, and cultural space (situation) in which the self is embedded. If this sounds far-fetched, consider the subjective experience of driving a car.

For experienced drivers, the car becomes an extension of the self. Statements such as "she's too close to my rear" or, worse, "he hit me" reveal the subjective sense of internalizing the dimensions of the car. This subjective recalibration of boundaries facilitates the greater sense of control experienced by good drivers.

From this point of view, it is important to distinguish between presence as process and presence as feeling. Presence as process is the continuous activity of the brain in separating "internal" and "external" within different kinds of afferent and efferent signals.

As emphasized by de Vignemont and Fourneret, the double sense of agency depends on the same mechanisms of action control: It results from the unconscious comparison between different kinds of afferent and efferent signals. Therefore, these monitoring systems allow one to automatically distinguish one's own actions and those of the other. Thus, presence as process can be described as a sophisticated form of monitoring of action and experience, transparent to the self but critical for its existence.

As Russell further clarified,Action-monitoring is a subpersonal process that enables the subjects to discriminate between self-determined and world- determined changes in input. It can give rise to a mode of experience (the experience of being the cause of altered inputs and the experience of being in control) but it is not itself a mode of experience.

For this reason, presence as feeling is not separated from the experience of the subject but is related to the quality of our actions. It corresponds to what Heidegger defined as "die interrupted moment of our habitual standard, comfortable being-in-the-world" Subjectively, a higher level of presence as feeling is experienced by the self as a better quality of action and experience.

However, sometimes we become aware of presence as a feeling of being separate from our being-in-the-world, as during either breakdowns or optimal experiences. Winograd and Flores refer to presence disruptions as breakdowns: A breakdown occurs when, during our activity, an aspect of our environment that we usually take for granted becomes part of our consciousness. If this happens, we shift our attention from action to the object or environment in order to cope with it.

To illustrate, imagine sitting outdoors engrossed in reading a book on a pleasant evening. As the sun sets and the light diminishes, one continues reading, engrossed in the story, until one becomes aware that the light is no longer suitable for reading. In such conditions, before any overt change in behaviour, what we experience is a breakdown in reading and a shift of attention from the book to the light illuminating the book.

It is interesting to consider why we experience such breakdowns. Our hypothesis is that breakdowns are a sophisticated evolutionary tool used to control the quality of experience, which ultimately enhances our chances of survival.

As a breakdown occurs, we experience a lower level of presence as feeling, which reduces the quality of experience and leads us to confront environmental difficulties.

On the other end of the spectrum are optimal experiences. According to Csikszentmihalyi, individuals preferentially engage in opportunities for action associated with a positive, complex, and rewarding state of consciousness known as optimal experience or flow.

There are some exceptional situations in real life in which the subject's activity is characterized by an unusually high level of presence. In these situations, the subject experiences a full sense of control and immersion.

When this experience is associated to a positive emotional state, the result is the feeling of flow. An example of flow is the case in which a professional athlete is playing exceptionally well (positive emotion) and achieves a state of mind in which all attention is focused on the game (high level of presence).

For Ghani and Deshpande, the two main characteristics of flow are total concentration on an activity and the enjoyment that one derives from the activity. Significantly, these authors identified two other factors that affect the experience of flow: a sense of control over one's environment and the level of challenge relative to a certain skill level.

TECHNOLOGY, PRESENCE, AND FLOW

A critical corollary of our vision of transformation of flow in rehabilitation is design-technologically mediated situations that elicit a state of flow by activating a high level of presence. In particular, we argue that VR and Ami are the best technologies for facilitating optimal flow experiences. In this section, we will explain the rationale behind this claim. Immersive VR is the medium most capable of activating the highest level of presence and allowing flow when connected to positive emotional experiences.

The work of Gaggioli supports this vision. Gaggioli compared the experience reported by a user immersed in a virtual environment with the experience reported by the same individual in daily situations.

To assess the quality of experience, the author used a procedure called the experience sampling method, which is based on repeated online assessments of the external situation and internal personal states of consciousness.

Results showed that VR experience was the activity associated with the highest level of optimal experience (22% of self-reports).

Reading, television viewing, and the use of other media-in the contexts of both learning and leisure activities-yielded lower percentages (15%, 8%, and 19% of self-reports, respectively) of optimal experiences.

The successful use of VR exposure in therapy highlights the possibility that a high level of presence elicited by the use of technology may help facilitate rehabilitation. VR has been used in a number of therapeutic contexts, including therapy for phobias, posttraumatic stress disorders, and pain reduction in burn patients.

Ami could be a powerful tool for increasing the level of presence in natural environments. This can be achieved by providing tools or cues that directly or indirectly support the action of the subject. Ami offers the user new tools or targeted cues that make his or her action simpler (e.g., an interactive map to make it easier to reach the clinician's office in the hospital).

It also offers indirect support by providing cues that improve the meaning given to the situation (e.g., a narrative describing the history of a church we are visiting, along with the times of church services and information about the congregation).

Authentic rehabilitation implies the active participation of patients in their contexts, their exposure to opportunities for action and development, and their freedom to select the opportunities that they perceive as most challenging and meaningful. In response to this vision, a critical asset potentially offered by VR to the rehabilitation process is the possibility of triggering optimal experiences.

Optimal experiences cultivate individual development within a given skill domain. As Massimini and Delle Fave noted, to replicate a flow experience, a person will search for increasingly complex challenges in the associated activities and will improve his or her skill, accordingly. This process has been defined as cultivation; it fosters the growth of complexity not only in the performance of flow activities but in individual behaviour as a whole.

This process can also be activated after a major trauma. As Delle Fave explained, to cope with dramatic changes in daily life and in accessing environmental opportunities for action, individuals may develop a strategy defined as transformation of flaw, a person's ability to build upon optimal experiences to identify and exploit new and unexpected resources and sources of involvement.

We hypothesize that it is possible to use VR and Ami to activate a transformation of flow to be used for rehabilitative purposes. The proposed approach begins with identification of an enriched environment that containsfanctional real-world demands.

The use of real-world demands is critical to creating a connection between subjective experience and true agency. Then, we use the technology to enhance the subjective level of presence in the environment and to induce an optimal experience. Linking agency and presence promotes cultivation by linking an optimal experience to particular abilities.

This transformation of flow not only provides positive experiences but also guides and motivates fuller engagement beyond the scope of particular VR sessions.

It is interesting to note that the proposed approach can be considered an advanced technological version of the multisensory environment approach used in the rehabilitation of the learning disabled and of older people with dementia.

Multisensory environments are purpose-built units or rooms utilized for the application of multisensory stimulation, whose goal is the stimulation of the primary senses to generate pleasurable sensory experiences in an atmosphere of trust and relaxation without the need for intellectual activity. Exposure to multisensory stimulation occurs through the agency of the care provider, nurse or therapist who facilitates the development of a relaxing and supportive environment.

The results from a recent randomized controlled trial (N = SO) showed the efficacy of this approach in the treatment of older people with dementia. In particular, the use of a multisensory environment appeared to have a greater influence on aspects of communication in comparison with one-to-one activity, and also appeared to lead to improvement in behaviour and mood at a 4-week follow-up.

We hypothesize that the VR experiences we propose will have a greater impact because they rely on the agency of the participant rather than on that of the care provider.

To verify the link between advanced technologies and optimal experiences, the V-Store project was recently carried out to investigate the quality of experience and the feeling of presence in a group of 10 patients with frontal lobe syndrome involved in VR-based cognitive rehabilitation.

On one hand, during the project the experience sampling method was used for repeated online assessments of these patients' external situations and the emotional, cognitive, and motivational components of their daily experience during 1 week, which included traditional cognitive rehabilitation and sessions of exposure to the V-Store VR environment. On the other hand, after the VR experience the ITC-Sense of Presence Inventory was used to evaluate the feeling of presence induced by the VR sessions.

Findings highlighted the association of VR sessions with both positive affect and a high level of presence. In particular, during the VR sessions "spatial presence"-the first scale of the ITC-Sense of Presence Inventory-was significantly correlated with the positive psychological feelings of "being free" and "being relaxed".

The transformation of flow may also exploit the plasticity of the brain, producing some form of functional reorganization. Optale and his team used a transformation-of-flow approach to treat male erectile disorders. They found that 30 of 36 patients with psychological erectile dysfunction and 28 of 37 clients with premature ejaculation maintained partially or completely positive response at a 6-month follow-up.

The most interesting aspect of their work is the PET scan analysis. Optale et al. used PET scans to analyse regional brain metabolism changes from baseline to follow-up in the experimental sample. The analysis of the scans showed different metabolic changes in specific areas of the brain connected with the erection mechanism.

These findings suggest that this approach may hasten the healing process and produce lasting neurological changes. The relationship between VR-based therapy and neurological functioning is an exciting avenue for further research.

Recent experimental results from the work of Hoffman and his group in the treatment of chronic pain also might be considered to foster this vision. Few experiences are more intense than the pain associated with severe burn injuries. In particular, daily wound care-the cleaning and removal of dead tissue to prevent infection-can be so painful that even the aggressive use of opioids (morphine-related analgesics) cannot control the pain.

However, it is well-known that distraction-for example, having the patient listen to music-can help to reduce pain for some people. Hoffman, Doctor, Patterson, Carrougher, and Furness conducted a controlled study of the efficacy of VR as an advanced distraction by comparing it with the efficacy of a popular Nintendo video game.

The results showed dramatic reductions in pain ratings during VR in comparison with those during the video game. Furthermore, using an fMRI scanner, they measured pain-related brain activity for each participant during conditions of VR and without VR in a study in which order was randomized.

The team studied five regions of the brain that are known to be associated with pain processing: anterior cingulate cortex, primary and secondary somatosensory cortex, insula, and thalamus. They found that during VR all these regions showed significant reductions in activity. In particular, they found direct modulation of pain responses within the brain during VR distraction. The degree of reduction in pain-related brain activity ranged from 50% to 97%.

DISCUSSION

In this chapter, we suggest the possibility of using two emerging communication technologies-Ami and VR for a new class of rehabilitative applications based on a strategy described as "transformation of flow." The vision underlying this concept arises from positive psychology. According to this vision, existing professional treatments should include positive peak experiences because they serve as triggers for a broader process of motivation and empowerment.

Within this context, transformation of flow can be defined as a person's ability to draw upon an optimal experience and use it to marshal new and unexpected psychological resources and sources of involvement.

We identified the feeling of "presence"-the feeling of being in a world that exists outside the self-as the theoretical link between the technology and transformation of flow. The technology is used to trigger a broad empowerment process within the flow experience induced by a strong sense of presence.

Two emerging technologies, VR and Ami, may facilitate these processes. By inducing a feeling of presence, VR and Ami may support a person's actions, allowing a greater subjective sense of personal efficacy.

An avenue of research that we are currently exploring concerns the use of this technologically based transformationof-flow protocol to fight the onset of Alzheimer's disease. In particular, we hypothesize that this approach could be used to target mild cognitive impairment, a pathological state that differs from normal aging characterized by objective evidence of memory impairment.

However, despite the significant advances in computer and graphic technology and the development of different VR and Ami applications, their rehabilitative use is still limited by the maturity of the systems available today. No off-the-shelf solutions are currently available.

Our experience is that rehabilitation research with VR and Ami requires much patience for dealing with conflicting hardware and software. Nearly every VR system requires a dedicated staffer at least one computer technician to keep the system running smoothly.

Testing the available technology is an important and ongoing process, so therapists and researchers must continue to investigate the application of these tools to their day to-day research and clinical practice. Finally, it is still the case that in most circumstances, today and in the foreseeable future, the clinical skills of the rehabilitator are the key factor in the successful use of any technology.

Job search is a concept that has attracted a lot of attention from scholars and practitioners. Most of the research on this issue has focused on processes and causes that determine the organizational choices of job searchers. Less research has attempted to examine the processes and determinants of what can be termed sectorial choice, namely choices between working in the public or the private sector regardless of the specific organization.

The issue of sectorial choice is an important one both for individuals seeking jobs and for policy makers in the public sector in search of qualified applicants. Yet, very little research has investigated the process of job search by looking at the sector rather than the organization as the main concept of inquiry. Two works are exceptional in this regard. Kilpatrick, Cummings and Jennings examined work values and image of employees in the Federal Service.

Their book attempted to shed some light on the issue of sectorial choice, but limited research directly followed the issues raised by it.

A more recent work by Blank examined and compared demographic characteristics of employees in the public and private sectors. The main finding of that paper was that groups protected by federal laws, such as minorities and veterans, tended to work in the public sector.

One goal of this study is to stimulate more research that may make conceptual as well as practical contributions. Instead of elaborating on the limitations of research on this topic, we adopted use some of the ideas of the two studies mentioned above. Kilpatrick et al.'s notion of the importance of the image of the public sector is applied here by using the concept of public sector image as one of the main determinants of tendency to work in the public sector.

Blank's study was the first to propose a model of factors that determines whether one is a public or private sector employee. Some of the determinants proposed by Blank are applied here. While Blank's model is based on demographic determinants, our model includes psychological as well as experience variables together in addition to the public sector image variables.

Although this study of final-year Israeli students was exploratory, three specific research questions were advanced and tested. First, what are the determinants of public sector image; second, what are the determinants of the tendency to work in the public sector; third, do the determinants of tendency to work in the public sector relate to it directly or indirectly through the mediating effect of the public sector image.

The answers to these research questions were expected to contribute to the literature by providing new data about an issue that has been inadequately examined. Beside the expectation that the findings of this study will stimulate more research on the issue, the data provided here may provide policy makers in the public sector with new ideas and ways to attract qualified applicants to the public sector.

CONCEPTUAL FRAMEWORK

The concept explained here is the tendency to work in the public sector. Ajzen and Fishbein and Ryan argued that intention to behave in a certain way is the linkage between attitudes and behaviour. That is, understanding the reasons for high versus low tendency to work in the public sector has important implications for understanding the actual decisions of applicants whether or not to work in a public sector organization.

A concept advanced by Perry and Wise, the closest concept to tendency to work in the public sector, is motivation to work in the public sector. Perry and Wise proposed three categories of reasons that are related to such motivation: rational motives, such as participation in the process of policy design, normative motives, such as willingness to serve the public interest, and emotional motives, such as commitment to the public sector resulting from an inner believe in its social importance.

The concept examined here, tendency to work in the public sector, is similar to the one proposed by Perry and Wise but is more suitable for our target population, namely final-year students. Because our interest here is what causes prospective employees to decide to work or not to work in the public sector, tendency to work in this sector seems to be a more appropriate concept for examination.

Another reason to prefer this concept is that the relationship between tendencies towards a given behaviour and the actual behaviour is not always close. Thus one may have a low tendency to work in the public sector, but in the absence of any real alternative in the private sector may decide to work in the public sector regardless. Note that a person may choose a job not in accordance with his or her preferences because when the organizational choice had to be made no employment alternatives existed in the preferred sector.

In this research we were particularly interested in the tendencies, not necessarily on the actual behaviour. We wished to explore possible reasons why job in the public sector seemed attractive. As stated, this in itself can provide scholars and policy makers with important information on how to attract employees to the public sector.

Once we determined that the concept of under investigation here was the tendency to work in the public sector, it was only natural that the conceptual framework for developing a model of proposed determinants of this tendency would be based on the literature of job search and job choice.

Moss and Frieze contended that the process of job choice has two main parts: first, early socialization, when the individual develop expectations and accumulates information on alternative jobs; second, the actual job search and job choice. Lord and Kerman argued that information on the prospective job and organization is collected before the entry into the organization.

Individuals collect and process information on different jobs from childhood onward. Gatewood et al. explained that the process of job choice is one of information evaluation. Individuals collect information from two main sources to decide whether to seek work in a given organization: (1) informal, such as family and friends; (2) formal, such as newspaper ads and employment agencies. Getewood et al. argued that information from informal sources is more important for people than that from formal sources.

The above studies suggest that the roots of decisions on employment in the public sector might be found very early in a person's life. An interesting research question in this regard is how the process of accumulation of information on employment alternatives affects one's image of the public sector. The role of socialization mentioned by Gatewood et al. seemed to be closely relevant to the research subject at hand, namely tendency to employment in the public sector, so aspects of socialization were examined in this respect.

The literature on job search and job choice has naturally concentrated on the organizational level. Two concepts from this research seemed to be most relevant to this research and were integrated into its conceptual model. The first is the concept of person-organization fit, which refers to the fit between one's personality, values and beliefs and the strategic needs, norms, and values of the organization.

The fit is created partly by the organization in the selection process and partly by the organizational socialization process. The literature has emphasized several aspects of fit between the individual and the organization: fit between one's knowledge, qualifications, and abilities and one's job requirements; fit between one's needs and the organizational structure as well as its support systems; fit between one's values and the organization's perceived image or personality.

The concept of person-organization fit provides the conceptual framework for this research. It leads to the idea that prospective employees gather information about the public sector and evaluate the fit between their characteristics and those of the public sector.

The outcomes of this evaluation affect their decisions whether to consider the public sector as an employment alternative favorably or not. This assumption is in line with Cable and Judge, who argued that the theory of person-organization fit can explain employment decisions of prospective employees. Bowen et al.'s approach to the concept of person-organization fit emphasizes the organizational image as an important component of the fit.

Organizational image is the second important concept adopted for this research from the job-choice literature. Rynes defined organizational image as a general impression of the attractiveness of the organization.

This impression is based on the amount of information the applicants have at the first stages of their job search, and it affects their preliminary decisions. The importance of the organizational image on employment decisions was emphasized by several scholars. The organizational image is determined by social and cultural processes. People are prepared for a realistic level of expectations of the job, and this preparation is accomplished done by a variety of socialization agencies such as school, home, community, and the media.

We are interested not so much in the organizational image as in the sectorial one, more specifically, in the image of the public sector. The literature on this issue is sparse, so some reliance on the organizational image literature was necessary. In analogy with Rynes's definition of organizational image, we defined sectorial image as a general impression of the attractiveness of the public sector, which affects employment decision.

The few studies that have looked into the issue of sectorial image are quite old, and rather limited in their methods. In some of these studies the public sector image was measured by one item and not by scales tested for their reliabilities and validated for their psychometric properties. Yet despite their limitations, the studies on sectorial image found in general that the image of the public sector was not favorable among American employees.

Jasper, who examined engineering graduates and novice engineers, concluded that the general feeling of the group appeared to be that government employment carried a stigma. The students pictured the engineer working for the government as primarily interested in security and felt that employees hired by the government were generally mediocre in ability.

The above studies found what seems to be a prevalent negative image/reputation of the public sector, particularly regarding its employees and work in its organizations.

RESEARCH MODEL AND HYPOTHESES

Following the literature, we anticipated that our research population, students before graduation, would develop expectations and gather information on various jobs. This stage is preparatory to the next, which is the actual selection. This study focused on one specific and defined question out of the many possible here, namely if there is a sectorial choice, and if so, what are some of its determinants.

Here we set out the research model and its hypotheses. Two of the main concepts of the model have been discussed above: the dependent variable, tendency to work in the public sector, and the mediating variable, public sector image. The independent variables will be described below, together with our hypotheses regarding their relationships with the mediator and the dependent variables.

The model consists of three groups of independent variables: demographic variables, background and experience variables, and personal- psychological variables. The first group of hypotheses concerns the relationship between the independent variables and the dependent variable, tendency to work in the public sector.

Because we anticipated that public sector image would be positively related to tendency to work in the public sector, we expected the same pattern of relationship between the independent variables and tendency to work in the public sector to prevail for the relationship between the independent variables and public sector image.

Therefore, in the hypotheses section we do not elaborate on the relationship between the dependent variables and public sector image but we analyse these relationships in the results section and discuss their implications in the discussion. The main hypothesis of this research was the anticipation of a mediating relationship. That is, sectorial image will mediate the relationship between the independent variables and the tendency to work in the public sector.

DEMOGRAPHIC VARIABLES

The main rationale to expect demographic characteristics to be related to tendency to work in the public sector is that deprived groups in society, such as minorities and women, will tend to work in an employment environment where they are more protected and less discriminated. The public sector is considered to be such an environment.

Arabs are a deprived minority in Israel and work in the public sector was found to assist them in earning higher wages and suffering less discrimination than in the private one. It was thus logical to expect a greater tendency to work in the public sector among Arab students than among Jewish students, and for Arab students to hold a more positive image of this sector.

By the same token it could be argued that immigrants students, those not born in Israel, would also prefer employment in the public sector. Immigrants constitute an unprotected social group that will search for employment that can provide them more job security and less discrimination, namely employment in the public sector.

Dolton, Makepeace, and Inchley argued that the public sector is one of the more popular employment choices among women. Their income there is higher than in the private sector and they are less discriminated there than in the private sector.

Women may be expected to demonstrate more positive image of the pubic sector and higher tendency to work there than men. Following this logic it could also be expected that married students would prefer employment in the public sector. Blank argued that the public sector attracts employees looking for job security, and married people are more vulnerable in terms of the costs of losing their jobs.

Therefore the public sector can be an attractive alternative for them. Finally it could be expected that older students would tend to work in a more stable environment and be less willing to take risks in their career than younger students.

Job security would be a stronger consideration for older students and this would impel them towards employment in the public sector. Thus, according to Hypothesis 1 (H1) Arabs, immigrants, females, married, and older students will have a more positive image of the public sector and higher tendency to work there.

BACKGROUND AND EXPERIENCE VARIABLES

The literature has emphasized the role of socialization in determining one's organizational choice. Most of the variables that follow represent earlier experiences of students that could shape and affect their attitudes to employment in the public sector. One of them is the major discipline studied by the student. The difference will be between students whose major is in the social sciences and those whose major is in humanities.

The importance of this factor was advanced by Kilpatrick et al. The rationale is that social sciences students feel that they have studied something of practical value that make them more attractive in the job market and can assist them in finding a job. Students in humanities feels that what they have studied has less practical value and relatively little to offer in the private sector, so they will prefer employment in the public sector, with its reputation of being less selective than the private.

Kilpatrick et al. also argued that the average grades of students also affect their decision to choose employment in the private or public sector. Students with higher grades have more alternatives and are more valuable in the employment market, considering that new graduates generally have no work experience.

This fact makes the average grades the main measure of quality graduates' as job applicants. Those with higher grades will feel more competent and confident to search for a job in the private rather than the public sector, so they will have a lower tendency to work in the latter.

Treadwell and Harrison emphasized the role of work experience as one of the main socialization agents. Students who have worked at part-time jobs in the public sector acquired a more realistic perception of the employment there, which probably be more positive than what they had before working in it.

They will have acquired more accurate information about employment there, including the sector's advantages and benefits. It was thus expected that students who had worked in the public sector would have a stronger tendency to work there and a more positive image of the employment there.

By the same token we posited that students also with work experience but with higher income have experienced its benefits, and because higher income is commonly associated with employment in the private sector, such students may be expected to prefer employment in that sector.

They would avoid the public sector, which is certainly not associated with high income. The role of the perception of alternative employment opportunities has been mentioned in the literature as an important criterion in the process of job search. Individuals who perceive that they have less employment alternatives and opportunities, regardless of the reasons, will tend to look for a job with more security.

In that way they will not have to go back to the job market, which is not promising for them as job seekers. Thus, according to Hypothesis 2 (H2) students whose major is in the social sciences, whose average grades are lower, who have had more work experience in the public sector, and a lower income, and who perceive that they have fewer alternatives in the job market, will have a more positive image of the public sector and will have a stronger tendency to work there.

PERSONAL PSYCHOLOGICAL VARIABLES

Leary, Wheeler, and Jenkins argued that personal characteristics are related to employment choices. Moss and Frieze explained that individuals choose the one that has the best fit with their needs.

The rationale of person-organization fit, the main conceptual framework of this research, also supports the inclusion of personal-psychological variables as determinants of tendency to work in the public sector. Several personal variables are included here.

Kilduff argued that people with low self-monitor will feel more comfortable in a work environment that emphasizes more autonomy, and more personal freedom, in comparison with people with high self-monitor who will prefer a more conformist environment. Those with low self-monitor will prefer an environment that has clear and formal expectations of their role in the organization.

Accordingly, we expected students with low self-monitor to prefer an environment with more autonomy and tolerating more self-expression, while students with high self-monitor would prefer employment in the public sector, which is considered a more conformist environment than that which they would probably find in the private sector.

It was also expected here that students with external locus of control would prefer employment in the public sector. Students with internal locus of control would attribute success to ability and performance.

This would strengthen their preference for employment in the private sector, which seems to emphasize effort and results.

A person with external locus of control attributes his or her success to external causes, and will prefer stable employment where the compensation and promotion systems are regulated by laws and formal procedures generated by the government.

A person with external locus of control will feel less vulnerable in employment in the public sector.

Two needs variables were also included in the group of personal-psychological determinants. First, students with low need for achievement would prefer employment in the public sector. The rationale is similar to the one outlined in the psychological variables mentioned above.

Students with high need for achievement are more ambitious and value competition in order to achieve their goals. Those with low need for achievement would prefer stability and security over competition, and the public sector is considered a stable and secure environment.

Finally, it was strongly expected that students with high need for security would prefer employment in the public sector. Blank argued that because the goal of the public sector is not profit it attracts job seekers with higher need for security.

Employees in the public sector are and feel more secure in terms of losing their job and it could be expected that students with a high need for need security would prefer employment in the public sector.

Thus according to Hypothesis 3 (H3) students with high self-monitor, external locus of control, low need for achievement and high need for security will have a positive image of the public sector and higher tendency to work there.

THE MEDIATING ROLE OF PUBLIC SECTOR IMAGE

The research model suggests that the relationship between the above-mentioned determinants and tendency to work in the public sector is not direct but mediated by the image of the public sector.

Kilpatrick et al. were among the very few researchers who examined and emphasized the concept of public sector image. Rynes in a more recent work defined public sector image as a general impression of the attractiveness of the sector, which affect employment choice.

Krau and Ziv argued that the image of employment in the public service mediates the relationship between the characteristics of employment there and the employment choice of individuals.

The expectation here for a mediated relationship is based on the following rationale.

Average students are in their early stages of job search, and without stable and permanent employment all they have developed is an image of different aspects of the public sector. Thus, the determinants mentioned above are related first to the perceived image of the public sector.

Demographic, work experience, and personal-psychological characteristics all function to shape the image of the public sector starting from childhood and during the years of study at university. The importance of the image is emphasized by the person-organization fit theory.

Prospective employees evaluate their characteristics and those of the organization, and choose the one that has the best fit with their characteristics. The image that is the result of these determinants is directly related to the tendency to work in the public sector. Thus according to Hypothesis 4 (H4) the relationship between the determinants and the tendency to work in the public sector will be mediated by the image of the public sector.

METHOD

The target population of this study was 1640 third-year undergraduate students of most of the departments at an Israeli university. Departments that were not included in the sample were Law, Social work, Art, Nursing, Occupational therapy, Department of Teaching and Teacher education. The reason for not including them is because in the Israeli setting the graduates of these departments do not have much of a sectorial choice.

Most of the available jobs for students in Law and Art departments are in the private sector and most of the available jobs for students in Social work, Occupational therapy, Teaching and Teacher education are in the public sector. In all the other departments graduates have more available jobs in both sectors and therefore it was decided to include in the sample only students from such departments. Therefore, all 1640 third-year students from these departments were defined as the target population and were asked to participate in the study.

Questionnaires were distributed by mail to the home address of each of them. After two waves of distributions, 660 usable questionnaires were returned, a response rate of 40%, which was acceptable considering that this was a mail survey.

A breakdown of respondents by their major subject showed that 76% of the sample were social sciences students, 64% were females, 86% were Jews, and 14% were Arabs. Respondents' average age was 25.8 years (s.d.= 4.1); 84% of them were born in Israel, 22% were married, 70% had a part- or a full-time jobs, and 50% had some experience in working in the public sector.

A comparison of the sample with some characteristics of the entire population as provided by the university administration, revealed that 64% were female in the target population, a percentage identical to that in the sample; 76% were Jews in the target population, compared with 86% in the sample; 57% were social sciences students in the target population, compared with 76% in the sample.

The differences are reasonable, so we may generalize from the sample to the target population.

DATA ANALYSIS

The main statistical analyses in this study were multiple and hierarchical regressions. To support the hypotheses regarding the mediated relationship between the independent variables and the dependent variable, we followed Baron and Kenny and James and Brett. According to them, a mediating relationship can be supported by one or more of the following methods:

- Regression analysis,
- ANOVA or MANOVA,
- Testing for interactions.

Nevertheless, Baron and Kenny elaborated on the simplicity and the effectiveness of regression analysis, compared with the limited test for mediation in other methods such as ANOVA. Accordingly, we applied the regression analysis method, in which, as described by Baron and Kenny, to test for mediation one estimates the following three regression equations.

First, the mediator is regressed on the independent variable, whereby the independent variable must affect the mediator. Second, the dependent variable is regressed on the independent variable, whereby the independent variable must affect the dependent variable.

Third, the dependent variable is regressed on both the independent variable and on the mediator, whereby the mediator must affect the dependent variable. If these conditions all hold in the predicted direction, then the effect of the independent variable on the dependent variable must be less in the third equation than in the second.

FINDINGS

First we examined the two scales for the public sector image to find whether the items of the two scales should be treated as multi-dimensional or unidimensional. Exploratory factor analysis of the 32 items of the two scales was performed, and produced three factors; 14 of the 15 items of the image of public sector employee loaded strongly on the first factor, and 13 of the 17 items of image of public sector employment loaded strongly on the second factor.

Three items of the employment image loaded on a third factor, and one item of employee image did not load on any of the factors. This finding supported in general the existence of two separate dimensions. But two other indications supported the treatment of the two dimensions as one scale. One of these was the relatively high correlation between the two scales (r=.66).

Note, however, that a correlation of.66 is still acceptable in terms of treating the two constructs as separate dimensions. The other indication was that the reliability of the 32 items was very high (.97) and supported the notion that the two scales were in fact one construct.

One can see that the findings above are not conclusive in terms of making a clear decision whether to treat public sector image as a unidimensional or a multidimensional construct. Therefore, we decided to analyse and present the data with the public sector image as a unidimensional and a multidimensional construct.

The findings show good reliabilities and good psychometric properties of research variables. The correlations among the independent variables were not high except for the correlation between employment status and income. These findings support the absence of multicollinearity.

Note that although the variables in this study were based on self-report data, allowing source bias or general method variance, the low correlations among the independent variables demonstrate the absence of common method error. The correlation matrix shows negative relationships between tendency to work in the public sector and the three public sector image scales.

Some consistency can be found in the relationships between the demographic variables and the public sector image variables as well as the tendency to work in the public sector. This is strongly supported for the variables ethnicity, country of origin, major studies, and average grade. The variable experience in the public sector is also related significantly to the image variables and to the variable tendency to work in the public sector.

Note, too, the lack of relationship between the personal-psychological variables and the image variables. Tendency to work in the public sector was related to two psychological variables (self-monitor and need for security). In short, the correlations provide some support for hypotheses 1 and 2 and weaker support for hypothesis 3.

In each of the equations the mediating variables (public sector image of employment, employee, and the total scale) were regressed on the independent variables. Also, the dependent variable was regressed on the independent variables. The findings generally support the two terms for mediation mentioned above.

First, significant relationships existed between the independent variables and the dependent variable. Variables representing each group of the independent variables (demographic, experiences, and psychological) were related to tendency to work in the public sector. As for the relationships between the mediating and the dependent variable, the findings showed significant relationships between the two that support the second term of mediation.

These relationships were stronger for the image of employee and for the total scale of image than for the image of employment. The general conclusion is that the findings meet the first and second requirement for mediation as described by Baron and Kenny.

Conceptually, the findings provide stronger support for hypotheses 1 and 2 than for hypothesis 3. Hypothesis 1 predicted that demographic variables would be related to public sector image and to tendency to work in the public sector.

While the demographic variables were not related to the image of employment in the public sector, the findings show that males and Arabs had a more positive image of employee in the public sector, and Arabs had a stronger tendency to work there than Jews. This provides some support for hypothesis 1.

Stronger support was found for hypothesis 2. Three of the experience variables were related to the image of the public sector. Students whose major was humanities had a more positive image of the public sector in all the three dimensions tested here. Students with higher grades had a more negative image of the public sector in all the dimensions.

Students with some work experience in the public sector had a more positive image of employee in the public sector. The above significant relationship was found for the total image scale but not the image of employment. Two of the experience variables were related to tendency to work in the public sector. Students whose major was in humanities and students with some work experience in the public sector had a stronger tendency to work there. Altogether, the findings seem to provide solid support for hypothesis 2.

Hypothesis 3 predicted that the psychological variables would be related to image of the public sector and to the tendency to work there, and it received partial support by the data. None of the psychological variables was related to any of the public sector images, and this finding was not expected. Hypothesis 3 was supported by the relationship of two of the psychological variables to tendency to work in the public sector.

As expected, students with low self-monitor, and with high need for security, had stronger tendency to work in the public sector. The variables locus of control and need for achievement were not related to the image variables or to tendency to work in the public sector. In all it may be concluded that hypothesis 3 was only partially supported by the data.

This two-step regression was proposed by Ferris, Frink, Bhawuk, and Zhou to allow a more sensitive evaluation of the third condition for mediation: the mediators must affect the dependent variable, and, more importantly, the effect of the independent variables on the dependent variable must be less in the last equation (the relationship between the independent variables and the dependent variable) than in the second steps.

As mentioned this was done twice, when first public sector was treated as multidimensional and when in a second set of equations the public sector image was analysed as one scale. The mediating factors were entered into the equation in the first step while all other independent variables were entered in the second one.

The findings provide empirical support for condition. First, the data strongly show that public sector image was strongly related to tendency to work in the public sector. Most of the variance in tendency to work in the public sector was due to the effect of public sector image, while all other variables contributed 10% or 11% to the total explained variance.

Although this estimation was not part of the research hypotheses one should note the significant effect of the mediators on tendency to work in the public sector. This finding supports the rationale of hypothesis 4, which expected strong relationships between public sector image, as mediating factors, and the dependent variable, tendency to work in the public sector.

The data strongly support hypothesis 4 when we compare the last equation with the two second step equations. The data clearly show that the effect of the independent variables was less in the regression equation than in the two regressions.

All these findings are much in line with the third condition for mediation of Baron and Kenny. In short, the findings provide empirical support for hypothesis 4, namely public sector image mediated the relationship between all the independent variables and tendency to work in the public sector.

DISCUSSION

One of the goals of this study was to draw more attention by scholars to an issue that has been overlooked for many years and to stimulate more research on this important topic. The findings of this study support most of the basic arguments advanced by this chapter. First, tendency to work in the public sector is a construct that has a meaning for students who are exploring their possibilities in the job market.

The same can be said about the concept of public sector image that was also advanced here. Moreover, the two concepts are related, and the image of the public sector mediated the relationship between the proposed determinants and tendency to work in the public sector. Thus, despite the somewhat exploratory nature of this study since, very little research has been conducted on the issue, the findings show that the topic examined offers a promising and challenging research agenda for the future.

The findings of this study provide general support to the very few and somewhat old studies on this issue. Kilpatrick et al. set out the notion that the image one has about the public sector can affect one's attitudes and behaviour.

This idea was elaborated here and tested by use of valid and reliable scales with more advanced methodology than that employed by Kilpatrick et al. The scales we proposed and tested captured two important dimensions of the public sector image: the image of its employees and the image of employment in the public sector.

The findings were not conclusive in determining whether public sector image is a multidimensional or unidimensional construct. While the relatively high correlation between the two suggests that perhaps they should be treated as unidimensional it seems that a multidimensional perspective was better supported by the data.

Some interesting differences between their determinants supported the notion that they are distinct. For example image of employment was related only to two experience variables while image of employee was related also to gender ethnicity and country of origin. Future research should test the scales proposed here to arrive to a more definite conclusion whether image of the public sector is a unidimensional or a multidimensional construct.

Regardless of this methodological aspect in both its unidimensional and multidimensional form, the findings here showed the potential of image of the public sector as a concept able to increase understanding of prospective employees' decision whether or not to work in the public sector.

The findings strongly supported the notion that public sector image mediates the relationship between determinants and tendency to work in the public sector. That is, demographic, background, and experience variables work to shape the image one has of the public sector, and this image determines one's tendency to work in that sector.

This process emphasizes the role of socialization in shaping one's image of the public sector, and supports Moss and Frieze's argument that socialization is an important component in the job search and job choice processes. The relationship between work experience in the public sector and the image of the public sector supports Lord and Kerman's argument that the information on the prospective job and organization is collected before entry into the organization.

The findings here show, as suggested by Gatewood et al., that the process of sectorial choice is one of information evaluation. Individuals collect information that assists them to decide whether to get an employment in a given organization, in this case the public sector.

The findings of this study also support earlier findings of Blank, who examined demographic determinants of workers' choice between employment in the public or private sector.

Blank's study differs from this one because it examined and compared employees from both the public and the private sectors, while ours examined tendency to work in the public sector among students. Yet some similarities between the findings of the two studies exist.

First, Blank's main findings showed that non-whites and veterans, groups protected by federal employment laws, preferred the public sector but women had no statistically distinguishable preference between the sectors. Blank's finding was supported in general by the findings here. Arab students, a relatively deprived minority in Israel, preferred employment in the public sector and had a more positive image of the public sector than Jewish students.

It may be concluded that minorities prefer employment in the public sector because they feel more protected by the laws and regulations in it, regardless of culture and country. Another interesting finding is that in both studies gender had no significant effect on employees' working in the public sector in Blank's study, or on students' tendency to work in the public sector here.

This finding showed that, regarding employment in the public sector, gender becomes less important in the process of making a sectorial choice.

Other characteristics affect females' decisions in both cultures whether or not to work in the public sector, not the anticipation that they will be more protected in the public sector. This conclusion needs to be tested in future research.

Another finding by Blank was that employees with lower education preferred the public sector, while those with higher education or more experience seemed to prefer the private sector. The logic of Blank's finding was in a way supported here.

Education represents human capital, and those with more of this resource felt more confident to compete in the private sector. In this study, grades and major subject represent human capital for students. It is not surprising that students whose major was in social sciences and who won higher grades thought that by having more human capital they had more options in the job market and could compete successfully in the private sector.

This was demonstrated here in the negative image that students with higher grades had of the public sector and in the stronger tendency of students whose major was in humanities to work in the public sector.

The findings here provide support for human-capital theory in the sense that prospective employees with more human capital do not perceive work in the public sector as employment that will enable them to capitalize on their resources. This study's contribution is to show that what Blank found for employees can be predicted prior to their joining the workforce. Our findings in the Israeli setting accord with those of Jasper for engineering graduates and novice engineers noted above.

The findings here, almost 40 years later and in another culture, seem to support those of Jasper. Note, however, that many differences exist between the above studies, particularly between Blank's work and this one. A major difference is the inclusion in our model of public sector image, which was strongly supported by the data.

Another notable finding is the relatively weak effect of the psychological variables. These had no effect on any of the public sector image forms. This finding emphasizes the role of socialization and not personality in shaping one's attitudes to employment in the public sector. But one cannot ignore the strong effect of personality on tendency to work in the public sector.

This was demonstrated in the significant effect of self-monitor and more especially need for security, on this tendency. This finding shows that certain personalities tend to look for employment in the public sector. The strong effect of need for security shows that not only is the public sector a better environment for protected groups such as minorities, but this pattern is also relevant for those who feel unprotected whether or not they are in a protected group. These finding needs to be replicated in future research before definite conclusions can be made.

The findings here strongly support the conceptual framework of person-organization fit as appropriate to understanding of the determinants of tendency to work in the public sector. This theory postulates that what determines one's choice is the fit between one's personality, values, and beliefs and the strategic needs, norms, and values of the organization.

The findings here emphasize the fit from the individuals' point of view. Prospective employees who are from a minority group (Arabs), who are not especially trained (major in humanities and not social sciences), who have some work experience in the public sector, whose personality leans towards a more conformist formalized and dependency environment, and above all who have a strong need for security, prefer to work in the public sector.

Support for the person-organizational fit framework is reinforced by the significant effect of two psychological variables on tendency to work in the public sector. This effect supports the approach emphasizing the fit between the individuals' personality and the perceived organizational image or personality. The effect of the psychological variables was not evident in the relationship between the psychological variables and image of the public sector.

This study offers some practical implications particularly for policy makers. While all will agree on the need to increase the quality of the workforce in the public sector, this study offers new insights into how to do it. Image was found here as a key concept affecting students=tendency to work in the public sector.

Some prospective employees will not choose the public sector because of its negative image. But this image can be shaped and influenced. For example, providing students with some experience in the public sector is one practical way to improve the image of the public sector and increase the tendency to work there.

Providing social sciences graduates with information on the advantages of working in the public sector is another way to attract them to the public sector. Improving the image of the public sector will probably attract more excellent students.

Person-organization fit theory postulates that the fit can be created by the organization in the selection or the socialization process. The effect of the variable experience in the public sector emphasizes the ability of public organizations to use the socialization process to attract qualified employees to the public sector.

The effect of the two psychological variables suggests that the selection process can be used to detect these psychological characteristics. But first a strategic decision has to be made by organizations: do they want employees with high selfmonitor and high need for security? If not, applicants possessing these two characteristics might be rejected. Image is one of the reasons why people who feel less confident about themselves choose to work in the public sector.

Improving the public-sector image will probably result in more quality applicants wishing to work in the public sector. This study showed some ways by which the image of the public sector can be enhanced, but much more work is needed to explore other factors that shape it.

Finally, several limitations of this study must be considered. First, because this research examined students, there may be limits to the generalizability of the findings to other populations, especially employees. second, the study relied on self-report data, allowing for the possibility of same-source bias, a common problem with cross-sectional, non-behavioral measurement.

Because the multivariate analysis considered the simultaneous effects of all variables, the extent of this problem was reduced. Third, much of the work on public sector employment has concentrated on American employees, which limits ability to generalize findings across other cultures and settings. While the American data are very important, there must be more diversity in the cultures and nations that are tested. This chapter has attempted to show the usefulness of such research in another culture, the Israeli one, and also to propose some directions for nature study.

Despite the limitations, this study has some important contributions. The findings here demonstrate the importance of public sector image and tendency to work in the public sector as important considerations for understanding sectorial choice of prospective employees. The proposed model has some important conceptual and practical implications that can direct future research. More research on this issue seems warranted in light of the findings and before solid conclusions can be made on the findings here. The contribution of this study is its proposing some promising directions for research on an interesting and important issue.

❐

Chapter - 6

Technology in Preparing Youth

Today, technology has become essential in almost every educational, employment, community, and recreational environment. Access to electronic and information technology can help students with a wide range of abilities and disabilities prepare for and succeed in adult life. Specifically, for people with disabilities, such access has the potential to maximize independence, productivity and participation in academic programmes, employment, recreation and other adult activities. In addition, for those who have the interest and aptitude, advanced technology skills can open doors to high tech career fields that were once unavailable to people with disabilities.

Although the benefits of technology may be even greater for people with disabilities than for people without disabilities, individuals with disabilities are less than half as likely as their non-disabled counterparts to own computers, and they are about one-quarter as likely to use the Internet. In addition, the design of many Web pages, instructional software programmes, productivity tools, telecommunications products, and other electronic and information technologies erects barriers for some individuals with disabilities.

For example, Web pages that do not include text alternatives that can be read by speech and Braille output systems limit information access by a student who is blind or is a poor reader; the content of a videotape that does not have captions is inaccessible to a viewer who is deaf; software with a high reading level may not be accessible to people with learning disabilities or developmental disabilities; and office equipment that cannot be operated from a seated position is inaccessible to an employee who uses a wheelchair for mobility.

Taking advantage of the power that technology offers in improving the precollege and postsecondary academic outcomes for individuals with experience far less career success than their non-disabled peers. However, these differences in achievement diminish between individuals as they gain more education.

For example, the employment rate for individuals with disabilities who do not complete high school is 15.6%; for those who complete high school it is 30.2%; for those with some postsecondary education it is 45.1%; and for those with four years of college it is 50.3%. Clearly, technology access that leads to greater success in precollege and postsecondary education has the potential to improve career outcomes for people with disabilities.

Today, individuals with disabilities are significantly underrepresented in postsecondary education and a significantly lower percentage of students with disabilities than those without disabilities eventually earn degrees. The largest and fastest growing disability among freshmen who report having disabilities is learning disability - 40.4% in 2000 as compared to 16.1% in 1988. Percentages of students with disabilities reporting other types of disabilities are 16.1% blindness or partial sight, 15.4% health-related impairments, 8.6% hearing impairments, 7.1% orthopedic impairments, 2.9% speech impairments, and 16.9% other impairments.

Even those who complete postsecondary studies are likely to have fewer work-based learning experiences than those who do not have disabilities. Lack of job skills and related experiences before graduation create additional barriers to employment for people with disabilities.

The poor employment figures for people with disabilities coupled with the positive impact of postsecondary education and work-related experiences make increasing their success in these activities an important goal. The cost of failure to reach this goal, to these individuals and to society, is high.

High-tech careers are particularly accessible to individuals with disabilities because of the combined effect of the increasing use of electronic and information technology and of the advancements in assistive technology that provide access to computers and other electronic equipment for people with a variety of disabilities. A bachelor's degree or higher is a prerequisite for many of these challenging careers.

Although few students with disabilities pursue high-tech postsecondary programmes and careers and the attrition rate is high, those who succeed in these fields demonstrate that opportunities do exist for people with disabilities who successfully overcome the barriers imposed by facilities, electronic and information technology inadequate academic preparation, lack of role models, and negative attitudes.

In order for students with disabilities to pursue postsecondary academic and career options, they must have access to the high-tech tools available to their nondisabled peers. These include computers, websites, telecommunications products, instructional software, and scientific equipment. Full access requires that built-in barriers to these tools and resources as well as facilities in which they are housed be removed and appropriate assistive technology be readily available.

Today, the full potential of using technology to prepare young people with disabilities for postsecondary education is not being realized. Funding is reported as the top barrier by service providers and policy experts. Consumers identify the two biggest barriers to be lack of knowledge of stakeholders about appropriate assistive technology and lack of funding to purchase assistive technology.

Many graduates of teacher education programmes are not adequately prepared in the general use of computer technology and in classroom applications. In addition, as reported by the National Council on Disability, "the rapid acquisition of educational technology has not sufficiently addressed the needs of students with disabilities. Access for students with disabilities is just beginning to be identified as an important factor when purchasing educational technology."

Consequently, products with inaccessible characteristics are often purchased, inaccessible electronic resources and educational software are developed and procured, and inaccessible facilities are constructed. Many computer support staff, regular education teachers, and special education teachers are not sufficiently trained to use mainstream and specialized equipment and on how these technologies can work together to maximize access to education for students with disabilities.

As summarized by Hasselbring and Glaser, "Lack of adequate teacher training has an especially strong impact on students with disabilities because technology is often a critical component in planning and implementing an educational programme for these students."

Other barriers to technology access for individuals with disabilities include lack of trained professionals to evaluate assistive technology, difficulties in locating assistive technology for testing by individuals with disabilities, confusion about existing laws and policies regarding assistive technology and accessible electronic and information technology, gaps in laws and policies that fund assistive technology, and the bureaucracy of public programmes and insurance companies.

In particular, because of differences in laws and funding for technology between precollege and college environments, even students who are lucky enough to gain access to empowering technology in precollege settings may not be allowed to take it with them when they exit high school.

Clearly, much work needs to be done before the full potential of today's technology to promote postsecondary academic and career success for students with disabilities is realized.

Although it is easier to agree on the problems that exist than the interventions that will overcome them, most would agree that the situation would be much improved if the following three conditions were assured.

- All individuals with disabilities have access to technology that promotes positive academic and career outcomes.
- People with disabilities learn to use technology in ways that contribute to positive postsecondary academic and career outcomes and self-determined lives.
- There is a seamless transition of availability of technology for all people with disabilities as they move from K-12 to postsecondary to career environments.

This chapter defines terminology related to the use of technology by people with disabilities. Then, it describes what specific roles technology can play in preparing young people with disabilities for postsecondary education and employment. Next, legal issues in precollege education, postsecondary academic, and employment settings are discussed.

After that, is a summary of key issues that must be addressed in order for young people with disabilities to gain the full benefits that technology has to offer as they make the transitions from precollege education to postsecondary education and employment. Finally, implications and recommendations are suggested.

TERMINOLOGY

Throughout this chapter, technology includes electronic and information technology and assistive technology that provides access to electronic and information technology. Information technology is defined as "any equipment or interconnected system or subsystem of equipment, that is used in the automatic acquisition, storage, manipulation, management, movement, control, display, switching, interchange, transmission, or reception of data or information.

The term information technology includes computers, ancillary equipment, software, firmware and similar procedures, services (including support services), and related resources." Electronic technology encompasses information technology, but also includes any equipment or interconnected system or subsystem of equipment that is used in the creation, conversion, or duplication of data or information.

Electronic technology includes telecommunications products such as telephones and office equipment such as copiers and fax machines. Many electronic and information technology products are designed in such a way that they are inaccessible to people with some types of disabilities.

For example, a person with a visual impairment may not be able to interpret instructions if they are presented only in a visual format; a person who is deaf cannot access content if it is only presented aurally; someone with who is a poor reader cannot access content that requires a high reading level. An important term to define is access, as it relates to the use of computer hardware, software, and other technology.

According to the National Science Foundation, "access implies the ability to find, manipulate and use information in an efficient and comprehensive manner". Too often even those individuals with disabilities who have a computer and Internet connection still cannot make full use of its capabilities because of the inaccessible features of hardware and/or software. They have technology, but do not have access to all of the benefits it delivers to others.

Assistive technology is defined as "any item, piece of equipment, or system, whether acquired commercially, modified, or customized, that is commonly used to increase, maintain, or improve functional capabilities of individuals with disabilities".

Assistive technology enables people with disabilities to accomplish daily living tasks; assists them in communication; and provides greater access to education, employment, and recreation. It can be used to maximize physical or mental functioning and minimize the impact of a disability. Examples of assistive technology include scooters and wheelchairs, alternative automobile controls, environmental controls, prostheses, communication aids, hand splints, hearing aids, and alternative input and output devices for computers.

An assistive technology service is defined as "any service that directly assists an individual with a disability in selection, acquisition or use of an assistive technology device". For this chapter, only assistive technology that interfaces with electronic and information technology and related services are relevant.

The process of creating products that are accessible to people with a wide range of abilities, disabilities, and other characteristics is called universal design. Universal design is defined by the National Centre for Universal Design at North Carolina State University as "the design of products and environments to be usable by all people, to the greatest extent possible, without the need for adaptation or specialized design".

At this Centre, a team of architects, product designers, engineers, and environmental design researchers established a set of principles of universal design to provide guidance in the design of environments, communications, and products. General principles include: the design accommodates a wide range of individual preferences and abilities; the design communicates necessary information effectively, regardless of ambient conditions or the user's sensory abilities; the design can be used efficiently and comfortably and with a minimum of fatigue; and appropriate size and space is provided for approach, reach, manipulation, and use regardless of the user's body size, posture, or mobility.

The concept of universal design has been applied to all teaching and learning activities. In particular, when producers apply universal design principles as they create electronic and information technology, the products are more usable by everyone, including people with disabilities.

They minimize the need for assistive technology and are compatible with commonly used assistive hardware and software. Below are a few examples of accessible electronic and information technology and its benefits to students with disabilities in educational settings.

- Accessible Web pages allow students with disabilities, including those who have sensory impairments and those with low reading skills, to access information; share their work; communicate with peers, teachers, and mentors; and take advantage of distance learning options.
- Accessible instructional software (on disks, CDs or other media) and documentation allow students with disabilities to participate side-by-side with their peers in computer labs and classrooms as they complete assignments; collaborate with peers; create and view presentations, documents, spreadsheets; and actively participate in simulations and other computer-based activities.

Accessible telephones make communication accessible to everyone, including people with cognitive, mobility, visual, and hearing impairments.

The following section provides examples of roles technology can play in the lives of individuals with disabilities.

ROLES OF TECHNOLOGY FOR STUDENTS WITH DISABIUTIES

The following examples demonstrate how electronic and information technology can be used by students with disabilities and contribute to their independence, productivity, and participation in academics and careers. Specifically, technology can help them in the following ways.

- Maximize independence in academic and employment tasks. Example: A student with a mobility impairment uses a hands-free keyboard and mouse to operate a computer to take class notes, access library resources, and complete papers rather than have an assistant write for her.
- Participate in classroom discussions. Example: A student who cannot speak uses a computer-based communication device to deliver speeches and participate in class discussions.
- Gain access to peers, mentors, and role models. Example: In a supported Internet community, a student who is deaf uses e-mail to chat with other teens, gain support for college and career transition from mentors, and meet role models.
- Self-advocate. Example: A student who is deaf uses a TTY and relay service to arrange appointments regarding internship accommodations with her supervisor.
- Gain access to the full range of educational options. Example: A student who is blind and uses speech output technology fully participates in an Internet-based distance learning course that employs universal design principles to assure access to people with disabilities.
- Participate in experiences not otherwise possible. Example: a young man with no functional use of his arms and legs experiences completing a chemistry experiment through a computer simulation and observing sea life while swimming in the ocean through virtual reality.
- Succeed in work-based learning experiences. Example: A student who has no use of his hands independently operates a computer to draft and edit articles in a journalism internship at the local newspaper office.
- Secure high levels of independent living. Example: A young person who has a developmental disability uses a cell phone to maintain regular contact with caregivers as he participates in community activities. Example: A teen with a mobility impairment uses a voice- controlled system to operate the television, turn lights on and off, open doors, and perform other tasks of daily life.
- Prepare for transitions to college and careers. Example: A student with a learning disability that makes it difficult for him to read uses a computer with a speech output system to explore internship and career opportunities, take self-paced career readiness and interest tests, and research the academic programmes and services for students with disabilities offered at colleges of interest.

- A girl who is blind and a boy who has no use of his hands work on the school newsletter with fellow journalism students; she uses speech output technology, he uses a voice recognition system, and other students use standard input and output devices on a local area network in the computer lab.
- Master academic tasks that they cannot accomplish otherwise. Example: A student with a learning disability uses a set of software tools to support her management of reading, writing, and study demands in a postsecondary setting.
- Enter high-tech career fields. Example: A child who shows interest in engineering at a young age, but does not have the fine motor skills to manipulate objects, gains technical knowledge using the Internet, operates computer simulations of engineering tasks, and develops a solid foundation for college studies and a career in engineering.
- Participate in community and recreational activities. Example: An adult who is blind can privately cast his vote for President of the United States because the voting booth is designed to be accessible to everyone.

These and countless other examples demonstrate the important roles electronic and information technology can play as young people with disabilities pursue postsecondary education and careers.

First, they realise the same benefits as individuals without disabilities - they write articles, develop spreadsheets, access Internet-based resources and services, work side-by-side with their peers. In addition to these benefits, however, some people with disabilities use technology as compensatory tools which allow them to do things that are otherwise impossible because of their disabilities.

For example, technology can provide a voice for those who cannot speak in the customary way; can allow people to write even though they do not have functional use of their hands; can make it possible for individuals to use the telephone even though they do not have the ability to hear. The following section summarizes key legislation related to technology access for people with disabilities in elementary and secondary schools, postsecondary institutions, and employment.

LEGISLATION

The Individuals with Disabilities Education Act mandates that each state provide a free and appropriate education for all children, regardless of their abilities or disabilities. It requires that individual education plans (IEPs) be developed for students with disabilities who meet certain criteria and that assistive technology and transition, among other things, be considered in the development of IEPs.

Section 504 of the Rehabilitation Act of 1973 prohibits discrimination against individuals with disabilities in federally-funded programmes and services that receive, which include the vast majority of educational institutions. The Americans with Disabilities Act of 1990 (ADA) reinforces and extends the requirements of section 504 to public programmes and services, regardless of whether or not they receive federal funds.

Precollege programmes must provide access to all children, regardless of disabilities; thus, all students with disabilities, regardless of whether they have IEPs, have a right to the same technology access that is provided to students without disabilities.

For qualified students who disclose their disabilities and present appropriate documentation, postsecondary institutions must provide reasonable accommodations to assure equal access to programme offerings.

Although the ADA does not specifically mention electronic and information technology, the United States Department of justice clarified that the ADA applies to Internet-based resources - "Covered entities that use the Internet for communications regarding their programmes, goods, or services must be prepared to offer those communications through accessible means as well". The ADA mandates nondiscrimination in employment as well, requiring reasonable accommodations for employees with disabilities; such accommodations may include the purchase of assistive technology.

Provisions of the Carl D. Perkins Vocational and Applied Technology Education Act of 1998, the Rehabilitation Amendments of 1992 and 1993, the School-to-Work Opportunities Act of 1994, and the Technology-Related Assistance for Individuals with Disabilities Act of 1988 further dictate programme access and support services that must be provided to people with disabilities.

Unfortunately, many elementary, secondary, and postsecondary educators and service providers have difficulty understanding and applying the maze of conflicting definitions, eligibility criteria, and policy implications of legislation that impacts the provision of technology access for individuals with disabilities.

Section 508 of the Rehabilitation Act requires that agencies of the federal government develop, purchase, and use electronic and information technology that is accessible to individuals with disabilities. The Architectural and Transportation Barriers Compliance Board (Access Board) developed standards to which these agencies must comply.

Even for those who are not covered entities under section 508, the standards developed by the Access Board provide a good starting point for organizations seeking to meet their ADA obligations. They include standards for (a) accessible desktop and portable computers, (b) Web-based resources, (c) video and multimedia products, (d) software and operating systems, and (e) selfcontained, closed systems such as photocopiers and fax machines.

Although educational institutions and employers have legal obligations to provide technology access to students and employees with disabilities, barriers still prevent people with disabilities from gaining full access to technologies that can help them reach their full potential.

DISCUSSION

Technology has the potential to improve the educational, career, and adult living outcomes for people with disabilities. However, this potential will not be realized unless barriers to reaching the following goals are overcome.

- All individuals with disabilities have access to technology that promotes positive academic and career outcomes.
- People with disabilities learn to use technology in ways that contribute to positive postsecondary academic and career outcomes and self-determined lives.
- There is a seamless transition of availability of technology for all people with disabilities as they move from K-12 to postsecondary to career environments.

The specific goals addressed in each discussion section are indicated in parentheses immediately after each question.

ACCOMMODATIONS VS. UNIVERSAL DESIGN

How can the creation of universal design of electronic and information technology be promoted? Designing inclusive environments that are accessible to everyone, with and without disabilities, minimizes the need for individual accommodations.

Employing the universal design approach to the development of technology devices, facilities, information resources, and services is a critical step towards ensuring that students with disabilities are provided with full access to programmes and activities in the school, workplace, and community.

Promoting the use of electronic and information technology standards established by the federal government can help educational and employment entities move closer to this goal. Librarians, educators, and others who purchase technology products for schools need to demand that accessibility considerations be included in the procurement process.

Similarly, distance learning programme providers must employ universal design principles to make courses accessible to potential students with a wide variety of abilities and disabilities, including those who are blind and use speech or Braille output systems.

A universal design approach to electronic and information technology selection and use in schools can help to reduce technology costs as well as facilitate the transfer of technology from secondary to postsecondary educational settings. It can promote compatibility in education and workplace settings; reduce stigma, cultural, and attitudinal barriers for students with disabilities; and make it easier for service providers to respond to the changing technology needs of students.

FUNDING

Who will assure funding so that children with disabilities can gain access to empowering technology? Funding is often cited as a barrier to technology access for people with disabilities. Although the cost of technology is often lower than anticipated and funding is sometimes suggested as a constraint when issues of selection and management are actually more challenging, technology does cost money and must be paid for in some way.

This issue is likely to grow increasingly important as elementary and secondary educators continue to be faced with implementing the assistive technology requirements of IDEA, as technology in general becomes more widely available as a tool for student learning, and as awareness of assistive technology becomes more widespread. Besides consideration of the overall costs, deciding who (e.g., school, government agency, insurance, family) should pay for technology under specific circumstances and who owns the technology as a person transitions between various levels of education and employment creates additional challenges to be overcome.

Technology choices for people with disabilities should be driven by both short-term and long-term needs. Besides initial purchase, questions about who is responsible for upgrades and technical support during all life stages must be answered.

Funding is needed for training personnel to deliver technology services at various academic and employment levels and during transition periods, as well as for increasing technology awareness among all key stakeholders, including parents, educators, librarians, service providers, employers, and people with disabilities.

SELECTION

Who will select appropriate technology and provide ongoing support for students with disabilities at various levels in the educational and career preparation process? The planning and implementation of effective technology for students with disabilities requires specialized knowledge and skills regarding legislation, policies, and technology applications and products by those in decision-making and support positions.

These individuals include special education teachers, occupational therapists, community service providers, students with disabilities, families, and technology professionals. Increasing the knowledge and skills of these individuals regarding the availability and potential uses of technology is a critical step towards ensuring that students are provided with the tools and supports that will increase readiness and motivation as they transition to postsecondary education and employment.

Service providers need to have the capacity to keep pace with the rapidly changing technology that can benefit students with disabilities. With the growing complexity of computing environments and number of commercially available assistive technology devices, staff at smaller institutions faces special challenges in acquiring and maintaining current information about technology options and the most appropriate applications for students with disabilities.

FULL PARTICIPATION IN ACADEMIC AND EMPLOYMENT OFFERINGS

How can general and special education teachers, career services staff, and employers be better trained to understand the capabilities and accommodation needs of students with disabilities and use technology to help people with disabilities fully participate in academic and employment offerings? Sometimes technology is used in a very limited way to enhance the education of students with disabilities.

For example, a computer might be available to a student in a computer lab, but not used by the student for test-taking because an individual teacher is not aware that the student can use this technology or because they are not sensitive to the need for students with disabilities to complete their work independently as they prepare for postsecondary studies and careers.

Similarly, assistive technology is not always readily available to a student who might, with this technology, be able to participate in work-based learning experiences, such as a summer internship.

This problem, in part, can be addressed with increased funding for assistive technology; greater awareness of the availability and potential uses of assistive technology on the part of stakeholders, including educators, career services staff, parents, and employers; and effective coordination between these individuals.

PEER AND MENTOR SUPPORT

How can students with disabilities employ technology to gain access to meaningful peer and mentoring relationships on the Internet? Potential role models who have disabilities and are experiencing success in college and careers are often separated from potential protégés by great distances and both potential mentors and protégés face more complex transportation challenges than individuals without disabilities.

Peer and mentor support can be provided via moderated discussion groups on the Internet. Supportive electronic communities can contribute to the self-sufficiency of people with disabilities. Such activities, however, incur administrative time and costs.

ANYTIME, ANYWHERE ACCESS TO TECHNOLOGY

How can educators and employers assure that appropriate technology is available when and where people with disabilities need it? Sometimes accessible technology is available to a student with a disability in a special education resource centre or other isolated location, when it is most needed in the classroom and at home. Often technology available to students at the secondary school level does not transition with them as they pursue postsecondary education and employment.

Funding and management strategies should be flexible enough to provide maximum benefit of technology access for each individual student. Coordinated education and community service systems are essential in ensuring that transfer of technology is a seamless process. This can be facilitated by the development of interagency and/or cost-sharing agreements that identify specific roles and responsibilities of agencies to address the technology needs of both students with disabilities who have IEPs and those who do not.

PROMOTION OF SELF-ADVOCACY, INDEPENDENCE, AND SELF-DETERMINATION

How can parents, educators, and service providers encourage students with disabilities to use technology to self advocate, perform daily tasks independently, and move towards self-determined lives? Successful transition is integral to a student's realization of postsecondary education, employment, and adult living objectives. Like all other aspects of the transition process, the role of technology should be addressed in a way that maximizes the involvement of the student.

Student transition plans should include self-advocacy objectives in the technology area so that students are able to articulate their technology needs to others (e.g., teachers, professors, employers) and access training and support throughout their lives. Ideally, by high school graduation, students with disabilities are experts on the types of technology that serve them best, the technical support requirements of their systems, and the resources available to them.

WORK-BASED LEARNING

How can students with disabilities gain access to hightech work-based learning experiences to prepare them for the world of work? Internships, job shadows, service learning, and other work-based learning experiences can help students with disabilities gain job skills, explore accommodation options, and learn to use technology in work settings.

Such experiences can improve their chances for a successful school-to- work transition. Individuals who coordinate work experiences for high school and college students as well as participating employers need greater awareness of the potential contributions and accommodation needs, including assistive technology, of students with disabilities.

Stakeholders should work together to assure that students have access to appropriate technology for employment settings and that students are included in the process in such a way that they gain the knowledge and self-advocacy skills they need for success in postsecondary education and careers.

LEGISLATION AND POLICY

How can the maze of confusing and conflicting laws, rulings, and policy be simplified? Policy makers and advocates should explore ways to clarify existing legislation and use consistent terminology and standards. Dissemination of current laws, policies, and resources should be tailored to the needs of various stakeholders and disseminated widely.

Differences that occur as students transition between academic levels and academic and career environments should be clearly addressed. Policy makers and advocates should also identify and correct inconsistencies and gaps in legislation and policies regarding the selection, funding, and support of assistive technology.

AWARENESS

How can we assure that key stakeholders have general knowledge of how technology can benefit individuals with disabilities?

To be assured that good decisions are made by IEP teams and other decision-makers, all stakeholder groups need to be aware of the types of technology options available to enhance the academic and career outcomes for individuals with disabilities.

These groups include general and special education teachers, occupational therapists, rehabilitation counselors, policymakers, paraprofessionals, pre- service and in-service trainers, employers, interagency and community service providers, students, families, technology professionals, postsecondary disabled student services staff, and medical equipment providers.

Individuals within these groups represent key stakeholders in the process of ensuring that students are provided with appropriate technology and support services as they pursue education and careers.

If stakeholders are not aware of how technology can support students with disabilities, these students will not have assistive technology adequately considered in the IEP process; they will not have access to the full school curriculum; they will not be provided with developmentally appropriate devices and services; they will fail to use technology effectively; and they will not become prepared to self-advocate regarding their technology needs in future stages of their lives.

Because of the large number of students with learning disabilities, stakeholder knowledge of how technology can promote the success of this group in educational and employment settings is especially important.

RESEARCH

How can we promote research that will improve our understanding of issues related to technology access for people with disabilities and its impact on post-school outcomes? Mainstream electronic and information technology and assistive technology are in a constant state of rapid development.

We cannot assume that what was impossible yesterday for people with disabilities is not possible today. The National Science Foundation, the Department of Defence, the U.S., Department of Education and other national and private funding agencies should be encouraged to support basic research and promising practices that employ technology to improve the postsecondary education and career outcomes for individuals with disabilities.

The current conditions, legal issues, potential applications, and challenges regarding the use of technology by individuals with disabilities discussed in this chapter thus far lead to the implications for practice listed in the next section.

IMPLICATIONS FOR PRACTICE

Federal legislation, demands by people with disabilities and their advocates that they be included in all life experiences, increased acceptance of diversity, improved medical care, and advancements in electronic and information technologies have contributed to higher expectations and improved preparation of students with disabilities for postsecondary academic programmes, careers, and community involvement.

As a result, young people with disabilities are better prepared to pursue higher education and ever-increasing numbers of students with disabilities are attending postsecondary academic institutions. Technology has an important role to play in promoting the success of people with disabilities in employment and careers.

However, legal mandates for computer access for students and employees with disabilities are not always reflected in practice, even within organizations that have developed access policies.

Stakeholders are not fully aware of technology options, legal issues, and advocacy strategies. These stakeholders include people with disabilities, parents and mentors, government entities, paraprofessionals, policy makers and administrators, precollege and postsecondary educators, librarians, technical support staff, and employers. These individuals must diligently work together if the following goals are to be reached.

- All individuals with disabilities have access to technology that promotes positive academic and career outcomes.
- People with disabilities learn to use technology in ways that contribute to positive postsecondary academic and career outcomes and self-determined lives.
- There is a seamless transition of availability of technology for all people with disabilities as they move from K-12 to postsecondary to career environments.

Promising practices to be considered in order to reach these goals include those that follow. Most recommendations support multiple goals.

- Administrators and policymakers should establish policies, standards, and procedures at all academic and employment levels to assure that accessibility is considered when electronic and information technology is procured.
- Administrators and policymakers should establish policies, standards, and procedures and provide training and support at all educational levels to assure that Web pages, library resources, computing and science labs, and distance learning programmes are accessible to everyone, including students with disabilities.
- Policymakers and administrators should assure that funding is available to purchase appropriate assistive technology at all levels of academic programmes, in employment settings, and during transition periods between these stages.
- Agencies should collaborate on planning, funding, selecting, and supporting assistive technology to assure continuous technology access and support as students with disabilities transition through academic levels and to employment.
- Educators, librarians, parents, support staff, computer lab managers, and other stakeholders should have access to training so that they will be able to design accessible facilities and activities;

select accessible computers and software; purchase appropriate assistive technology; and assure that students with disabilities use technology for their maximum benefit as they pursue academics, careers, and self-determined lives.

- Legislators and policy makers should take steps to clarify existing legislation; disseminate information about current laws, policies, and resources tailored to the needs of various stakeholders; and use consistent terminology and standards. They should identify and correct inconsistencies and gaps in legislation and policies regarding the selection, funding, and support of assistive technology, especially as individuals transition between all academic and employment levels.
- Students with disabilities should be included at all stages of technology selection, support, and use so that they learn to self-advocate regarding their needs for accessible technology in the classroom and workplace.
- Students with disabilities should be taught to use technology in ways that 1) maximize their independence, productivity, and participation in all academic and employment activities, 2) facilitate successful transitions between all academic and employment levels, and 3) lead to successful, self determined adult lives. Technology should be used to support mentoring relationships, access to electronic information, participation in science labs, communication in class discussions, self-advocacy practice, independent living tasks, work-based learning opportunities, and other academic and career preparation activities.
- Students with disabilities at high school and college levels should participate in internships and other work-based learning experiences where they can practice using technology in work settings.

Besides taking immediate steps to assure that technology is accessible and appropriately used by individuals with disabilities, there is a need for ongoing research to inform future practice.

❒

Chapter - 7

Media Participation in Explaining Internet Needs

Mass media in forming and reflecting public opinion, connecting the world to individuals and reproducing the self-image of society. Critiques in the early-to-mid twentieth century suggested that media weaken or delimit the individual's capacity to act autonomously — sometimes being ascribed an influence reminiscent of the telescreens of the dystopian novel 1984. Mid

20th-century empirical studies, however, suggested more moderate effects of the media.

Current scholarship presents a more complex interaction between the media and society, with the media on generating information from a network of relations and influences and with the individual interpretations and evaluations of the information provided, as well as generating information outside of media contexts.

The consequences and ramifications of the mass media relate not merely to the way newsworthy events are perceived (and which are reported at all), but also to a multitude of cultural influences that operate through the media. The media have a strong social and cultural impact upon society. This is predicated upon their ability to reach a wide audience with a strong and influential message.

Marshall McLuhan uses the phrase "the medium is the message" as a means of explaining how the distribution of a message can often be more important than content of the message itself. It is through the persuasiveness of media such as television, radio and print media that messages reach their target audiences. These have been influential media as they have been largely responsible for structuring people's daily lives and routines. Television broadcasting has a large amount of control over the content society watches and the times in which it is viewed.

This is a distinguishing feature of traditional media which New media have challenged by altering the participation habits of the public. The internet creates a space for more diverse political opinions, social and cultural viewpoints and a heightened level of consumer participation. There have been suggestions that allowing consumers to produce information through the internet will lead to an overload of information.

The extent to which an audience engages with a media text can be roughly split into three degrees. The first of these is primary involvement, in which the audience is solely concentrating on consuming the media text. For example, sitting down solely to watch a favourite programme on television.

Secondary involvement is when an audience's concentration is split between the media text and another distraction. For example, working on the computer while watching television. Tertiary involvement is when the media text is merely in the background, with no real concentration upon it at all. For example, glancing at a newspaper on a crowded train. While this theory is somewhat simplistic, it provides a clear and probable explanation as to the changes in audience reception.

Perhaps the most widely accepted theory on audience reception is Denis McQuail's Uses and Gratifications model. This places emphasis on the reasons audiences consumes media. The first reason outlined in the model is the need to reinforce ones own behaviour by identifying with roles, values and gender identities presented in the media.

Secondly, consumers need to feel some kind of interaction with other people which is offered by text such as a soap opera or a lifestyle magazine. The third reason is the need for security. Media offer a window to the world that allows education and the acquisition of information. The final reason is the need for entertainment through both escapism, and the need for emotional release, such as laughter. A strength of the Uses and Gratifications theory is the emphasis on the audience as active in the reception of media.

However, this would suggest no passivity within the audience whatsoever. A person may, for example, be too lazy to turn off their television and as a result consume any media that is available, regardless of need. This theory also pays little attention to the short term and long term effects of media on the audience.

Since, its inception, the Internet has been hailed because it is convenient, informative, resourceful, and entertaining. It has been estimated that over 54 million Americans go online each day. That number is still growing. It is of theoretical and practical significance to examine dependency on the Internet. First, this line of study should further researchers' theoretical understanding of media and Internet dependency, and shed light on the relationship between people and new technologies.

Second, research on Internet dependency should help integrate the study of interpersonal and mass communication, and provide insight into mediated communication. In this study, the authors examined the influence of key factors, especially motivation and involvement, on Internet dependency.

Investigating relationships among motivation, involvement, and dependency contributes to understanding of the Internet in several ways. First, although each construct has received extensive inquiry in the past, research investigations have been independent of each other so that links among these constructs are not clear.

In particular, the role of involvement in relation to motivation and dependency in the new technology environment remains sketchy. Second, to facilitate researchers' understanding of new media, an inspection of the formative process of communication outcomes is essential. Nonetheless, a lack of empirical evidence supporting such a formative process mitigates researchers' conceptualization of media outcomes such as Internet dependency. Understanding media dependency warrants consideration of the possible influence of motivation and involvement in the process. Third, as Greenwald and Leavitt argued, different media have "different potential for boosting involvement".

The unique attributes of the Internet (e.g., combining personal and mediated channels), for example, may help enhance or mitigate effects on involvement. Fourth, researchers have disagreed about how to conceptualize and operationalize constructs such as involvement and dependency in the Internet context. There is a need to clarify the systematic links among these concepts to advance the theorizing of new media research.

Below, relevant literature on motivation, involvement, and dependency are first reviewed. Second, based on the literature, the authors elaborate the rationale for the relationship among these constructs and propose specific research questions and hypotheses. Third, method and results are examined and discussed.

MOTIVATION

Investigators have suggested the effectiveness of combining interpersonal and media motives to examine media use, especially the uses of newer media such as computers and the Internet. Several researchers have suggested that people use the Internet to fulfill interpersonal and media needs.

Flaherty, Pearce, and Rubin, for example, argued that people use the

Internet to satisfy interpersonal needs (e.g., affection), needs traditionally gratified by the media (e.g., entertainment), and newer media needs (e.g., meeting others). These different types of needs drive a variety of motives for using the Internet.

INTERNET MOTIVES

Research has shown that traditional media motives explain a significant portion of why people use the Internet. Ferguson and Perse found people watching television for diversion also tend to use the World Wide Web for diversion. Kaye compared Web use motives and television viewing motives and found similarities among them.

Six prominent motives were identified for using the Internet: entertainment, social interaction, pass time, escape, information, and Web site preference. In a later study, Kaye and Johnson found people who obtained political information used the Internet for guidance, information seeking/ surveillance, entertainment, and social utility.

People, though, might have greater incentive for using the Internet than for using traditional media. Ebersole, for instance, found college students used the Internet for research and reading, for easy access to entertainment, for communication and social interaction, to relieve boredom, to access material otherwise unavailable, to obtain product information and technology support, to access games and sexually explicit sites, and to conduct consumer transactions. Sjoberg identified four popular reasons why Swedish teenagers use the Internet: surfing the Net, looking for information, chatting with others, and downloading programmes.

MEDIA INVOLVEMENT

In media research, involvement pertains to media users' relationships with messages conveyed by media or with media, media personae, or other media users. A. M. Rubin and Perse conceptualized media involvement as "cognitive, affective, and behavioral participation during and because of exposure".

The concept of media involvement places the locus of involvement within the individual rather than within messages.

Moreover, media involvement stresses the interaction between audiences and external factors such as messages or media. This emphasis corresponds with Andrews, Durvasula, and Akhter's argument that consumers, not products, are the foci of involvement with advertising.

To understand involvement, one needs to understand audiences, as involvement is vital for explaining the "role of active interactants in communication".

INVOLVEMENT AND AUDIENCE ACTIVITY

The concept of audience activity has been a focus of many audience studies. The connection between activity and involvement is evident. Lin explained that audience activity is a construct describing audiences' media motives (i.e., utility), selectivity, and involvement with messages.

Levy and Windahl identified two dimensions of audience activity: the orientation dimension included selectivity, involvement, and use; the temporal dimension covered activities before, during, and after exposure. They argued audience activity varies across different periods of media exposure.

Levy and Windhal focused on three types of activity: selectivity before exposure, involvement during exposure, and use after exposure. The first type of activity speaks to motives for using the media. The second type speaks to psychological engagement. The third type speaks to media utility and effects. Because these types of activities operate along a temporal dimension, such a relationship between motives, involvement, and uses should hold in a temporal order: media motives [right arrow] involvement [right arrow] media use and effects.

MEDIA INVOLVEMENT AS A MEDIATOR

Several researchers have investigated relationships among media motives, involvement, and effects. Perse found instrumental viewing motivation positively related to elaboration, whereas ritualistic viewing motivation positively related to engaging in distracting behaviors.

In other words, cognitive involvement was linked to instrumental motives more than to ritualistic motives. Perse also found utilitarian motives for viewing local news were linked to cognitive involvement and angry feelings, and diversionary motives were related to happy feelings. In addition, A. M. Rubin and Step observed that information-seeking and entertainment motives were positive predictors of involvement with television talk-show content. And, Perse found instrumental motivation predicted cognitive and affective involvement (i.e., positive reactions) with television viewing. Ritualistic motivation predicted affective involvement (i.e., negative reactions), but not cognitive involvement.

Research has shown that cognitive involvement and affective involvement are interrelated and influence media use and outcomes. Perse suggested that people who were cognitively involved and experienced positive affect were less likely to change television channels when viewing. On the other hand, those who were less cognitively involved and experienced negative affect were more likely to change channels.

Examining other links between involvement and media use, Henning and Vorderer found that people with a low need for cognition and unhappy feelings usually watched television more often than did their counterparts. They argued television viewing requires less thinking and cognition than other media, such as reading the newspaper; therefore, people who do not enjoy thinking are more likely to watch television. This suggests that cognition and affects influence media use.

In line with this thinking and research, the relationship between media motives, cognitive and affective involvement, and media use and outcomes can be illustrated as follows: media motives [right arrow] cognitive and affective involvement [right arrow] media use/effects. Here, cognitive involvement and affective involvement function as mediators between media motives and media use/effects.

MEDIA DEPENDENCY

Investigators have suggested that media dependency is a relation reflecting how individuals' goals are conditional upon the resources media afford. This conceptualization is crystallized as the individual media dependency (IMD) theory. Moreover, media dependency cannot be simplified as goals because dependency stresses a relation, whereas goals reflect an attribute.

IMD theory ties in with uses and gratifications theory (UGT), but also is at variance with such research in some respects. Grant et al. commented that both perspectives address the question "what do people do with media?" They argued uses and gratifications focuses on where individuals go to satisfy their needs, and IMD focuses on why an individual accesses this medium to achieve a goal.

Ball-Rokeach contended that the formation of individual media dependency is determined by structural or macro factors, and social psychological factors of individuals. However, early work on media dependency within the sociological framework may underestimate the role of social psychological factors such as individual needs in the formation of media dependency. Examining media dependency from a uses and gratifications perspective should help illuminate these relationships.

The differing foci of the two approaches have led to distinct operationalization of certain key concepts. For example, media dependency is often treated as a single variable assessing the extent of one's reliance on a medium to achieve goals, whereas uses and gratifications often focuses on dimensions of media experience and outcomes.

Further, using a measure to assess one's "global dependency" on a medium has no equivalent in uses and gratifications research. Therefore, it is reasonable to argue media dependency is conceptually and operationally distinct from traditional concepts in uses and gratifications.

Past research has shown consistent support for the conceptualization and operationalization of media dependency. Also, the conceptual domain of prior media dependency research is consistent and comparable across studies and media.

For example, Loges demonstrated the conceptualization of media dependency is valid across media types including newspapers, radio, magazines, and television. Thus, it is reasonable to define Internet dependency as a relation reflecting one's reliance on the Internet to achieve goals.

Some become dependent on the Internet as a source of information, entertainment, and interpersonal connection. Researchers have traditionally conceptualized media dependency as a manifestation of one's dependence on media for play, orientation, and understanding. Play speaks to entertainment needs, understanding to information-seeking needs, and orientation to interpersonal connection needs.

LINKS AMONG MOTIVATION, INVOLVEMENT AND DEPENDENCY

Media System Dependency (MSD) theory and UGT help explicate the relationships among motivation, involvement, and Internet dependency. Ball- Rokeach argued that MSD is a theory of media power instead of media effects. Dependence is the flip side of power, and hence, a dependence relationship strengthens when a party to the relationship is motivated to seek another's resources.

In other words, whether one is motivated to use a medium will influence the intensity of the user-medium dependency relationship. Seen from MSD, Internet dependency speaks to the power-dependency relations between users and the Internet. That dependency relation is also responsive to individuals' motivational investment, which is equivalent to involvement as identified in UGT.

According to MSD, the individual media dependency relation is asymmetrical. This means that people are less pivotal to the media system's needs than the media system is to an individual's needs.

Such an asymmetrical relation is relatively stable at the individual media dependency level. Put differently, people's needs, which drive motivations, play a significant role in the individual media dependency relation. As A. M. Rubin and Windahl argued, individuals' needs and motives cannot be separated; both are precursors of media dependency. Further, in the Uses and Dependency Model, A. M. Rubin and Windahl noted that the media system, societal system, and audience combine to influence people's motives for using media, which correspondingly influence their use of media and functional alternatives.

In addition, media use including consumption, message processing, interpretation, and other activity (e.g., involvement), produce media effects or consequences. Researchers have suggested media dependency often occurs in conjunction with traditional media effects.

For instance, the intensity of media dependency relations often makes persuasion or attitude change more salient. In other words, media dependency is a media effect that is contingent on audience involvement with media or media content.

Ball-Rokeach explained that individual media dependency relationships vary along three conceptual dimensions: intensity, goal scope, and referent scope. As for Internet dependency, the first dimension refers to how one perceives the Internet to help fulfill goals or needs; the second dimension refers to goals of understanding (social and self), orientation (interaction and action), and play (social and solitary); and the third dimension refers to the number of Internet functions a user adopts.

Logically, changes in people's motivation for using the Internet should result in variation of individual Internet dependency along the three dimensions. First, the stronger and wider one's motivation to use the Internet, the more likely one would perceive the Internet to be helpful (i.e., intensity). Second, the more diverse one's Internet motives are, the wider the scope of the goals.

Third, the more diverse one's Internet use motives, the wider the referent scope of Internet dependency. Specifically, if an individual is motivated to use the Internet for a range of reasons (e.g., entertainment, information seeking, interpersonal communication), that person is more likely to access a wider spectrum of Internet functions such as e-mail, Web browsing, and online games.

Therefore, motivation for using the Internet might predict Internet dependency along all dimensions, with involvement (i.e., motivation investment) being a precursor of Internet dependency.

Furthermore, as noted earlier, involvement is a motivated activity, which serves as a mediator between motivation and media outcomes. Therefore, it is legitimate to propose the following relationship: media motives [right arrow] cognitive and affective involvement [right arrow] Internet dependency.

RESEARCH QUESTIONS AND HYPOTHESIS

The main objective was to examine Internet dependency through a uses and gratifications lens, highlighting the centrality of communication motivation and involvement. In addition, the nature of personal dependency on media is goal-related. Therefore, investigating audience uses and effects requires consideration of the links among communication motivation, involvement, and media dependency.

Although previous Internet motive studies have shown some consistent findings, identifying a comprehensive and generalizable Internet motive typology is a complicated issue. First, the samples used in previous research vary. For example, Katz and Aspden used a national random telephone sample, whereas Papacharissi and Rubin and Charney and Greenberg used college-student samples.

Second, with the rapid development of Internet technology and changes in media environments, researchers may identify additional Internet motives. For instance, Internet access is now easier and less costly, so more people are likely to use the Internet to achieve different goals. Third, researchers have used different measures of Internet motives. Because reliability and validity vary across instruments, it becomes more difficult for researchers to reproduce the same Internet motive typology.

Consequently, the aim is to employ an Internet motives typology that reflects a contemporary portrait of Internet use. Because constructing instruments for measuring Internet motives is still in an early stage, examining the typology of Internet motives should provide insight into measurement issues.

Communication motivation is central to understanding media uses and effects, but has not received sufficient attention in newer media research. Media use, which describes individuals' selecting, consuming, processing, and interpreting media and their content, is a key variable in media effects.

One of the current authors' purposes was to examine how motivation relates to typical uses of the Internet. Focusing on typical use facilitates understanding Internet use because the variety of Internet functions complicates individuals' use patterns. Moreover, establishing a connection between motivation and typical Internet use should reveal why people use the Internet differently.

As A. M. Rubin and Windahl argued, people's motives predict media use, which is constrained and shaped by societal structures and conditions. Examining individuals' typical Internet use enhances understanding of the user-Internet relationship because Internet use leads to media outcomes such as Internet dependency. Therefore, the first research question asked:

[RQ.sub.1]: Which motives best explain individuals' typical uses of the Internet?

Research suggests involvement mediates the relationship between media motives and outcomes. Eveland (2001) found cognitive involvement (e.g., attention and elaboration) mediated the relationship between motivation for using media for surveillance reasons and gaining political knowledge from the media. In terms of MSD, Ball-Rokeach explained that people's motivational investment is a precursor of media dependency. Similarly, from a UGT perspective, A. M. Rubin asserted, involvement is motivated activity.

Thus, both MSD and UGT support the proposition that involvement is an antecedent of media dependency.

Moreover, as noted earlier, theoretically, media motives precede media involvement in a temporal order. Examining the role of involvement in Internet dependency adds information about activity in the newer media environment. The current authors sought to examine how involvement mediates the process leading to Internet dependency. This hypothesis was:

[H.sub.1]: Cognitive involvement and affective involvement mediate the relationship between Internet motivation and Internet dependency.

Media dependence follows from heightened needs or motivation to use the media. In line with UGT, a host of intervening variables (e.g., involvement) affect the process from motivation to media outcomes. Because involvement is a motivated activity, it is difficult to separate from media motives. To explain Internet dependency as a result of antecedent factors and mediating variables, and to assess the precise unique contribution of these factors, the second research question asked:

[RQ.sub.2]: What is the relative contribution of motivation and involvement to predicting Internet dependency?

METHOD

Design and Procedure

Research assistants enrolled in a liberal education-required communication class at a large midwestern university were trained to locate male and female participants representing four broad age classifications: 18 to 29, 30 to 39, 40 to 49, and 50 and over. Each assistant was required to contact two male and two female participants. Of these four participants, one participant needed to be within each age group. Following Human Subjects Review Board approval, research assistants attended a training session in which the principal researcher or colleagues discussed research ethics and provided precise instructions for distributing and collecting questionnaires. Research assistants received four blank questionnaires and four envelopes, and were asked to return those finished questionnaires sealed in envelopes with participants' initials across the seal.

SAMPLE

Overall, 471 questionnaires were subjected to data analysis. The sample was 46.9% male (n = 221) and 53.1% female (n = 250); 2.5% of the participants had not completed high school (n = 12); 21.9% were high school graduates (n = 103); 35.2% completed some college (n = 166); 26.8% were college graduates (n = 126); and 13.6% attended or completed graduate school (n = 64). There were 129 participants between 18 and 29 years old (27.4%), 116 between 30 and 39 years (24.6%), 112 between 40 and 49 years (23.8%), and 114 between 50 and 74 years (24.2%); M age = 38.93, SD = 13.38. There were 398 Caucasians (84.5%), 44 African Americans (9.3%), 3 Asian Americans (0.6%), 3 Hispanics/ Latinos (0.6%), 2 Native Americans (0.4%), and 21 others (4.5%).

MEASUREMENT

Typical Internet Use

Participants were asked to bear in mind their typical use of the Internet when completing the questionnaire. Descriptive statistics showed 44.2% of the participants typically used e-mail (n = 208), 36.1% typically used general Web browsing (n = 170), 6.8% typically downloaded music or games (n = 32), 6.8% typically used other Internet functions (n = 32), 3.0% typically used newsgroups/bulletin boards/listservs (n = 14), 2.3% typically shopped online (n = 11), and 0.8% typically used chatrooms (n = 4).

So, 80.3% of the participants identified e-mail or Web browsing as their typical use of the Internet. Fewer than 20% of the participants identified the other Internet functions as their typical use.

Given the variety and complexity of Internet functions, the focus was on the most salient typical Internet uses rather than all uses.

The nature of this study warranted examining the prominent characteristics of participants' typical Internet use. Because the most salient typical use patterns were e-mail and Web browsing, when examining the relationship between factors such as motivation and typical Internet use, the focus was on e-mail and general Web browsing.

Internet Motives

The CMC Motives Scale constructed by Papacharissi and Rubin was used to measure people's Internet use motives. They culled a majority of items from the Interpersonal Communication Motives Scale, and the Television Viewing Motives Scale.

The CMC Motives Scale assessed motivation on a 5-point Likert scale ranging from 1 (not at all) to 5 (exactly) "likes my reason for using the Internet." There were several reasons to conduct principal components analysis with the Internet motive typology. First, this study was exploratory in nature. Researchers have not reached consensus about how to measure involvement and Internet motives.

At this stage, it was difficult to say which measure was better, and hence, it was safer to use exploratory instead of confirmatory techniques. Second, prior research on the latent structure of motives is relatively clear. So, the focus of this study was not to uncover the latent motive structure, but rather to reduce the measured variables to a smaller number of composite components.

As Grant et al. argued, the focus of uses and gratifications research is to create a small set of variates from a large set of variables. To that end, principal components analysis was more appropriate than exploratory factor analysis.

Moreover, the objective of the study was not to examine the interrelationships among different motives. Motivation was treated as an independent variable for explaining other variables.

The principal components analysis technique helps retain as much information as possible in the original variables. Third, due to a lack of the differentiation between motivation, involvement, and affect in past research, it is necessary to achieve a simple structure of the constructs. For that purpose, varimax rotation was a better choice compared to other alternatives.

The analysis yielded five factors accounting for 55.6% of the total variance. Responses to items loading on each factor were averaged to form the motive indexes. Factor 1, Substitution, accounted for 31.9% of the total variance after rotation. The factor included all three pass-time items, all three relaxation items, one habit item, one escape item, and one inclusion/companionship item. The factor reflected a leisure motivation or amotivation, meaning users lacked a very clear intent or purpose. This 9-item factor reflected Internet use as a displacement activity because there was no better alternative.

Factor 2, Information, accounted for 9.6% of the total variance. It consisted of all three information items, one convenience item, one economy item, and one surveillance item. This 6-item factor reflected using the Internet for information searching. It was the most salient factor.

Factor 3, Social Interaction, explained 6.4% of the total variance. It included two social interaction items, two surveillance items, one inclusion/companionship item, and two expressive need items. This 7-item factor depicted using the Internet to interact with others and to get others' views. Factor 4, Convenience, accounted for 4.4% of the total variance. It consisted of one social interaction item, one time control item, and one economy item.

This 3-item factor reflected using the Internet because it was a convenient communication medium. Factor 5, Control, explained 3.4% of the total variance. It included two control items and one affection item. This 3-item factor depicted using the Internet to get others to do something. It was the least salient factor.

COGNITIVE INTERNET INVOLVEMENT

The 5-item Elaboration Scale was used to measure cognitive involvement. Response options ranged from 1 (strongly disagree) to 5 (strongly agree). Items in this scale (e.g., "while I am using the Internet, I think about how the online information relates to other things I know") are more applicable to the Internet environment than the other two subscales (i.e., attention, recognition) sometimes used in prior studies. Moreover, elaboration implies attention, and is an appropriate assessment of cognitive involvement.

Eveland and Dunwoody adapted the elaboration scale to assess elaboration of online information. Eveland, Seo, and Marton adapted the elaboration scale to measure people's learning from television news, newspapers, and online news. In the present study, the mean of the five items was used as an index of cognitive involvement.

AFFECTIVE INTERNET INVOLVEMENT

The adapted MACL contains 20 adjectives describing various moods. There are 10 adjectives to measure positive affect (i.e., amused, at ease, calm, cheerful, content, delighted, happy, pleased, relaxed, satisfied) and 10 adjectives to measure negative affect (i.e., angry, ashamed, bored, depressed, embarrassed, fearful, gloomy, miserable, sad, worried). Response options ranged from 1 (strongly disagree) to 5 (strongly agree) with each mood descriptor.

As mentioned before, due to the exploratory nature of the current study, in particular, the disagreement of measuring involvement in an online context, the present researchers used principal components analysis with varimax rotation on the 20 affective involvement items. By using a 60/40 factor loading rule with a minimum eigen value of 1.00 per factor, two interpretable factors were retained. These two factors explained 57.8% of the total variance.

Factor 1, Positive Affect, explained 30.7% of the total variance after rotation. It included all 10 positive affect items. This 10-item factor reflected Internet users' positive affective involvement.

Factor 2, Negative Affect, explained 27.0% of the total variance after rotation. It included eight of the original negative affect items. The two omitted items were "I feel angry" and "I feel bored." The 8-item factor reflected Internet users' negative affective involvement.

INTERNET DEPENDENCY

To date, researchers have not precisely clarified how to measure Internet dependency. A review of prior research suggests disagreement in constructing such a measure. One reason is that researchers differ in their understanding of Internet dependency. For example, researchers often interchange terms such as Internet dependence, heavy use, and addiction without referring to their conceptual differences.

In addition, research has seldom examined whether it is possible to apply relevant measures of assessing traditional media dependency to the newer media context. Such an attempt, however, is a practical way for constructing an Internet dependency measure, and provides insight into measuring audiences in different media contexts. More importantly, as noted before, the conceptual domain and operationalization of media dependency have been consistent and comparable across different media.

Therefore, the most recent version of the Television Dependency Scale developed by Grant was adapted to measure Internet dependency. Grant found the 18 items to be reliable for assessing dependency on different types of media. The revised Internet Dependency Scale includes six dimensions: action orientation, interaction orientation, self-understanding, social understanding, solitary play, and social play.

Sample items include: "In your daily life, how helpful is the Internet to..." (a) "get ideas about how to approach others in important or difficult situations?" (b) "have something to do when nobody is around?" (c) "stay on top of what is happening in the community?" (d) "keep up with world events?" (e) "figure out what to buy?" (f) "decide where to go for services such as health, financial, or household?" and (g) "plan where to go for evening and weekend activities?" Through its wording, the instrument enhanced the "correspondence between the media dependency relational concept and its measurement".

Response options ranged from 1 (not at all helpful) to 5 (extremely helpful). Grant explained that the six dimensions of this scale are highly correlated, and Grant et al. found it was valid and reliable to use all six dimensions to measure media dependency. Thus, combining the six dimensions produced a global measure of media dependency. The mean response to the 18 items was the index of Internet dependency.

DATA ANALYSIS

Data analysis proceeded in several steps. First, the current authors computed descriptive statistics and conducted reliability analyses of all scales. Second, because linear regression was used, data were examined to see whether linear-regression assumptions were violated.

Normality, linearity, and homoscedasticity were examined by plotting the residual scores against the predicted scores. Examining these assumptions insured that linear regression, instead of nonlinear techniques, was suitable for the data. The scatter plot indicated these assumptions were not violated with dependency as the dependent variable.

HYPOTHESIS

The current authors posited that cognitive and affective involvement would mediate the relationship between Internet motives and dependency. There were zero-order product-moment correlations of.63 between substitution motivation and Internet dependency,.52 between information motivation and Internet dependency,.62 between social interaction motivation and Internet dependency,.37 between convenience motivation and Internet dependency, and.48 between control motivation and Internet dependency.

After controlling for cognitive involvement and affective involvement, the third-order partial correlations were.41 between substitution motivation and Internet dependency,.42 between information motivation and Internet dependency,.41 between social interaction motivation and Internet dependency,.26 between convenience motivation and Internet dependency, and.28 between control motivation and Internet dependency.

Therefore, controlling for involvement (a) reduced the correlation between substitution motivation and dependency by a magnitude of.22, (b) reduced the correlation between information motivation and dependency by.10, (c) reduced the correlation between social interaction motivation and dependency by.21, (d) reduced the correlation between convenience motivation and dependency by.11, and (e) reduced the correlation between control motivation and dependency by a magnitude of.20. Taken as a whole, then, cognitive involvement and affective involvement mediated the relationship between Internet motives and Internet dependency.

The path analysis provides additional information about this mediation effect. Substitution motivation directly affected cognitive involvement, positive affect, and negative affect. Cognitive involvement, positive affect, and negative affect directly influenced Internet dependency.

Taken as a whole, involvement mediated the relationship between substitution motivation and Internet dependency. But, motivation, except the convenience motive, also had a direct effect on Internet dependency. This suggests that involvement partially mediated the relationship between motivation and Internet dependency, generally supporting the hypothesis.

DISCUSSION

Consistent with prior research, over 80% of the participants typically used the Internet for e-mail or general Web browsing.

The results support Eveland and Dunwoody's proposition that the Web as "a system of information delivery can be used to influence information processing". Papacharissi and Rubin observed that information-seeking motivation positively predicted Web browsing but negatively predicted e-mail use. Their finding is consistent with the results of the current study. It is legitimate to argue that the Web serves as a better information tool than does e-mail.

Similar to Teo's finding, women were more likely to use e-mail than were men. Men were more likely than women to use the Internet for Web browsing. As a communication tool, e-mail affords opportunities to express oneself and interact with others. Teo explained that men are more likely to be interested in using the Internet for learning, whereas women are more interested in communicating with others on the Internet. Teo also suggested that women tended to perceive computer-mediated communication more favorably than did men.

The results also provide insight into the "gratification opportunities" a medium can provide, that is, a medium's beneficial attributes. Researchers have shown that the gratification opportunities e-mail affords (e.g., fast speed, convenience, less expensive) are important reasons for people's preference for using e-mail.

In addition, Westmyer, DiCioccio, and Rubin found that being motivated to control others influenced one's evaluation of the effectiveness and appropriateness of communication channel choice. They observed that people rated oral channels such as the telephone more effective and appropriate to fulfill their control needs than written channels such as e-mail.

Although e-mail was not compared with other communication channels in this study, it makes sense that people use e-mail to seek to control others. One can control whether or not to reply and when to reply to others' e-mail. Also, e-mail use might be related to saving face. If one does not want to confront another person directly for the sake of saving face, e-mail may offer more control compared to other channels such as the telephone.

The second research question asked about the relative contribution of antecedent factors to predicting Internet dependency. Demographics accounted for a small proportion of the variance. Younger people were more likely to exhibit Internet dependency than older participants. Again, this might link to the "built-in bias" of the Internet. Some people are more "technologically savvy" than others. Younger people are more likely than older people to be at the frontline of technological developments.

Motivation and involvement were more important predictors of Internet dependency than were demographics. This is consistent with uses and gratifications' emphasis on the role motivation and involvement play in the media effects process. As A. M. Rubin stated, media dependency develops from people's communication motives, attitudes, media use patterns, and available functional alternatives.

Among the various Internet use motives, substitution, information seeking, and social interaction were most salient in explaining and predicting Internet dependency. Substitution motivation reflected a ritualized orientation to fill time, relax, and escape, whereas information seeking and social interaction motivation reflected a more instrumental, goal-directed orientation focusing on informational content of the Internet.

HYPOTHESIS

The results of this study are consistent with the literature. Both cognitive and affective involvement mediates the relationship between one's motives to communicate and media outcomes. Involvement and affect play an important role in media outcomes, including dependence on the Internet. The findings support the proposition that a range of intervening orientations may influence the relationship between audience motivation and media outcomes. The present findings also are consistent with the uses and gratifications argument that audience activity "plays an important intervening role in the effects process". An interesting finding is that motives to interact socially and to control others' behaviour were strong predictors of cognitive involvement, and the motive to fill time, relax, and escape was a strong predictor of positive affect, that is, feeling cheerful, pleased, delighted, calm, relaxed, and at ease. As noted earlier, social interaction and control motivations reflect an instrumental orientation, and substitution motivation reflects a ritualized orientation for using the Internet.

The finding makes sense within the uses and gratifications framework. An instrumental orientation speaks to an active use of media and suggests involvement with media content, whereas a ritualized orientation speaks to a less active use of media and suggests affinity with the medium. The current findings suggest that an instrumental Internet orientation aligns closely with greater cognitive involvement and a ritualized orientation aligns more with affective involvement.

LIMITATIONS

There are several limitations that might influence the generalizability of these findings. First, the cross-sectional data employed in this study do not warrant a claim of any causal relationships among motivation, involvement, and Internet dependency.

Indeed, panel data might be a better choice for examining such relationships. A cursory review of extant uses and gratifications literature also attests to a lack of panel data.

Moreover, the quota sample, which excluded people under the age of 18, might restrict the generalizability of findings; more people under age 20 have come online. Research assistants were asked to select an equal number of male and female participants. This was not wholly achieved, nor was the precise quota for age. The Internet population, though, might not be so gender and age balanced.

Second, operationalizing some constructs might limit the scope of the study. For example, although the Internet motives scale and media dependency scale often appear in prior research, some items of these two instruments appear to be similar.

To some extent, such a seeming repetition results from the nature of dependency relationships which implicate motivation. As mentioned before, though, dependency cannot be reduced to motivation or goals because the former is a relation and the latter is an attribute. Accounting for a temporal dimension in a longitudinal design might help future researchers empirically distinguish constructs such as motivation, involvement, and dependency.

Third, the operationalization of typical Internet use provided a viable empirical portrait to examine the research questions and hypothesis, but might not precisely reflect the complexity of an individual's use patterns. It is likely that each individual uses several Internet functions each day.

Researchers would benefit from developing a mechanism for capturing the complexity of the Internet and user patterns. Fourth, there are no single, agreed-upon instruments to measure cognitive involvement, affective involvement, and dependency in the context of Internet use.

Although the adapted scales were reliable, their construct validity deserves further examination in Internet settings. Perse, for example, measured cognitive involvement along three dimensions: attention, recognition, and elaboration.

In this study, the current authors used the elaboration subscale to measure cognitive involvement, and the MACL to measure affective involvement. It is possible that Internet users have other emotional reactions during Internet use beyond the 20 moods identified in the MACL. Renewed efforts to conceptualize and measure affective involvement are warranted.

FUTURE DIRECTIONS

The Internet affords a variety of functions. To obtain an in-depth understanding of the Internet, researchers may take a close look at dependency on a specific Internet function such as e-mail or instant messaging, or on a combination of Internet functions. Although in this study participants' typical uses of the Internet were e-mail and Web browsing, it could be illuminating to analyse the profile of those who usually use other Internet functions such as chatrooms and bulletin boards.

Comparing those whose typical use of the Internet is different from each other could provide further data about the relationship between individual differences and Internet dependency. As Oliver stated, researchers should pay more attention to individual differences in media effects research; neglecting this might lead to an underestimate or biased assessment of media effects.

This study suggests various forms of involvement are important mediating factors in Internet uses and dependency. Although the relationship between cognitive involvement and affective involvement was not the focus, it is possible that Internet users could shift from cognitive involvement to affective involvement, or vice versa. Moreover, involvement is variable rather than constant.

To understand involvement better, researchers need to investigate changes in involvement during Internet use, and over time. For example, when will users initially become involved with the content and mechanism of the Internet? When and why will they stop being involved? Investigating such processes will further illuminate the mediating role of involvement, and help clarify how motivation and involvement affect Internet dependency.

We are grateful for Professor C. Edwin Baker's lively response to our article and for the opportunity to clarify the important issues he raises, chiefly about the relationship between theory and evidence in media regulation specifically and law generally. We appreciate in particular his praise of our article's "innovative statistical techniques," given that our primary aim was to provide a new approach to empirically measure substantive viewpoint diversity.

Our empirical measures and methods help to address long-standing questions about whether media consolidation leads to convergence in viewpoints (the "convergence hypothesis"). We are glad that Baker agrees that the article makes progress in the empirical understanding of the media and that it is "far superior methodologically to most empirical studies that [he] ha[s] seen."

At the same time, Baker "denies the policy relevance" of our article. At heart, Baker asserts that empirical evidence about viewpoint diversity is "entirely irrelevant" to media regulation. In the place of empirical inquiry, we should conduct "value-based enquir[ies]" (for example, in the form of the theory he espouses) and, he argues, "anecdotal tales of seriously objectionable past abuses by media moguls could be much more informative" than statistical inquiry.

As a result, Baker argues that the FCC should aim to maximize the number of media owners ("source diversity"), as opposed to "viewpoint diversity." We write here to defend the role of empirical research in law, as well as the conclusions of our article. As we explain below, Baker's view suffers from deep ambiguity and internal inconsistency, ignores the empirical turn in communications law, and adopts the extreme position that normative theory should displace what he calls "law schools' recent romance with statistical empiricism [and] welfare economics," which Baker views as "malignant" to the "hermeneutic discipline" of law.

Most disconcerting is Baker's call for anecdotal tales and normative theory to take the place of—and preclude any role for—empirical scholarship (as well as positive and economic theory) in law. Our original article was entirely in that pluralistic spirit, invoking legal analysis and social science, qualitative and quantitative evidence, and drawing positive and normative inferences. Empirical inquiry has the potential to resolve parts of public policy problems that would be irresolvable on normative grounds alone. Its promise is not endless—a point we expressly highlight in our article—but it surely is not "entirely irrelevant."

CLARIFYING THE MUDDLE

OUR CONTRIBUTION

Our Stanford Law Review article makes four contributions to the broad question of federal regulation of media ownership. First, we document a trend that the FCC and numerous commentators have noted, namely the sharp empirical turn that the law on structural media ownership regulations has taken over the past twenty years.

The Telecommunications Act of 1996 requires that the FCC periodically "determine whether any of such [ownership] rules are necessary in the public interest as the result of competition." Under arbitrary and capricious review (review as a matter of administrative—not constitutional—law), the courts have increasingly required the FCC to provide evidence of the convergence hypothesis, and the FCC responded in 2002 by commissioning an unprecedented number of empirical studies on the connection between ownership and viewpoint diversity.

Second, our article surveys existing work and highlights serious limitations to extant measures of viewpoint diversity. For example, editorial endorsements of Democratic presidential candidates result in little variation between media outlets in a two-party system.

Alternatively, conventional reading and coding of "bias" of news articles (content analysis) can be fraught with lack of transparency and replicability, as is widely acknowledged (indeed by Baker himself). Third, given limitations of existing empirical approaches, our major contribution is to provide a new, transparent, and replicable measure of editorial viewpoint diversity by capitalizing on rapid advances in statistical measurement methodology.

Much like the concept of "intelligence," the idea of a "viewpoint" is complex and cannot be readily observed in a direct fashion. Nonetheless, intelligence and viewpoints do have observable implications. In educational testing, the measurement of intelligence is commonly dealt with through standardized testing—most importantly, the administration of common questions to place students on a common scale. Our approach capitalizes on that insight to look for instances where newspapers opine on common issues, namely Supreme Court decisions.

For over a year, with the help of a research team of fourteen Harvard and Stanford undergraduate and law students, we engaged in exhaustive data collection to collect every editorial written on Supreme Court decisions across twenty-five newspapers from 1988-2004, personally reading over 1,600 editorial positions in the process.

Adapting finely-tuned statistical methods (to account for differences across Justices, outlets, questions, and time) allows us to scale the newspapers on a substantively meaningful dimension of the Supreme Court Justices and to examine the evolution of editorial viewpoints during mergers and acquisitions.

Our results show stability in viewpoints for three conglomerate acquisitions, convergence for the case of the merger of the Atlanta Journal and the Atlanta Constitution to form the Atlanta Journal-Constitution, and divergence for the New York Times's acquisition of the Boston Globe. In short, consolidation does not inexorably lead to convergence or divergence.

This purposely adopts a broad view of empirical inquiry as encompassing both quantitative and qualitative research. Indeed, we devote an entire section of the article to an in-depth view of these two cases, drawing on a range of qualitative (e.g., detailed reading of editorials and phone calls with editors from every newspaper in our dataset) and quantitative (e.g., subscriber databases and census data) sources to complement our measures of viewpoint diversity and draw out complexities of these cases.

Fourth, we provide brief, but specific, policy implications based on the difficulty of empirical inquiry. Appellate interpretation of the 1996 Act holds that, unless the FCC finds that an ownership regulation continues to serve the public interest (typically involving evidence of convergence), the FCC shall repeal or modify it.

Our results point to a deep tension in this statutory reading between empirical justification and deregulation—the call for empirical verification subject to a high evidentiary standard may be tantamount to wholesale deregulation. Instead, incremental modification of ownership regulations may better facilitate empirical evaluation while heeding appellate interpretation.

We propose that the FCC collaborate with researchers to incorporate policy evaluation into regulation. Lastly, our case studies also highlight the crucial roles of editorial policies, editorial board organizational structure, and critical distinctions between mergers and acquisitions.

BAKER'S POSITION

Baker's response comes in two sections. In the first, he restates in a substantially similar form to previous writings his normative theory of media consolidation: "The three major reasons to oppose media concentration in general, and mergers in particular, can be labeled: (i) the democratic distribution value; (ii) the democratic safeguard value; and (iii) the media quality value...."

The democratic distribution value posits that everyone should have an "equal voice" in the same fashion of the one person, one vote requirement familiar from election law. Under Baker's view this "lead[s] inexorably to the recommendation of a maximum dispersal of media power... represented ultimately by ownership" so that "everyone [is] able to experience some media as her own."

"Increasing ownership dispersal always works in the direction of equalizing the distribution of media power among groups."

The democratic safeguard value posits that ownership dispersal guards against the "danger of demagogic power." Baker relies on a number of illustrations, largely from his other writings, of the problems of media concentration: the support of a media conglomerate for Adolf Hitler; mentioning by news programmes of an affiliate quiz show (Who Wants to Be A Millionaire?); pharmaceutical threats against the New York Times for exposes in affiliated magazines; Knight-Ridder's muting of Miami Herald editorial criticism of Edwin Meese due to pending approval of a joint operating agreement; Atlantic Richfield influencing editorial policy at the British Observer; and Richard Nixon's White House conversation about possible retaliation against the Washington Post via its broadcast licenses.

Despite these illustrations, he concludes that "empirical measurement of the effect of interest conflicts is predictably uninformative" as it would be difficult to observe such conflicts:

Any informed sense of the degree of danger will likely reflect a structural examination of the possibilities of and incentive for this "corruption" combined with qualitative or ethnographic investigations and, possibly, quantitative surveys of editors' and journalists' self-reports, though with recognition that ingrained, unconscious practices will often be the repositories of the corrupting incentives.

The media quality value stems from Baker's belief that "most conglomerates focus almost exclusively on the bottom line," which, he argues, uniformly undermines quality journalism. Since, positive externalities of democratic deliberation and accountability flow from healthy media, Baker favors the following policy to promote quality journalism:

The owners who are most likely to favour journalism over profits include several predictable types:

- Smaller, usually local, owners who take identity from their firms' contributions to their community or from the journalistic product they create;
- Workers who take professional pride in the quality of their product;
- Non-profit entities whose goals include service to their community. Each category justifies policy moves to increase its ranks.

Because these three values (democratic distribution, democratic safeguard, and media quality) are, evidently, sufficient reasons "to oppose media concentration," Baker concludes that our empirical assessment of whether media consolidation reduces viewpoint diversity is entirely irrelevant.

The second section of Baker's response more directly addresses our article. First, Baker points to limitations in our study, namely that

- News reporting "may be more significant for democratic discourse than editorial positions";
- Our study focuses only on the top twenty-five newspapers;
- Our study only contains "a sample of five mergers"; and
- "The relevant diversity should be qualitative, not simply quantitative."

He hypothesizes that in theory some local newspapers may see convergence in news, but divergence in editorial positions, upon merging.

Second, Baker argues that "[t]he democratic quality of discourse is not measured by the amount of diversity actually occurring" but by three other factors:

- That views are not suppressed,
- That views are not subject to suppression, and
- "That there are meaningful efforts to develop relevant information and perspective."

Lastly, Baker argues that the "problem" with our article "lies in its potentially misdirecting policy discussion by purporting to give an empirical but actually irrelevant basis for deregulation." He ruminates at great length as to whether our "error of not considering the real reasons to oppose concentration... is explicable." He hypothesizes:

- That we were "misled" by "the confusion of other scholars and of the FCC itself,"
- That we are "anti-regulatory advocates strategic[ally],... pick[ing] up on the term 'diversity'" and "then interpret[ing it] in commodified terms" in order to move the discussion to "a battleground on which [we] have the greatest chance to win," and/or
- That our error reflects "economists' occupational inclination to see value in what can be purchased in markets... and a corresponding bias in [our] resulting political recommendations."

Most broadly, he argues that "[l]aw aspires to legitimacy, which in turn ultimately is a matter of values and reasons, not a matter of deductive logic or fact or mere instrumental rationality" and that our major methodological error may stem from, amongst other reasons, "a false image of science, an ingrained fearful desire of originally untenured academics to steer clear of controversy," or "an immature craving to escape uncertainty and indeterminacy." His conclusion is sweeping:

The Court's recent call for empirical evidence while avoiding explanations of how or why it is relevant... and many law schools' recent romance with statistical empiricism, following up on the Court's earlier affair with welfare economics, reflects these impulses [to avoid value judgments].

These hopes of interpretive value avoidance and tendencies towards instrumentalist reductionism are malignant. Economics and empiricism are the easy parts of legal scholarship, appropriate only as handmaidens to its real vocation.

Legal scholarship and inquiry, like all hermeneutic disciplines, though clearly in need of knowledge of the world, have traditionally been at their best when they understood themselves as value-based inquiries.

Given these provocative arguments, which indict the entirety of welfare economics and empirical legal studies in a few brushstrokes, we are compelled to respond. Notwithstanding the colorful rhetoric—relegating economics and empiricism as "only handmaidens" to legal scholarly inquiry—we share at least three key agreements with Baker.

First, what Baker terms the "democratic safeguard value" is an important and relevant underlying consideration in media regulation. As we squarely acknowledged in our article, the media plays an important role in the functioning of a healthy democracy. Yet one primary way the FCC has incorporated this concern is precisely via viewpoint diversity: diverse viewpoints foster democratic deliberation and, at least in theory, ultimately, accountability.

We agree that policymakers should carefully evaluate the risk to democracy posed by potential changes of federal communications law. Nonetheless, our more modest aim was to respond to the recent empirical demands of media law and scholarship. Further, as we elaborate below, most such careful risk evaluations will likely contain an important empirical component.

Second, many aspects of media output beyond editorial positions of the top twenty-five newspapers are relevant. None of these are new concerns that Baker raises.

Our article was entirely clear about these limitations and sought to improve on existing empirical work. We explained: "because we only examine major newspapers, our measures may ignore the types of newspapers whose viewpoints are most threatened by media consolidation" and "our focus on editorial positions ignores news reporting."

Of course, convergence in the top newspapers is still of interest—indeed, three of Baker's illustrations of democratic safeguards revolve around top newspapers (each in our dataset): the New York Times, the Washington Post, the Detroit Free Press, and the Miami Herald.

As to news, methods similar to ours may be adapted to study news reporting, and we show below—and in other work—that editorial viewpoints are strongly correlated with news slant.

Our focus on editorial viewpoint diversity is a direct response to the fact that both scholars and the Commission have pointed out editorials as relevant.

Third, we agree with a weak version of Baker's concern, namely that we must recognize the limitations of empirical inference. Our article went on at great length to highlight the difficulties of direct policy evaluation of the ownership rules. Given that there is little variation in ownership regulations, it is extremely difficult to directly assess the causal effect of these regulations.

Yet the fact that empirical inquiry is limited does not mean that it is worthless. To the contrary, across disciplinary fields, empirical inquiry has advanced scholarship and produced tremendous knowledge, which surely explains in part the enthusiasm—not shared by Baker—about empirical legal studies. While we agree on these three major points, Baker's response goes astray in numerous directions.

A VULNERABLE THEORY

The first part of Baker's response, which rehashes in substantially identical form (and with the same examples) the theory already spelled out in his book and another article, is entirely outside the scope of our work. He views his unique normative theory as the sufficient reason to oppose media consolidation. Since, the theory, at least according to Baker, has no observable implications, and cannot be proven wrong with data, we do not dwell on it here.

We merely note that it is difficult to have a complete theoretical answer in an empirical vacuum. One could easily question the theoretical grounds: does the theory provide any way to draw the tradeoff between benefits and costs of ownership regulations when his theory provides only reasons to oppose media consolidation?

Does the theory provide any sense of when ownership regulations may be too great when federal law could mandate, for example, that every single individual should own a broadcast station? How does the democratic distribution analogy to one person, one vote operate when social choice theory highlights the difficulties of preference aggregation, which could similarly plague aggregation of voices by media outlets?

Moreover, why doesn't the analogy to election law undercut the notion that empirical evidence is "irrelevant" when election law commonly deals with evidence of vote dilution, fraud, and the effects of electoral rules?

How are the value of democratic distribution and the policy implication of maximum dispersal of media power not a matter of tautology when valuing equal voices "inexorably" leads to more owners of media? It is one matter to state values and another to see how to achieve them—how does Baker's view avoid conflating ends and means?

Although the theory may not be vulnerable to empirical verification, it is vulnerable to each of these deep theoretical ambiguities. We leave it for others to resolve the persuasiveness of these claims. This sought to examine what empirical evidence exists for the convergence hypothesis with a reliable and valid measure of editorial viewpoints, responding directly to the empirical turn in the law and scholarship. We thereby address why systematic empirical inquiry into viewpoint diversity matters and respond to Baker's specific assertions about our article.

THE FCC AND THE COURTS

One of the fundamental misconceptions, Baker argues, is our focus on substantive viewpoint diversity. Instead, he argues, "[m]any FCC policies are most explicable if based on a concern for source diversity without the requirement of any degree of actual content or viewpoint diversity." By source diversity, Baker means the number of owners. In focusing on viewpoint diversity, he argues, we "overread" sources and are "misled" by "the confusion of other scholars and of the FCC itself."

As support for the idea that source diversity is not a means to viewpoint diversity, he cites to a 1970 FCC Multiple Ownership Order (despite the "confusion of... the FCC") and the Supreme Court's 1978 decision in FCC v. National Citizens Committee for Broadcasting (NCCB). This view suffers from two fatal flaws. First, neither the 1970 Multiple Ownership Order nor the NCCB case support the idea that source diversity is to be valued independently—or to the exclusion—of viewpoint diversity. From the 1970

Multiple Ownership Order, Baker selectively quotes the FCC (and omits the last portion of the sentence, relevant since, it highlights what was at least perceived as a natural limit in broadcast spectrum): "A proper objective is the maximum diversity of ownership that technology permits in each area." Although that language might suggest source diversity, the same order goes on to say the following:

Although the principal purpose of the proposed rules is to promote diversity of viewpoints in the same area, and it is on this ground that our above discussion is primarily based, we think it clear that promoting diversity of ownership also promotes competition....... Simply stated, the fundamental purpose of this facet of the multiple ownership rules is to promote diversification of ownership in order to maximize diversification of programme and service viewpoints as well as to prevent any undue concentration of economic power contrary to the public interest.

From the NCCB case, Baker admits that the Supreme Court highlighted viewpoint diversity, but argues that the Court also recognized source diversity when it noted the interest in "preventing undue concentration of economic power."

This language itself is vague and does not necessarily implicate source diversity, but more telling is Justice Marshall's discussion for the majority, which at each juncture connects ownership with viewpoint diversity:

[The FCC's] policy judgement was certainly not irrational and indeed was founded on the very same assumption that underpinned the diversification policy itself and the prospective rules upheld by the Court of Appeals and now by this Court—that the greater number of owners in a market, the greater the possibility of achieving diversity of programme and service viewpoints.

Second, even disregarding the 1970 Multiple Ownership Order and NCCB, what is most telling is that Baker fails to discuss any authority within the last twenty years for the primacy of source diversity. Indeed, that would be difficult, as the courts and FCC could not be clearer. In its 2002 Biennial Order, the FCC states:

The Commission has sought, therefore, to diffuse ownership of media outlets among multiple firms in order to diversify the viewpoints available to the public....... We therefore continue to believe that broadcast ownership limits are necessary to preserve and promote viewpoint diversity.

"Source diversity" refers to the availability of media content from a variety of content producers. The Notice explained that source diversity can contribute to our 'retail" goals of viewpoint diversity and programme diversity.... The record before us does not support a conclusion that source diversity should be an objective of our broadcast ownership policies.

The Commission adopted the newspaper/broadcast cross-ownership rule because it believed that diversification of ownership would promote diversification of viewpoint.

In short, the FCC explicitly rejected Baker's position that source diversity is an independent objective. As we stated in our article, the conventional justification for the ownership regulations is as "a means to the ultimate end of furthering substantive viewpoint diversity." Similarly, the D.C. Circuit noted in a series of cases:

The only support the Commission offered for regulation based on this possibility was the idea that every additional chance for a programmer to secure access would enhance diversity.

The stated purpose of the seven-station rule was 'to promote diversification of ownership in order to maximize diversification of programme and service viewpoints' and 'to prevent any undue concentration of economic power.'

The only recent evidence Baker alludes to is from comments filed by the public in the 2002 Biennial Review, which he conjectures may have been animated by concerns about source diversity.

Of course, what was in the mind of each of some 500,000 plus parties filing comments is a matter of pure speculation. Suffice it to say that Commissioner Adelstein, who dissented from the 2002 Biennial Order and highlighted the comments, notes the importance of viewpoint diversity when stating that "[t]he public has a right to be informed by a diversity of viewpoints so they can make up their own minds." Baker's sharp separation of source and viewpoint diversity is an artifact of his own normative theory and has no basis in current law.

THE EMPIRICAL TURN OF THE LAW

Beyond asserting the irrelevance of viewpoint diversity, Baker argues that our statement that "[c]ourts and in turn the Commission have increasingly mandated some form of empirical evidence" is a claim with "unfortunate lack of citation" that may "represent a willingness merely to assume a nonexistent legal mandate that... would require [our] expertise." Indeed, he concludes, "I can find no specific support for their claim that 'measuring viewpoint diversity is... mandated by law.'"

Such a charge is severe. But it plainly misreads the thrust of our article, which had an entire section devoted to the empirical turn in the law of media, documented by dozens of references with copious discussion of the case law. We showed that starting with cases such as Schurz Communications, Inc. v. FCC, Time Warner Entertainment Co. v. FCC, Fox TV Stations, Inc. v. FCC, Sinclair Broadcast Group, Inc. v. FCC, and culminating in the 2002

Biennial Order, courts and the FCC have increasingly required evidence to sustain the convergence hypothesis, instead of deferring as the NCCB court did several decades earlier.

Little else would account for why the FCC, in an unprecedented fashion, commissioned twelve empirical studies on localism and diversity in its 2002 biennial review, specifically seeking comment on "whether th[e] longstanding presumed link between ownership and viewpoint could be established empirically," and affirmatively stating in that context that "[t]o fulfill our biennial review obligation, we will first define our goals and the ways we will measure them."

Moreover, it would be a strange position for the courts and the FCC not to mandate at least some evidence. After all, the public interest determination under the 1996 Act has to be made every few years. If we are to rely exclusively on normative theory, as Baker desires, what could possibly change every few years about the values (and not evidence) of media quality and democratic distribution and safeguards?

When the Commission makes a policy determination to rescind the newspaper/broadcast cross-ownership rule—adopted initially "because it believed that diversification of ownership would promote diversification of viewpoint"—some record evidence must sustain the policy determination under standard administrative law principles.

Indeed, our description of the empirical turn in the law would be hard to refute. Describing none other than Baker's position, Christopher Terry and Professors David Pritchard and Paul Brewer note that "[s]ome advocates of strict limits on media cross-ownership argue that this kind of empirical evidence is 'simply irrelevant' to media ownership policy, but even they acknowledge that the FCC and the courts require such evidence."

They, in turn, refer to the following passage by Baker: "Recently in the media context, some courts and some policy makers routinely ask for empirical evidence to support governmental policies.... [The] request for more evidence emboldened some lower courts to strike down sensible media laws and regulations for lack of the empirical support that some individual judges wrongly believed relevant to constitutional legitimacy."

This language may also reveal where Baker misconceives the case law: evidence is not required as a matter of constitutional (First Amendment) law, but rather as a matter of administrative law: namely, the Court's application of arbitrary and capricious review.

Lastly, Baker does not appear to distinguish between types of evidence (e.g., qualitative and quantitative empirical evidence). The Supreme Court in Turner remanded for more development of evidence per se, and Baker equates this with "empirical evidence." Whether the empirical turn is normatively desirable is a different matter—a tension explicitly addressed in our discussion of policy implications—but Baker misunderstands our positive description of the empirical turn in the law, one which is resoundingly echoed in assessments by media scholars (and, strangely, by Baker himself elsewhere).

THE DANGERS OF ANECDOTALISM

Given that evidence as to viewpoint diversity plays a central role in media regulation, how do we know what inference the evidence sustains? The key is that the process of gathering evidence has to be articulated. Such formalization of the research process is a chief virtue of well-conducted empirical studies. This for example, articulated each step of the research process, making it transparent how the data was acquired, how observations were chosen, and thereby what inferences could be drawn.

By contrast, Baker's selective use of a handful of "anecdotal tales," which he argues are more informative than statistical inquiry, violates basic rules of inference and fails the fundamental research standard of replicability. Key questions go unanswered about the case he provides to illustrate the democratic safeguard concern: what's the population of units to which he is drawing inferences? How were the cases chosen?

By what process were they observed? How could his theory be falsified? We recognize that Baker, on one level, does not aspire to put forth a falsifiable theory. However, the deep tension is that his normative theory is laden with empirical propositions for which Baker offers only single cases as illustrations. Baker dismisses empirical studies for the following reasons:

Caution...dictates consideration of whether these empirical studies reflect not only particular historical but potentially changeable circumstances. It also dictates a consideration of whether they adequately conceptualize the issue under examination, remove effects of (hold constant) potentially competing, alternative, or additional causes, properly treat any indeterminacy in the findings, consider alternative explanations of the data, and so forth.

Each of these methodological challenges presents a valid concern, but applies a fortiori to the selective use of empirical examples by unarticulated criteria. When drawing a reliable inference from evidence it is no defence to say that the evidence is qualitative: basic rules of inference apply. To illustrate these points, we discuss several of Baker's cases and show the danger of drawing inferences from anecdotal tales alone. A. Who Wants to Be A Millionaire?

To illustrate how conglomerate ownership concentration can undermine journalistic integrity, Baker points to a study by economics Professor James Hamilton that ABC's affiliates mentioned the show Who Wants to Be a Millionaire? In over 80 per cent of local news programmes while no NBC affiliate found the ABC programme newsworthy.

While this case appears indicative of network self-promotion, Baker—unlike Hamilton—tells us nothing about how he chose this case.

Hamilton actually examined several instances of soft news, such as the reporting by network affiliates of Toy Story 2, an episode involving a lesbian kiss on Ally McBeal, and an interview by Barbara Waiters of Monica Lewinsky promoting her book.

The figure demonstrates that Baker singled out the extreme outlier that happened to be consistent with his views.

Worse, Baker has not articulated how Millionaire is even relevant to his theory of democratic safeguards and how it exemplifies that conglomerate ownership undermines journalistic integrity. First, only one of the cases studied by Hamilton—Toy Story 2—is about conglomerate ownership (involving Disney and ABC), and that case does not support the claim that conglomerate ownership influences soft news coverage. The observations are centered around the origin, indicating indistinguishable coverage rates by affiliates and non-affiliates of Toy Story 2 or its stars, Tim Allen and Tom Hanks.

Second, is network self-promotion about Millionaire or Ally McBeal's kiss truly relevant to the grave concerns about democratic deliberation and legitimacy? As we argued, one of the major benefits of empirical measurement is that it forces scholars to conceptualize more concretely what is meant by complex concepts, such as viewpoint diversity and distortion of journalism.

Reasonable people may disagree as to whether the evening news lead-in (e.g., "Coming up next: Millionaire") is innocuous, but measurement itself clarifies what we mean by quality of journalism. Lastly, if they are relevant, that comes into tension with the position that the costs to concentration cannot be measured.

CONGLOMERATE SUPPORT OF FASCISM

To illustrate how the "existence of... concentrated power within the public sphere creates a real danger of abuse," Baker points to a sobering example of the first German media conglomerate's support of Adolf Hitler. "No democracy should accept that risk" of "abuse of the concentrated power implicit in conglomerate media ownership," and ownership regulations, he argues, would guard against such atrocious outcomes of fascism.

As we stated, we agree with the underlying concern of democratic safeguards. Yet Baker also appears to make an empirically falsifiable claim when he states that "at least since, the first major German media conglomerate supported the rise of Hitler, various countries... have experienced demographic abuse of the concentrated power implicit in conglomerate media ownership," namely that conglomerate media outlets are more likely to support the abuse of power or fascism.

Unfortunately, we are given little information about the single example he provides (what sources he consulted, what other cases he considered, etc.). What if the only example provided was one of a small, non-conglomerate newspaper supporting Hitler? Would that support the contrary theory? A cursory examination of German media history reveals much more evidence by which one can assess the validity of this conglomerate-fascism connection, as many more newspapers existed.

The fact that the only conglomerate supported Hitler may be due to pure chance alone, especially if newspaper support of Hitler was widespread. This might weaken the inference that conglomerate status affected fascist support. Of course, drawing an inference about conglomerates when only one exists is fraught with peril.

The fascism theory may have another observable implication: if concentration matters, perhaps circulation should be associated with support of Hitler. Across three newspapers with small, medium, and large circulation, the lack of correlation remains the same. Of course, we have not said anything about how these cases were chosen. And that is precisely the point.

With more data, representative of a population, we might be able to examine the validity of Baker's hypothesis. The Hugenberg case illustrates the failure to heed basic principles of inference: articulate how observations were gathered, collect as much information as possible, and extract all possible observable implications of the theory.

Baker discusses two more cases to illustrate the "abuse of the concentrated power implicit in conglomerate media ownership." In 1976, the New York Times published several articles on medical malpractice that evidently angered the medical industry.

Medicine-related advertisers threatened to withdraw advertisements from Times-owned medical magazines, which were later sold, arguably in consideration of the threat. Baker argues that the advertising threat demonstrates the danger of conglomerates.

Two problems present themselves in connection with the first case. First, the relationship between medical magazines and the New York Times has nothing to do with extant cross-ownership rules. This is, of course, acceptable if it might inform us more generally about the impact of common ownership.

More importantly, the New York Times did, in fact, run this expose of medical malpractice, which may cut against Baker's strong assumption that conglomerates favour profits over journalism. Indeed, one of the major arguments about the benefits of consolidation is that news resources can be pooled to engage in more investigative journalism.

More generally, recall Baker's supposition:

The owners who are most likely to favour journalism over profits include several predictable types: (a) smaller, usually local, owners who take identity from their firms' contributions to their community or from the journalistic product they create; (b) workers who take professional pride in the quality of their product; (c) non-profit entities whose goals include service to their community.

These assertions appear inconsistent with the New York Times and the Washington Post examples. Worse, one strains for how to interpret this statement. Does statement (a) mean that smaller owners are more likely to "take identity" from their journalistic product than larger owners?

Or is the statement simply true by tautology (i.e., owners "most likely to favour journalism over profits" are "owners who take identity... from the journalistic product they create" and "workers who take professional pride in the quality of their product")? Can we define this in a falsifiable way? It is no defence that the theory isn't offered for positive scholarship—for policy purposes the implementation of Baker's rule would require decisionmakers to operationalize these categories.

Decidedly lacking from this statement are citations to vast amounts of empirical work on the topic of conglomerate and chain ownership of newspapers.

The Watergate example suggests that a relevant outcome is coverage of political scandals, and we might consult this literature to see whether smaller newspapers are generally more likely to cover political scandals. Examining the exact opposite, namely, "[o]verall coverage of scandals is significantly higher for newspapers with higher circulation" and "[n] ewspapers with higher circulation systematically devote more coverage to political scandals, at least in the news section."

Of course, we have not done a formal examination of all empirical works on this question (metaanalysis), and one may quibble with the exact design and how closely it tracks Baker's conjecture—but that is precisely the virtue of empirical work in helping to clarify theory.

THE RULES OF INFERENCE

Our examination of these cases is not to suggest that case studies are not worthwhile. To the contrary, well-chosen case studies can be tremendously illuminating. Indeed, recall that our article entailed a lengthy exposition of two case studies. The lesson from Baker's cases is that one must be careful about research design, principles of inference, and the dangers of anecdotalism.

In the end, for all the rhetoric about empirical studies being "irrelevant," there is a deep, unanswered tension in Baker's position. He suggests that ethnographic surveys and journalist self-reports (i.e., empirical studies) may be probative evidence of the corruption of concentrated media (and relies on one example from Hamilton's book chock full of empirical results), but dismisses other empirical studies as irrelevant. Further, he says:

I am a great admirer of empirical research. At places where I make empirical predictions—for example, that mergers typically reduce the quality of media performance—I have looked to see if empirical studies support... my claim, in this case finding that, although evidence is meagre, apparently mergers did have this negative effect.

Such a statement gets it exactly wrong. Social scientists are not advocates scouring for empirical studies that happen to support the favored position. To the contrary, social scientists look for every reason to falsify their theory, so as to ascertain the truth of the matter.

The very study that Baker looked to for support of his claim contains distinct findings that contradict his view on ownership.

That study concludes: "The data offer some evidence to support the argument favoring cross ownership." To draw an inference from scholarly literature, one cannot selectively choose results by unarticulated criteria.

One should look for all evidence that may be inconsistent with one's theory.

Only after such vetting can a researcher (or reader) be persuaded that some rival explanation does not account for observed phenomena. Anecdotalism is unlikely to take us far. Systematic measurement is crucial.

SYSTEMATIC MEASUREMENT

THE IMPORTANCE OF EMPIRICAL EVIDENCE WITH CALAMITOUS RISKS

It is precisely because the media plays an important role that empirical inquiry is warranted. Baker argues that evidence is entirely irrelevant due to the strength of his normative theory. Moreover, "empirical measurement... is predictably uninformative" and the "search for empirical evidence" is "misguided."

The danger to democracy is so strong that "[e]ven if, in the past, the risk had never led to bad results (which would make the danger hard to measure by normal statistical techniques), good institutional design—like good structural design of nuclear power plants—should not unnecessarily risk calamitous results."

The example of nuclear power is telling. If anything, it contradicts Baker's privileged and exclusive role for normative theory. While we may not observe many calamitous results of nuclear failure, observable indicators of structural design exist, such as the robustness of the containment structure, shutdown margins, and other operational controls.

How else would we discover what "good structural design" entails, or whether a design imposes "unnecessary risk"? It cannot be the case that empirical evidence is "simply irrelevant" for these determinations. Evidence, science, and expertise should and do inform the design of nuclear power plants.

The analogy is further illuminating because nuclear power presents a kind of "dread risk" feared by the public, but this perception diverges significantly from expert assessments of nuclear risk. Divergence between popular and expert assessments may well be present in the media context as well.

Calamitous disasters are not impervious to empirical scrutiny. One luminary of data visualization, Professor Edward Tufte, cogently argued that the reticence to appropriately examine data may well have contributed to the Challenger space shuttle disaster. While NASA was in possession of compelling evidence that low temperatures were associated with O-ring erosion (the cause of the shuttle explosion), it failed to examine the data in a sufficiently clear form to set off alarm.

As Tufte argued, irrelevant icons of side rocket boosters, inscrutable legends of damage, and chronological organization of shuttles distort the relevant relationship in the data between temperature and O-ring failure. The data exhibit a sharp pattern: O-ring erosion on previous shuttle flights occurred overwhelmingly at lower temperatures. Every shuttle below sixty- six degrees experienced erosion.

No failures occurred above seventy degrees. The only instance with three erosions occurred at the lowest observed temperature of fitly-three degrees.

And the temperature forecast for the day of the Challenger takeoff was some twenty degrees lower than any previous shuttle flight. Regardless of the exact relationship, extrapolating the pattern should have set off alarm bells. The risk of "calamitous results" warrants more examination—subject to principles of inference—of evidence, not less.

THE ENTERPRISE OF MEASUREMENT

The purpose of systematic measurement is to overcome the speculative nature of anecdotal tales. Yet Baker argues that "the relevant diversity should be qualitative, not simply quantitative." "The democratic quality of discourse is not measured by the amount of diversity," but by (1) the fact that views are not subject to or actually suppressed, and by (2) meaningful efforts to develop relevant information and perspective.

He argues that our measures of viewpoint diversity are "commodified," and thereby we commit a basic error: since, consumers value commodities (such as viewpoints) on the market, we miss "non-commodified" democratic values. We agree that there are other relevant media outputs that may be affected by media consolidation. But Baker's charge that viewpoints are irrelevant because they are "commodified" misunderstands the enterprise of measurement.

First, the enterprise of measurement is to capture meaningful outcomes. Prior to our research, indirect and inadequate proxies for substantive viewpoints were used. Statements about whether the Los Angeles Times became more "conservative" upon acquisition by the Tribune Company (or Baker's characterization of the Wall Street Journal as having a "reactionary" editorial stance) were hence, difficult to evaluate.

Our approach provides a transparent and neutral way to do this, addressing Baker's charge prior to our work that "the claims of content variation are bedeviled by intrinsic methodological measurement problems that cannot be solved in a value-neutral way." We disagree, and take it that Baker also retreats from the prior conclusion that measurement cannot be solved when he says that our study is "far superior methodologically."

Essentially, our measure recovers what a reasonable person would infer about the viewpoint of a newspaper if she read all editorials about the Supreme Court and learned about all votes cast by the Justices for a ten-year period. The latent scale represents the "distance" between the Justices based on voting patterns and analogous differences between newspapers based on "phantom" votes on Supreme Court cases, and can be interpreted as running from "liberal" to "conservative."

For example, the New York Times exhibits a phantom jurisprudence just to the left of Justice Stevens, and the Investor's Business Daily is closest in opinion to Justice Scalia. Moreover, the intervals capture the uncertainty in distinguishing newspapers: the San Francisco Chronicle and the Boston Globe are indistinguishable from each other (and closest to Justice Ginsburg). Our measurement approach thereby turned what was likely a subjective assessment into something transparent.

Second, the fact that quality matters does not mean that quality cannot be measured. If observable, it is by definition measurable. In addition, Baker mistakenly assumes that "media quality" cannot be measured in quantitative terms. It may be more challenging, but addressing that challenge was precisely what our measurement approach achieved. While our estimated measure is quantitative, the underlying data is qualitative as to whether a newspaper editorialized in favour of each Supreme Court decision or not. As Edward Lee Thorndike, a founder of educational psychology, stated:

Our ideals may be as lofty and as subtle as you please, but if they are real ideals, they are ideals for achieving something; and if anything real is ever achieved, it can be measured. Not perhaps now, and not perhaps fifty years from now; but if a thing exists, it exists in some amount; and if it exists in some amount, it can be measured.

Third, Baker's assertions—that our measure is market-based and that as "market apologists, [we] then interpret diversity in commodified terms—obfuscate rather than clarify. Our measures are not "market measures" in any classical sense (such as measures from contingent or hedonic valuation studies. The issue is not one of "commodification," but of measurement.

This becomes clear when he argues "[t]ypical market measures provide no direct way to measure purported contributions of separation of powers and legislative bicameralism to improving democratic deliberations and to reducing risks to liberty."

It is unclear what he means by "market measures," but both bicameralism and separation of powers have been studied voluminously by social scientists, including measures precisely relevant to broad concerns of liberty and deliberation, including effects on political accountability, judicial and congressional decision-making, executive appointments, government duration, fiscal deficits, majoritarian tyranny, policy stability, length of legislative bargaining, and the cohesion of a ruling coalition.

To say that this thriving research—studying and measuring the various dimensions of separation of powers and bicameralism—is irrelevant because it uses "market measures" (perhaps because a formal theoretic or quantitative empirical approach is adopted?) is misinformed. The incantation of an arguably ill-defined concept of "commodification" is not talismanic. If media quality has observable outcomes, they are measurable.

Indeed, Baker implicitly measures quality every time he invokes an illustration of the effects of concentration on media. Our methods empower such measurement. Fourth, our measure plausibly incorporates certain elements of Baker's media quality (notwithstanding the fact that it remains loosely articulated).

Viewpoint suppression, such as Tribune-company influence over the Los Angeles Times editorial board, would be captured, at least in part, by changes in substantive editorial viewpoints. And few other items on the pages of a newspaper are as relevant to the notion of "perspective" as editorializing.

Baker's argument effectively reduces to: you've missed something, yet I won't tell you exactly what it is, because it's not measurable. Indeed, it is ironic that he faults the courts for calling for empirical evidence "while avoiding explanations of how or why it is relevant." Yet clarification is precisely a major benefit of formal measurement: it forces the researcher to concretize concepts that are diffuse in the abstract and to refine what exactly it is that we mean by elusive terms such as "viewpoint diversity" and "quality." For example, one might argue that Supreme Court editorials miss "local diversity."

Thinking about how to measure local diversity forces one to conceptualize "diversity," when, for example, each newspaper might endorse candidates in completely different local races. Does the lack of editorial opposition to candidates in given local races still mean diversity (perhaps temporally or across subscription areas)? Measurement serves to clarify concepts and crystallize theory.

THE ROLE OF EDITORIALS AND NEWS

Baker validly points out that our focus on editorials does not capture news reporting. Yet he goes further in arguing that "news may be more significant for democratic discourse than... editorial positions" and that "[c]ritics of the media seldom bemoan a paper's editorial position. Rather, their chorus alleges slanted news presentation and, even more importantly, misguided choices—whether due to ideological bias or structural economic considerations—in not covering certain stories."

While we agree that news should be independently examined (which is possible—albeit with some complications—by adapting measurement methods similar to ours), we take issue with Baker's slapdash dismissal of the relevance of studying editorial viewpoint diversity. First, whether or not news reporting is "more significant" than editorializing is speculation. (Baker admits as much in stating that news "may be more significant for democratic discourse.")

Our contribution was to study editorial viewpoints, which serve a crucial role in the development of perspectives on public policy issues. Recall that one of Baker's indicators of "quality" is "meaningful efforts to develop relevant information and perspective." Editorials are at least one crucial output of such efforts to develop relevant perspective.

Second, Baker's own illustrations demonstrate that editorials play a central role. Knight-Ridder's reported influence over Miami Herald's criticism of Edwin Meese manifested itself precisely through editorials.

And although Baker discusses Atlantic Richfield in the context of incentives to "report favorably," at least according to the only source Baker cites, the company intervened in the writing of editorial columns. Moreover, Baker's example of a media conglomerate's "abuse of... concentrated power" is that of Alfred Hugenberg's support of Hitler, but again, one major channel of influence was via editorial policy and newspaper endorsements of Hitler. The very illustrations that Baker invokes are inconsistent with the notion that critics "seldom bemoan a paper's editorial position."

Third, even ignoring Baker's own inconsistency, it is simply untrue that critics seldom focus on editorial positions. None other than Ben Bagdikian, the "dean of American media critics," laments the homogenization of content due to media concentration. He discusses editorials on the fairness doctrine, the uniformity of editorial endorsements of political candidates, and instances of executive pressure influencing editorial endorsement decisions—something we expressly discussed in our article. And of course, as we have already noted, the FCC and existing scholarship consider editorial viewpoints important.

Fourth, Baker's conjecture that consolidation amongst local newspapers might cause convergence in news and divergence in editorials is intriguing, but a red herring. Baker offers not a shred of evidence upon which to assess its validity. One might conjecture the exact opposite: that upon acquisition, local newspapers fire the editorial board and run wire editorials (thereby converging in editorial viewpoints), while devoting resources to local news (thereby diverging in news reporting).

The Palo Alto Daily News, which is owned by the Bay Area News Group, for example, follows pretty much this practice of wire op-eds and local news. Since, we have provided exactly one more data point than Baker has, one might even argue that our conjecture is more plausible than his. Yet such conjectures become verifiable only with a measure of editorial viewpoint diversity—such as in the approach we have provided—and more systematic empirical investigation beyond anecdotes.

Lastly, our measures of editorial viewpoint diversity in fact offer considerable insight into news reporting, as they are highly correlated with news output. The measures are highly correlated, with the exception of the Wall Street Journal, which is known to have a conservative editorial desk and a liberal news desk. Of course, one might argue about the precise much about news reporting as well.

In the end, Baker is right to point to news as important, but his arguments that editorials are seldom at issue are internally inconsistent and unsupported. Conjecture cannot replace the hard work of developing a method of measuring editorial viewpoint diversity that is transparent, replicable, substantively interpretable, accounts for measurement uncertainty, and is, in principle, adaptable for the study of news diversity.

INFORMATION VERSUS SAMPLE SIZE

A remaining deficiency of our measurement approach, according to Baker, is that it has "a sample size of five." This is plainly wrong. Our data consisted of 10,598 votes by 13 Justices and 1,618 editorial positions by 25 newspapers across 1,186 cases from 1988 to 2004. While there are five mergers and acquisitions, these represent every one that occurred in the sample for this observation period, providing comparisons between some eleven newspapers before and after the transaction.

Moreover, we collected large amounts of information about each newspaper pre- and post-transaction and augmented this data with evidence from county-level circulation statistics, detailed studies of editorial board composition, and qualitative study of the editorials themselves.

By Baker's count, studying the effect of the collapse of the Soviet Union on mass political attitudes by conducting pre- and post-surveys of hundreds of respondents would count as a sample size of one.

Fixation on effective sample size is misguided. A sample size of one individual can be greatly informative when mapping the human genome, while a sample size of one million can be irrelevant when the causal factor of interest does not vary.

Similarly, a sample of twenty randomly selected individuals with randomly assigned treatment can be far more informative than a non-random sample of 5,000 individuals who have self-selected into treatment. The purpose of research design is not to maximize the number of observations, but to maximize leverage over quantities of interest so that we can meaningfully learn about the world.

THE NORMATIVE AND THE PERSONAL

While we greatly appreciate the lively response, it is oddly consumed with dissecting our personal motivations and presumed normative pre-commitments. Baker charges that as "anti-regulatory advocates," we "purport to give an empirical... basis for deregulation."

Nowhere do we do so. First, we did not start from a normative pre-commitment. To the contrary, at the outset of this research, we had no preconception as to what to expect about the evolution of viewpoints before and after mergers and acquisitions. And our results do not lend themselves to ready simplification of favoring regulation or deregulation, as we find evidence for convergence, divergence, and stability in light of newspaper consolidation.

Second, nowhere did our policy implications endorse deregulation and, if anything, made exactly the opposite point. We showed that "repealing the rules would exacerbate the already profound difficulties of empirical justification about the effects of a rule."

Further, we highlighted an implicit tension between the mandates of the 1996 Act for the FCC to (1) make a public interest determination (wrought by the difficulties of empirical evaluation), and (2) repeal or modify ownership regulations if they no longer serve the public interest.

We expressly argued that the difficulties of empirical inference militate in favour of incremental modification, rather than wholesale deregulation, which would accord with federal law when strong evidence sustaining the convergence hypothesis is lacking. To overcome the difficulties of the public interest determination, we suggested the FCC collaborate with research groups to design programme evaluation and field experiments to facilitate such evaluation.

Nowhere did we "purport to give an empirical... basis for deregulation." Baker oddly imputes implications where they do not exist. Most strangely, Baker's response makes a number of ad hominem claims and conjectures as to why we were personally "misled" and our "inexcusable" errors of failing to articulate his preferred theory.

As answers, he charges us with "making the same mistake" as scholars "driven by free-market ideology," and argues that we suffer of "economists' occupational inclination to see value in what can be purchased in markets" and "a corresponding bias in [our] resulting political recommendations."

In addition, with what he admits to be "intentionally inflammatory" rhetoric, he charges that our empirical measure fails to capture the media reporting about the connection between Saddam Hussein and Osama Bin Laden and argues that we miss the fact that the rise of Hitler had some association with conglomerate media ownership. And (as if that were not enough), our work may suffer from the "ingrained fearful desire of originally untenured academics to steer clear of controversy, [and] an immature craving to escape uncertainty and indeterminacy."

Most disturbing about these charges and this rhetoric is that they miss a fundamental point about scholarly research: ad hominem attacks have no role in scholarship. (Not to mention the fact that these accusations are each factually incorrect—neither of us is an economist, nor does welfare economics share the same intellectual history of statistics, nor do welfare economics and statistics have a corresponding political bias, nor could anyone accurately describe us as "anti-regulatory advocates," nor do we (hopefully) have an immature craving to escape uncertainty.

The merits of an empirical investigation stand apart from the author. Scholarly exchange is not about individuals—who are not "advocates" looking to confirm their favored theories, and are, rather, researchers seeking knowledge of the world—but about the research.

Our article started from the empirical turn that scholarship and the law have taken over the course of the past twenty years. Far from shying away from questioning that turn, our policy implications flowed from what we highlighted as the difficulties of empirical evaluation. Without having engaged in that inquiry, it would be impossible to ascertain the limits of empirical evaluation.

THE VIBRANT ROLE OF EMPIRICAL LEGAL STUDIES

In the end, we agree with Baker on the central contribution of our article: that our study moves forward the empirical literature on the media. Moreover, we appreciate the opportunity Baker has provided to address basic concerns over the role of theory—normative and positive—and empirics in law. Our conclusion is much more limited than Baker's sweeping indictment of welfare economics and empirical legal studies as "malignant" tendencies and as "only handmaidens" within the legal academy.

While we recognize the limits of empirical inquiry, we see a fruitful role for empirical investigation (and positive theory) as complementary to, and synergistic with, value-based inquiry in law. If policy decisions are to be made solely on normative theoretical grounds, as Baker desires, we may give up opportunities to forge consensus on contentious issues based on growing evidence.

Empirical evidence can inform value-laden decisions, particularly in administrative law and regulation where the factual issues become complex. Evidence that airbags save lives surely is useful for safety standards administered by the National Highway Traffic Safety Administration. Evidence that tailpipe emissions contribute to global warming surely is useful for the setting of motor vehicle standards by the Environmental Protection Agency.

And, similarly, evidence of whether viewpoints converge with media consolidation surely is relevant for the regulations administered by the FCC, as recognized by the FCC, appellate courts, and a large number of scholars.

In the end, our most basic disagreement is with the notion that empirical evidence is "entirely irrelevant." Value judgments are crucial to legal decisionmaking, but that does not mean we should operate in affirmative isolation of evidence. Baker charges that the empiricist is "a person on hands and knees looking for her keys under the street light despite her belief that she lost them on a dark stretch further down the street."

That may characterize some empirical research. But, to extend the analogy, the aim of our work was to capitalize on statistical methods to build new light poles to conduct new inquiries for where the keys may, in fact, lie. That is the crucial role of statistical methodology in a discipline where experiments simply cannot be run to obtain policy-relevant knowledge.

Legal scholars cannot, and should not, shut their eyes to evidence that can be brought to bear on policy questions of interest. Tools that have been first crafted outside of law, such as the methods we adapt from psychometrics and political science, can powerfully help to address policy questions and resolve disagreement that otherwise would be left to pure theory.

The deep irony in Baker's view—one that espouses pure normative, value-based theory that cannot be falsified—is that, in the end, it amounts to little more than "trust me." For all the rhetoric about democratic values (and diversity), Baker prefers a mode of legal scholarship for philosopher kings to the exclusion of all empirical (and positive) inquiry.

The burgeoning field of empirical legal studies plays in many ways the opposite role: by providing transparent, widely-accepted rules of inference. Science and empirical inquiry democratize the accumulation of knowledge.

One need not be a philosopher king to contribute to knowledge about the legal world, and anyone can be proven wrong by data. The democratization of knowledge about the law, the accumulation of wisdom about how it operates on the ground, and no one's exclusive claim to being right are what we view as progress.

Gauntlett goes on to criticize studies that focus on children by stating that they do not utilize adults as a control group, and that the studies are conducted primarily to further a "barely-concealed conservative ideology." He counters the premise of these studies with the concept that not all depictions of violence are even bad to witness. M.I.T. Professor Henry Jenkins, for instance, suggested in his speech to congress that The Basketball Diaries utilizes violence in a form of social commentary that provides clear social benefit.

David Gauntlett explains further that objects defined as "violent" or "anti-social" may not be judged as such in the minds of the viewer and tend to be viewed in artificial circumstances. These objects are furthermore based on previous studies with flawed methodology, and are not grounded in theory. Additionally, he claims that the effects model makes no attempt to understand the meanings of media.

- Historical criticisms situate the 'meta-narrative' of effects theory within a long history of distrust of new forms of media, dating as far back as Socrates's objections to the deleterious effects due to the written alphabet.
- Political criticisms pose an alternative conception of humans as rational, critical subjects who are alert to genre norms and adept at interpreting and critiquing media representations, instead of passively absorbing them.

Supporters of effects theory contend that commercials, advertising and voter campaigns prove that media influence behaviour. In the 20th century, aggressive media attention and negative coverage of trials involving celebrities like Roscoe Fatty Arbuckle or Michael Jackson have influenced the general public's opinion, before the trials effectively started. However, these critics do point out that while the media could have an effect on people's behaviour this isn't necessarily always the case.

Critics of the media effects theory point out that many copycat murders, suicides and other violent acts nearly always happen in abnormal upbringings. Violent, emotionally neglectful or aggressive environments influence behaviour more than watching certain programmes, films or listening to certain music. Most people who carry out these acts are also mentally unstable to begin with.

Critics also point out that just because an audience sees acts of violence in media, this does not mean they will actually commit them. Of the millions of people who watch violent films, only a small number have carried out acts of violence as a direct result. People regularly exposed to violent media usually grow up to be completely normal people. If there are any effects from media, they only affect a very small number of people. ❐

Chapter - 8

Media and Public Relations in Advertising

Advertising is a form of communication intended to persuade an audience to take some action. It usually includes the name of a product or service and how that product or service could benefit the consumer, to persuade potential customers to purchase or to consume that particular brand. Modern advertising developed with the rise of mass production in the late 19th and early 20th centuries.

Commercial advertisers often seek to generate increased consumption of their products or services through branding, which involves the repetition of an image or product name in an effort to associate related qualities with the brand in the minds of consumers. Different types of media can be used to deliver these messages, including traditional media such as newspapers, magazines, television, radio, outdoor or direct mail; or new media such as websites and text messages.

Advertising may be placed by an advertising agency on behalf of a company or other organization. Non-commerical advertisers that spend money to advertise items other than a consumer product or service include political parties, interest groups, religious organiz-ations and governmental agencies. Nonprofit organizations may rely on free modes of persuasion, such as a public service announcement.In 2007, spending on advertising was estimated at more than $150 billion in the United States and $385 billion worldwide.

HISTORY

Egyptians used papyrus to make sales messages and wall posters. Commercial messages and political campaign displays have been found in the ruins of Pompeii and ancient Arabia. Lost and found advertising on papyrus was common in Ancient Greece and Ancient Rome.

Wall or rock painting for commercial advertising is another manifestation of an ancient advertising form, which is present to this day in many parts of Asia, Africa, and South America. The tradition of wall painting can be traced back to Indian rock art paintings that date back to 4000 BC. History tells us that Out-of-home advertising and billboards are the oldest forms of advertising.

As the towns and cities of the Middle Ages began to grow, and the general populace was unable to read, signs that today would say cobbler, miller, tailor or blacksmith would use an image associated with their trade such as a boot, a suit, a hat, a clock, a diamond, a horse shoe, a candle or even a bag of flour. Fruits and vegetables were sold in the city square from the backs of carts and wagons and their proprietors used street callers (town criers) to announce their whereabouts for the convenience of the customers.

As education became an apparent need and reading, as well as printing, developed advertising expanded to include handbills. In the 17th century advertisements started to appear in weekly newspapers in England. These early print advertisements were used mainly to promote books and newspapers, which became increasingly affordable with advances in the printing press; and medicines, which were increasingly sought after as disease ravaged Europe.

However, false advertising and so-called "quack" advertisements became a problem, which ushered in the regulation of advertising content. As the economy expanded during the 19th century, advertising grew alongside. In the United States, the success of this advertising format eventually led to the growth of mail-order advertising.

In June 1836, French newspaper La Presse was the first to include paid advertising in its pages, allowing it to lower its price, extend its readership and increase its profitability and the formula was soon copied by all titles. Around 1840, Volney Palmer established a predecessor to advertising agencies in Boston. Around the same time, in France, Charles-Louis Havas extended the services of his news agency, Havas to include advertisement brokerage, making it the first French group to organize. At first, agencies were brokers for advertisement space in newspapers. N. W. Ayer & Son was the first full-service agency to assume responsibility for advertising content. N.W. Ayer opened in 1869, and was located in Philadelphia.

At the turn of the century, there were few career choices for women in business; however, advertising was one of the few. Since, women were responsible for most of the purchasing done in their household, advertisers and agencies recognized the value of women's insight during the creative process. In fact, the first American advertising to use a sexual sell was created by a woman – for a soap product. Although tame by today's standards, the advertisement featured a couple with the message "The skin you love to touch".

In the early 1920s, the first radio stations were established by radio equipment manufacturers and retailers who offered programmes in order to sell more radios to consumers. As time passed, many non-profit organizations followed suit in setting up their own radio stations, and included: schools, clubs and civic groups. When the practice of sponsoring programmes was popularised, each individual radio programme was usually sponsored by a single business in exchange for a brief mention of the business' name at the beginning and end of the sponsored shows. However, radio station owners soon realised they could earn more money by selling sponsorship rights in small time allocations to multiple businesses throughout their radio station's broadcasts, rather than selling the sponsorship rights to single businesses per show.

This practice was carried over to television in the late 1940s and early 1950s. A fierce battle was fought between those seeking to commercialise the radio and people who argued that the radio spectrum should be considered a part of the commons – to be used only non-commercially and for the public good. The United Kingdom pursued a public funding model for the BBC, originally a private company, the British Broadcasting Company, but incorporated as a public body by Royal Charter in 1927. In Canada, advocates like Graham Spry were likewise able to persuade the federal government to adopt a public funding model, creating the Canadian Broadcasting Corporation. However, in the United States, the capitalist model prevailed with the passage of the Communications Act of 1934 which created the Federal Communications Commission. To placate the socialists, the U.S., Congress did require commercial broadcasters to operate in the "public interest, convenience, and necessity". Public broadcasting now exists in the United States due to the 1967 Public Broadcasting Act which led to the Public Broadcasting Service and National Public Radio.

In the early 1950s, the DuMont Television Network began the modern practice of selling advertisement time to multiple sponsors. Previously, DuMont had trouble finding sponsors for many of their programmes and compensated by selling smaller blocks of advertising time to several businesses. This eventually became the standard for the commercial television industry in the United States. However, it was still a common practice to have single sponsor shows, such as The United States Steel Hour. In some instances the sponsors exercised great control over the content of the show— up to and including having one's advertising agency actually writing the show. The single sponsor model is much less prevalent now, a notable exception being the Hallmark Hall of Fame.

The 1960s saw advertising transform into a modern approach in which creativity was allowed to shine, producing unexpected messages that made advertisements more tempting to consumers' eyes. The Volkswagen ad campaign—featuring such headlines as "Think Small" and "Lemon" (which were used to describe the appearance of the car)—ushered in the era of modern advertising by promoting a "position" or "unique selling proposition" designed to associate each brand with a specific idea in the reader or viewer's mind. This period of American advertising is called the Creative Revolution and its archetype was William Bernbach who helped create the revolutionary Volkswagen ads among others. Some of the most creative and long-standing American advertising dates to this period. The late 1980s and early 1990s saw the introduction of cable television and particularly MTV. Pioneering the concept of the music video, MTV ushered in a new type of advertising: the consumer tunes in for the advertising message, rather than it being a by- product or afterthought. As cable and satellite television became increasingly prevalent, specialty channels emerged, including channels entirely devoted to advertising, such as QVC, Home Shopping Network, and ShopTV Canada.

Marketing through the Internet opened new frontiers for advertisers and contributed to the "dot-com" boom of the 1990s. Entire corporations operated solely on advertising revenue, offering everything from coupons to free Internet access. At the turn of the 21st century, a number of websites including the search engine Google, started a change in online advertising by emphasizing contextually relevant, unobtrusive ads intended to help, rather than inundate, users. This has led to a plethora of similar efforts and an increasing trend of interactive advertising.

The share of advertising spending relative to GDP has changed little across large changes in media. For example, in the US in 1925, the main advertising media were newspapers, magazines, signs on streetcars, and outdoor posters. Advertising spending as a share of GDP was about 2.9 per cent. By 1998, television and radio had become major advertising media. Nonetheless, advertising spending as a share of GDP was slightly lower—about 2.4 per cent.

A recent advertising innovation is "guerrilla marketing", which involve unusual approaches such as staged encounters in public places, giveaways of products such as cars that are covered with brand messages, and interactive advertising where the viewer can respond to become part of the advertising message.

Guerrilla advertising is becoming increasing more popular with a lot of companies. This type of advertising is unpredictable and innovative, which causes consumers to buy the product or ideà. This reflects an increasing trend of interactive and "embedded" ads, such as via product placement, having consumers vote through text messages, and various innovations utilizing social network services such as MySpace.

Public Service Advertising

The same advertising techniques used to promote commercial goods and services can be used to inform, educate and motivate the public about non-commercial issues, such as HIV/AIDS, political ideology, energy conservation and deforestation.

Advertising, in its non-commercial guise, is a powerful educational tool capable of reaching and motivating large audiences. "Advertising justifies its existence when used in the public interest—it is much too powerful à tool to use solely for commercial purposes." Attributed to Howard Gossage by David Ogilvy.

Public service advertising, non-commercial advertising, public interest advertising, cause marketing, and social marketing are different terms for (or aspects of) the use of sophisticated advertising and marketing communications techniques (generally associated with commercial enterprise) on behalf of non-commercial, public interest issues and initiatives.

In the United States, the granting of television and radio licenses by the FCC is contingent upon the station broadcasting a certain amount of public service advertising. To meet these requirements, many broadcast stations in America air the bulk of their required public service announcements during the late night or early morning when the smallest percentage of viewers are watching, leaving more day and prime time commercial slots available for high-paying advertisers. Public service advertising reached its height during World Wars I and II under the direction of several governments.

TYPES OF ADVERTISING

Virtually any medium can be used for advertising. Commercial advertising media can include wall paintings, billboards, street furniture components, printed flyers and rack cards, radio, cinema and television adverts, web banners, mobile telephone screens, shopping carts, web popups, skywriting, bus stop benches, human billboards, magazines, newspapers, town criers, sides of buses, banners attached to or sides of airplanes ("logojets"), in-flight advertisements on seatback tray tables or overhead storage bins, taxicab doors, roof mounts and passenger screens, musical stage shows, subway platforms and trains, elastic bands on disposable diapers, doors of bathroom stalls, stickers on apples in supermarkets, shopping cart handles (grabertising), the opening section of streaming audio and video, posters, and the backs of event tickets and supermarket receipts. Any place an "identified" sponsor pays to deliver their message through a medium is advertising.

Television

The TV commercial is generally considered the most effective mass-market advertising format, as is reflected by the high prices TV networks charge for commercial airtime during popular TV events. The annual Super Bowl football game in the United States is known as the most prominent advertising event on television.

The average cost of a single thirty-second TV spot during this game has reached US$3 million . The majority of television commercials feature a song or jingle that listeners soon relate to the product.

Virtual advertisements may be inserted into regular television programming through computer graphics. It is typically inserted into otherwise blank backdrops or used to replace local billboards that are not relevant to the remote broadcast audience.

More controversially, virtual billboards may be inserted into the background where none exist in real-life. Virtual product placement is also possible.

Infomercials

An infomercial is a long-format television commercial, typically five minutes or longer. The word "infomercial" is a portmanteau of the words "information" and "commercial". The main objective in an infomercial is to create an impulse purchase, so that the consumer sees the presentation and then immediately buys the product through the advertised toll-free telephone number or web site.

Infomercials describe, display, and often demonstrate products and their features, and commonly have testimonials from consumers and industry professionals.

Radio Advertising

Radio advertising is a form of advertising via the medium of radio. Radio advertisements are broadcasted as radio waves to the air from a transmitter to an antenna and a thus to a receiving device.

Airtime is purchased from a station or network in exchange for airing the commercials. While radio has the obvious limitation of being restricted to sound, proponents of radio advertising often cite this as an advantage.

Press Advertising

Press advertising describes advertising in a printed medium such as a newspaper, magazine, or trade journal. This encompasses everything from media with a very broad readership base, such as a major national newspaper or magazine, to more narrowly targeted media such as local newspapers and trade journals on very specialized topics.

A form of press advertising is classified advertising, which allows private individuals or companies to purchase a small, narrowly targeted ad for a low fee advertising a product or service.

Online Advertising

Online advertising is a form of promotion that uses the Internet and World Wide Web for the expressed purpose of delivering marketing messages to attract customers.

Examples of online advertising include contextual ads that appear on search engine results pages, banner ads, in text ads, Rich Media Ads, Social network advertising, online classified advertising, advertising networks and e-mail marketing, including e-mail spam.

Billboard Advertising

Billboards are large structures located in public places which display advertisements to passing pedestrians and motorists. Most often, they are located on main roads with a large amount of passing motor and pedestrian traffic; however, they can be placed in any location with large amounts of viewers, such as on mass transit vehicles and in stations, in shopping malls or office buildings, and in stadiums.

MOBILE BILLBOARD ADVERTISING

Mobile billboards are generally vehicle mounted billboards or digital screens. These can be on dedicated vehicles built solely for carrying advertisements along routes preselected by clients, they can also be specially- equipped cargo trucks or, in some cases, large banners strewn from planes.

The billboards are often lighted; some being backlit, and others employing spotlights. Some billboard displays are static, while others change; for example, continuously or periodically rotating among a set of advertisements.

Mobile displays are used for various situations in metropolitan areas throughout the world, including:

- Target advertising
- One-day, and long-term campaigns
- Conventions

- Sporting events
- Store openings and similar promotional events
- Big advertisements from smaller companies
- Others

In-store Advertising

In-store advertising is any advertisement placed in a retail store. It includes placement of a product in visible locations in a store, such as at eye level, at the ends of aisles and near checkout counters, eye-catching displays promoting a specific product, and advertisements in such places as shopping carts and in-store video displays.

Covert Advertising

Covert advertising, also known as guerrilla advertising, is when a product or brand is embedded in entertainment and media. For example, in a film, the main character can use an item or other of a definite brand, as in the movie Minority Report, where Tom Cruise's character John Anderton owns a phone with the Nokia logo clearly written in the top corner, or his watch engraved with the Bulgari logo.

Another example of advertising in film is in I, Robot, where main character played by Will Smith mentions his Converse shoes several times, calling them "classics," because the film is set far in the future. I, Robot and Spaceballs also showcase futuristic cars with the Audi and Mercedes-Benz logos clearly displayed on the front of the vehicles.

Cadillac chose to advertise in the movie The Matrix Reloaded, which as a result contained many scenes in which Cadillac cars were used. Similarly, product placement for Omega Watches, Ford, VAIO, BMW and Aston Martin cars are featured in recent James Bond films, most notably Casino Royale. In "Fantastic Four: Rise of the Silver Surfer", the main transport vehicle shows a large Dodge logo on the front. Blade Runner includes some of the most obvious product placement; the whole film stops to show a Coca-Cola billboard.

Celebrities

This type of advertising focuses upon using celebrity power, fame, money, popularity to gain recognition for their products and promote specific stores or products. Advertisers often advertise their products, for example, when celebrities share their favourite products or wear clothes by specific brands or designers. Celebrities are often involved in advertising campaigns such as television or print adverts to advertise specific or general products.

The use of celebrities to endorse a brand can have its downsides, however. One mistake by a celebrity can be detrimental to the public relations of a brand. For example, following his performance of eight gold medals at the 2008 Olympic Games in Beijing, China, swimmer Michael Phelps' contract with Kellogg's was terminated, as Kellogg's did not want to associate with him after he was photographed smoking marijuana.

MEDIA AND ADVERTISING APPROACHES

Increasingly, other media are overtaking many of the "traditional" media such as television, radio and newspaper because of a shift towards consumer's usage of the Internet for news and music as well as devices like digital video recorders (DVRs) such as TiVo.

Advertising on the World Wide Web is a recent phenomenon. Prices of Web-based advertising space are dependent on the "relevance" of the surrounding web content and the traffic that the web site receives.

Digital signage is poised to become a major mass media because of its ability to reach larger audiences for less money. Digital signage also offer the unique ability to see the target audience where they are reached by the medium.

Technology advances has also made it possible to control the message on digital signage with much precision, enabling the messages to be relevant to the target audience at any given time and location which in turn, gets more response from the advertising. Digital signage is being successfully employed in supermarkets. Another successful use of digital signage is in hospitality locations such as restaurants. and malls.

E-mail advertising is another recent phenomenon. Unsolicited bulk E- mail advertising is known as "e-mail spam". Spam has been a problem for e- mail users for many years. Some companies have proposed placing messages or corporate logos on the side of booster rockets and the International Space Station.

Controversy exists on the effectiveness of subliminal advertising, and the pervasiveness of mass messages. Unpaid advertising (also called "publicity advertising"), can provide good exposure at minimal cost. Personal recommendations ("bring a friend", "sell it"), spreading buzz, or achieving the feat of equating a brand with a common noun (in the United States, "Xerox" = "photocopier", "Kleenex" = tissue, "Vaseline" = petroleum jelly, "Hoover" = vacuum cleaner, "Nintendo" (often used by those exposed to many video games) = video games, and "Band-Aid" = adhesive bandage)— these can be seen as the pinnacle of any advertising campaign.

However, some companies oppose the use of their brand name to label an object. Equating a brand with a common noun also risks turning that brand into a genericized trademark - turning it into a generic term which means that its legal protection as a trademark is lost.

As the mobile phone became a new mass media in 1998 when the first paid downloadable content appeared on mobile phones in Finland, it was only a matter of time until mobile advertising followed, also first launched in Finland in 2000. By 2007 the value of mobile advertising had reached $2.2 billion and providers such as Admob delivered billions of mobile ads.

More advanced mobile ads include banner ads, coupons, Multimedia Messaging Service picture and video messages, advergames and various engagement marketing campaigns. A particular feature driving mobile ads is the 2D Barcode, which replaces the need to do any typing of web addresses, and uses the camera feature of modern phones to gain immediate access to web content. 83 per cent of Japanese mobile phone users already are active users of 2D barcodes.

A new form of advertising that is growing rapidly is social network advertising. It is online advertising with a focus on social networking sites.

This is a relatively immature market, but it has shown a lot of promise as advertisers are able to take advantage of the demographic information the user has provided to the social networking site.

Friendertising is a more precise advertising term in which people are able to direct advertisements towards others directly using social network service. From time to time, The CW Television Network airs short programming breaks called "Content Wraps," to advertise one company's product during an entire commercial break. The CW pioneered "content wraps" and some products featured were Herbal Essences, Crest, Guitar Hero II, CoverGirl, and recently Toyota.

Recently, there appeared a new promotion concept, "ARvertising", advertising on Augmented Reality technology.

CRITICISM OF ADVERTISING

While advertising can be seen as necessary for economic growth, it is not without social costs. Unsolicited Commercial E-mail and other forms of spam have become so prevalent as to have become a major nuisance to users of these services, as well as being a financial burden on internet service providers. Advertising is increasingly invading public spaces, such as schools, which some critics argue is a form of child exploitation. In addition, advertising frequently uses psychological pressure (for example, appealing to feelings of inadequacy) on the intended consumer, which may be harmful.

Hyper-commercialism and the Commercial Tidal Wave

Criticism of advertising is closely linked with criticism of media and often interchangeable. They can refer to its audio-visual aspects (e. g. cluttering of public spaces and airwaves), environmental aspects (e. g. pollution, oversize packaging, increasing consumption), political aspects (e. g. media dependency, free speech, censorship), financial aspects (costs), ethical/moral/social aspects (e. g. sub-conscious influencing, invasion of privacy, increasing consumption and waste, target groups, certain products, honesty) and, of course, a mix thereof. Some aspects can be subdivided further and some can cover more than one category.

As advertising has become increasingly prevalent in modern Western societies, it is also increasingly being criticized. A person can hardly move in the public sphere or use a medium without being subject to advertising. Advertising occupies public space and more and more invades the private sphere of people, many of which consider it a nuisance. "It is becoming harder to escape from advertising and the media. ... Public space is increasingly turning into a gigantic billboard for products of all kind. The aesthetical and political consequences cannot yet be foreseen." Hanno Rauterberg in the

German newspaper 'Die Zeit' calls advertising a new kind of dictatorship that cannot be escaped.

Ad creep: "There are ads in schools, airport lounges, doctors offices, movie theaters, hospitals, gas stations, elevators, convenience stores, on the Internet, on fruit, on ATMs, on garbage cans and countless other places. There are ads on beach sand and restroom walls." "One of the ironies of advertising in our times is that as commercialism increases, it makes it that much more difficult for any particular advertiser to succeed, hence, pushing the advertiser to even greater efforts." Within a decade advertising in radios climbed to nearly 18 or 19 minutes per hour; on prime-time television the standard until 1982 was no more than 9.5 minutes of advertising per hour, today it's between 14 and 17 minutes. With the introduction of the shorter

15-second-spot the total amount of ads increased even more dramatically. Ads are not only placed in breaks but e. g. also into baseball telecasts during the game itself. They flood the internet, a market growing in leaps and bounds.

Other growing markets are "product placements" in entertainment programming and in movies where it has become standard practice and "virtual advertising" where products get placed retroactively into rerun shows. Product billboards are virtually inserted into Major League Baseball broadcasts and in the same manner, virtual street banners or logos are projected on an entry canopy or sidewalks, for example during the arrival of celebrities at the 2001 Grammy Awards. Advertising precedes the showing of films at cinemas including lavish 'film shorts' produced by companies such as Microsoft or DaimlerChrysler. "The largest advertising agencies have begun working aggressively to co-produce programming in conjunction with the largest media firms" creating Infomercials resembling entertainment programming.

Opponents equate the growing amount of advertising with a "tidal wave" and restrictions with "damming" the flood. Kalle Lasn, one of the most outspoken critics of advertising on the international stage, considers advertising "the most prevalent and toxic of the mental pollutants. From the moment your radio alarm sounds in the morning to the wee hours of late- night TV microjolts of commercial pollution flood into your brain at the rate of around 3,000 marketing messages per day. Every day an estimated twelve billion display ads, 3 million radio commercials and more than 200,000 television commercials are dumped into North America's collective unconscious". In the course of his life the average American watches three years of advertising on television.

More recent developments are video games incorporating products into their content, special commercial patient channels in hospitals and public figures sporting temporary tattoos. A method unrecognisable as advertising is so-called "guerrilla marketing" which is spreading 'buzz' about a new product in target audiences. Cash-strapped U.S., cities do not shrink back from offering police cars for advertising. A trend, especially in Germany, is companies buying the names of sports stadiums. The Hamburg soccer Volkspark stadium first became the AOL Arena and then the HSH Nordbank Arena. The Stuttgart Neckarstadion became the Mercedes-Benz Arena, the Dortmund Westfalenstadion now is the Signal Iduna Park. The former SkyDome in Toronto was renamed Rogers Centre. Other recent developments are, for example, that whole subway stations in Berlin are redesigned into product halls and exclusively leased to a company. Düsseldorf even has 'multi- sensorial' adventure transit stops equipped with loudspeakers and systems that spread the smell of a detergent. Swatch used beamers to project messages on the Berlin TV-tower and Victory column, which was fined because it was done without a permit. The illegality was part of the scheme and added promotion.

It's standard business management knowledge that advertising is a pillar, if not "the" pillar of the growth-orientated free capitalist economy. "Advertising is part of the bone marrow of corporate capitalism." "Contemporary capitalism could not function and global production networks could not exist as they do without advertising."

For communication scientist and media economist Manfred Knoche at the University of Salzburg, Austria, advertising isn't just simply a 'necessary evil' but a 'necessary elixir of life' for the media business, the economy and capitalism as a whole. Advertising and mass media economic interests create ideology. Knoche describes advertising for products and brands as 'the producer's weapons in the competition for customers' and trade advertising, e. g. by the automotive industry, as a means to collectively represent their interests against other groups, such as the train companies.

In his view editorial articles and programmes in the media, promoting consumption in general, provide a 'cost free' service to producers and sponsoring for a 'much used means of payment' in advertising. Christopher Lasch argues that advertising leads to an overall increase in consumption in society; "Advertising serves not so much to advertise products as to promote consumption as a way of life."

Advertising and Constitutional Rights

Advertising is equated with constitutionally guaranteed freedom of opinion and speech. Therefore criticizing advertising or any attempt to restrict or ban advertising is almost always considered to be an attack on fundamental rights (First Amendment in the US) and meets the combined and concentrated resistance of the business and especially the advertising community.

"Currently or in the near future, any number of cases are and will be working their way through the court system that would seek to prohibit any government regulation of... commercial speech (e.g. advertising or food labelling) on the grounds that such regulation would violate citizens' and corporations' First Amendment rights to free speech or free press." An example for this debate is advertising for tobacco or alcohol but also advertising by mail or fliers (clogged mail boxes), advertising on the phone, in the internet and advertising for children. Various legal restrictions concerning spamming, advertising on mobile phones, addressing children, tobacco, alcohol have been introduced by the US, the EU and various other countries. Not only the business community resists restrictions of advertising.

Advertising as a means of free expression has firmly established itself in western society. McChesney argues, that the government deserves constant vigilance when it comes to such regulations, but that it is certainly not "the only antidemocratic force in our society....corporations and the wealthy enjoy a power every bit as immense as that enjoyed by the lords and royalty of feudal times" and "markets are not value-free or neutral; they not only tend to work to the advantage of those with the most money, but they also by their very nature emphasize profit over all else....

Hence, today the debate is over whether advertising or food labelling, or campaign contributions are speech...if the rights to be protected by the First Amendment can only be effectively employed by a fraction of the citizenry, and their exercise of these rights gives them undue political power and undermines the ability of the balance of the citizenry to exercise the same rights and/or constitutional rights, then it is not necessarily legitimately protected by the First Amendment."

In addition, "those with the capacity to engage in free press are in a position to determine who can speak to the great mass of citizens and who cannot". Critics in turn argue, that advertising invades privacy which is a constitutional right. For, on the one hand, advertising physically invades privacy, on the other, it increasingly uses relevant, information-based communication with private data assembled without the knowledge or consent of consumers or target groups.

For Georg Franck at Vienna University of Technology advertising is part of what he calls "mental capitalism", taking up a term (mental) which has been used by groups concerned with the mental environment, such as Adbusters. Franck blends the "Economy of Attention" with Christopher Lasch's culture of narcissm into the mental capitalism: In his essay "Advertising at the Edge of the Apocalypse", Sut Jhally writes: "20. century advertising is the most powerful and sustained system of propaganda in human history and its cumulative cultural effects, unless quickly checked, will be responsible for destroying the world as we know it.

The price of Attention and Hidden Costs

Advertising has developed into a billion-dollar business on which advertising. In Germany, for example, the advertising industry contributes 1.5% of the gross national income; the figures for other developed countries are similar. Thus, advertising and growth are directly and causally linked. As far as a growth based economy can be blamed for the harmful human lifestyle (affluent society) advertising has to be considered in this aspect concerning its negative impact, because its main purpose is to raise consumption. "The industry is accused of being one of the engines powering a convoluted economic mass production system which promotes consumption."

Attention and attentiveness have become a new commodity for which a market developed. "The amount of attention that is absorbed by the media and redistributed in the competition for quotas and reach is not identical with the amount of attention, that is available in society. The total amount circulating in society is made up of the attention exchanged among the people themselves and the attention given to media information.

Only the latter is homogenised by quantitative measuring and only the latter takes on the character of an anonymous currency." According to Franck, any surface of presentation that can guarantee a certain degree of attentiveness works as magnet for attention, e. g. media which are actually meant for information and entertainment, culture and the arts, public space etc.

It is this attraction which is sold to the advertising business. The German Advertising Association stated that in 2007 30.78 billion Euros were spent on advertising in Germany, 26% in newspapers, 21% on television, 15% by mail and 15% in magazines. In 2002 there were 360.000 people employed in the advertising business. The internet revenues for advertising doubled to almost 1 billion Euros from 2006 to 2007, giving it the highest growth rates.

Spiegel-Online reported that in the US in 2008 for the first time more money was spent for advertising on internet (105.3 billion US dollars) than on television (98.5 billion US dollars). The largest amount in 2008 was still spent in the print media (147 billion US dollars). For that same year, Welt-Online reported that the US pharmaceutical industry spent almost double the amount on advertising (57.7 billion dollars) than it did on research (31.5 billion dollars). But Marc-André Gagnon und Joel Lexchin of York University, Toronto, estimate that the actual expenses for advertising are higher yet, because not all entries are recorded by the research institutions. Not included are indirect advertising campaigns such as sales, rebates and price reductions. Few consumers are aware of the fact that they are the ones paying for every cent spent for public relations, advertisements, rebates, packaging etc., since, they ordinarily get included in the price calculation.

Influencing and Conditioning

The most important element of advertising is not information but suggestion more or less making use of associations, emotions (appeal to emotion) and drives dormant in the sub-conscience of people, such as sex drive, herd instinct, of desires, such as happiness, health, fitness, appearance, self-esteem, reputation, belonging, social status, identity, adventure, distraction, reward, of fears (appeal to fear), such as illness, weaknesses, loneliness, need, uncertainty, security or of prejudices, learned opinions and comforts. "All human needs, relationships, and fears – the deepest recesses of the human psyche – become mere means for the expansion of the commodity universe under the force of modern marketing. With the rise to prominence of modern marketing, commercialism – the translation of human relations into commodity relations – although a phenomenon intrinsic to capitalism, has expanded exponentially." 'Cause-related marketing' in which advertisers link their product to some worthy social cause has boomed over the past decade. Advertising exploits the model role of celebrities or popular figures and makes deliberate use of humour as well as of associations with colour, tunes, certain names and terms. Altogether, these are factors of how one perceives himself and one's self-worth.

In his description of 'mental capitalism' Franck says, "the promise of consumption making someone irresistible is the ideal way of objects and symbols into a person's subjective experience. Evidently, in a society in which revenue of attention moves to the fore, consumption is drawn by one's self- esteem. As a result, consumption becomes 'work' on a person's attraction.

From the subjective point of view, this 'work' opens fields of unexpected dimensions for advertising. Advertising takes on the role of a life councillor in matters of attraction. The cult around one's own attraction is what Christopher Lasch described as 'Culture of Narcissism'."

For advertising critics another serious problem is that "the long standing notion of separation between advertising and editorial/creative sides of media is rapidly crumbling" and advertising is increasingly hard to tell apart from news, information or entertainment. The boundaries between advertising and programming are becoming blurred. According to the media firms all this commercial involvement has no influence over actual media content, but, as McChesney puts it, "this claim fails to pass even the most basic giggle test, it is so preposterous."

Advertising draws "heavily on psychological theories about how to create subjects, enabling advertising and marketing to take on a 'more clearly psychological tinge'. Increasingly, the emphasis in advertising has switched from providing 'factual' information to the symbolic connotations of commodities, since, the crucial cultural premise of advertising is that the material object being sold is never in itself enough.

Even those commodities providing for the most mundane necessities of daily life must be imbued with symbolic qualities and culturally endowed meanings via the 'magic system of advertising. In this way and by altering the context in which advertisements appear, things 'can be made to mean "just about anything"' and the 'same' things can be endowed with different intended meanings for different individuals and groups of people, thereby offering mass produced visions of individualism."

Before advertising is done, market research institutions need to know and describe the target group to exactly plan and implement the advertising campaign and to achieve the best possible results. A whole array of sciences directly deal with advertising and marketing or is used to improve its effects.

Focus groups, psychologists and cultural anthropologists are '"de rigueur"' in marketing research". Vast amounts of data on persons and their shopping habits are collected, accumulated, aggregated and analysed with the aid of credit cards, bonus cards, raffles and internet surveying. With increasing accuracy this supplies a picture of behaviour, wishes and weaknesses of certain sections of a population with which advertisement can be employed more selectively and effectively.

The efficiency of advertising is improved through advertising research. Universities, of course supported by business and in co-operation with other disciplines, mainly Psychiatry, Anthropology, Neurology and behavioural sciences, are constantly in search for ever more refined, sophisticated, subtle and crafty methods to make advertising more effective.

"Neuromarketing is a controversial new field of marketing which uses medical technologies such as functional Magnetic Resonance Imaging (fMRI)— not to heal, but to sell products. Advertising and marketing firms have long used the insights and research methods of psychology in order to sell products, of course.

But today these practices are reaching epidemic levels, and with a complicity on the part of the psychological profession that exceeds that of the past. The result is an enormous advertising and marketing onslaught that comprises, arguably, the largest single psychological project ever undertaken. Yet, this great undertaking remains largely ignored by the American Psychological Association." Robert McChesney calls it "the greatest concerted attempt at psychological manipulation in all of human history."

Dependency of the Media and Corporate Censorship

Almost all mass media are advertising media and many of them are exclusively advertising media and, with the exception of public service broadcasting are privately owned. Their income is predominantly generated through advertising; in the case of newspapers and magazines from 50 to 80%. Public service broadcasting in some countries can also heavily depend on advertising as a source of income (up to 40%). In the view of critics no media that spreads advertisements can be independent and the higher the proportion of advertising, the higher the dependency. This dependency has "distinct implications for the nature of media content.... In the business press, the media are often referred to in exactly the way they present themselves in their candid moments: as a branch of the advertising industry."

In addition, the private media are increasingly subject to mergers and concentration with property situations often becoming entangled and opaque. This development, which Henry A. Giroux calls an "ongoing threat to democratic culture", by itself should suffice to sound all alarms in a democracy. Five or six advertising agencies dominate this 400 billion U.S., dollar global industry.

"Journalists have long faced pressure to shape stories to suit advertisers and owners .... the vast majority of TV station executives found their news departments 'cooperative' in shaping the news to assist in 'non-traditional revenue development." Negative and undesired reporting can be prevented or influenced when advertisers threaten to cancel orders or simply when there is a danger of such a cancellation. Media dependency and such a threat becomes very real when there is only one dominant or very few large advertisers. The influence of advertisers is not only in regard to news or information on their own products or services but expands to articles or shows not directly linked to them. In order to secure their advertising revenues the media has to create the best possible 'advertising environment'. Another problem considered censorship by critics is the refusal of media to accept advertisements that are not in their interest. A striking example of this is the refusal of TV stations to broadcast ads by Adbusters. Groups try to place advertisements and are refused by networks.

It is principally the viewing rates which decide upon the programme in the private radio and television business. "Their business is to absorb as much attention as possible. The viewing rate measures the attention the media trades for the information offered. The service of this attraction is sold to the advertising business" and the viewing rates determine the price that can be demanded for advertising.

"Advertising companies determining the contents of shows has been part of daily life in the USA since, 1933. Procter and Gamble (P&G) .... offered a radio station a history-making trade (today know as "bartering"): the company would produce an own show for "free" and save the radio station the high expenses for producing contents. Therefore the company would want its commercials spread and, of course, its products placed in the show. Thus, the series 'Ma Perkins' was created, which P&G skilfully used to promote Oxydol, the leading detergent brand in those years and the Soap opera was born ..."

While critics basically worry about the subtle influence of the economy on the media, there are also examples of blunt exertion of influence. The US company Chrysler, before it merged with Daimler Benz had its agency, PentaCom, send out a letter to numerous magazines, demanding them to send, an overview of all the topics before the next issue is published to "avoid potential conflict". Chrysler most of all wanted to know, if there would be articles with "sexual, political or social" content or which could be seen as "provocative or offensive". PentaCom executive David Martin said: "Our reasoning is, that anyone looking at a 22.000 $ product would want it surrounded by positive things.

There is nothing positive about an article on child pornography." In another example, the USA Network held top-level, off-the-record meetings with advertisers in 2000 to let them tell the network what type of programming content they wanted in order for USA to get their advertising." Television shows are created to accommodate the needs for advertising, e.g. splitting them up in suitable sections. Their dramaturgy is typically designed to end in suspense or leave an unanswered question in order to keep the viewer attached.

The movie system, at one time outside the direct influence of the broader marketing system, is now fully integrated into it through the strategies of licensing, tie-ins and product placements.

The prime function of many Hollywood films today is to aid in the selling of the immense collection of commodities. The press called the 2002 Bond film 'Die Another Day' featuring 24 major promotional partners an 'adventure' and noted that James Bond "now has been 'licensed to sell'" As it has become standard practise to place products in motion pictures, it "has self-evident implications for what types of films will attract product placements and what types of films will therefore be more likely to get made".

Advertising and information are increasingly hard to distinguish from each other. "The borders between advertising and media .... become more and more blurred.... What August Fischer, chairman of the board of Axel Springer publishing company considers to be a 'proven partnership between the media and advertising business' critics regard as nothing but the infiltration of journalistic duties and freedoms".

According to RTL-executive Helmut Thoma "private stations shall not and cannot serve any mission but only the goal of the company which is the 'acceptance by the advertising business and the viewer'.

The setting of priorities in this order actually says everything about the 'design of the programmes' by private television." Patrick Le Lay, former managing director of TF1, a private French television channel with a market share of 25 to 35%, said: "There are many ways to talk about television. But from the business point of view, let's be realistic: basically, the job of TF1 is, e.g. to help Coca Cola sell its product. (...) For an advertising message to be perceived the brain of the viewer must be at our disposal.

The job of our programmes is to make it available, that is to say, to distract it, to relax it and get it ready between two messages. It is disposable human brain time that we sell to Coca Cola." Because of these dependencies a widespread and fundamental public debate about advertising and its influence on information and freedom of speech is difficult to obtain, at least through the usual media channels; otherwise these would saw off the branch they are sitting on.

"The notion that the commercial basis of media, journalism, and communication could have troubling implications for democracy is excluded from the range of legitimate debate" just as "capitalism is off-limits as a topic of legitimate debate in US political culture".

An early critic of the structural basis of US journalism was Upton Sinclair with his novel The Brass Check in which he stresses the influence of owners, advertisers, public relations, and economic interests on the media. In his book "Our Master's Voice – Advertising" the social ecologist James Rorty wrote: "The gargoyle's mouth is a loudspeaker, powered by the vested interest of a two-billion dollar industry, and back of that the vested interests of business as a whole, of industry, of finance.

It is never silent, it drowns out all other voices, and it suffers no rebuke, for it is not the voice of America? That is its claim and to some extent it is a just claim..."

It has taught us how to live, what to be afraid of, what to be proud of, how to be beautiful, how to be loved, how to be envied, how to be successful.. Is it any wonder that the American population tends increasingly to speak, think, feel in terms of this jabberwocky? That the stimuli of art, science, religion are progressively expelled to the periphery of American life to become marginal values, cultivated by marginal people on marginal time?"

THE COMMERCIALISATION OF CULTURE AND SPORTS

Performances, exhibitions, shows, concerts, conventions and most other events can hardly take place without sponsoring. The increasing lack arts and culture they buy the service of attraction. Artists are graded and paid according to their art's value for commercial purposes. Corporations promote renown artists, therefore getting exclusive rights in global advertising campaigns. Broadway shows, like 'La Bohème' featured commercial props in its set.

Advertising itself is extensively considered to be a contribution to culture. Advertising is integrated into fashion. On many pieces of clothing the company logo is the only design or is an important part of it. There is only little room left outside the consumption economy, in which culture and art can develop independently and where alternative values can be expressed. A last important sphere, the universities, is under strong pressure to open up for business and its interests.

Competitive sports have become unthinkable without sponsoring and there is a mutual dependency. High income with advertising is only possible with a comparable number of spectators or viewers. On the other hand, the poor performance of a team or a sportsman results in less advertising revenues. Jürgen Hüther and Hans-Jörg Stiehler talk about a 'Sports/Media Complex which is a complicated mix of media, agencies, managers, sports promoters, advertising etc., with partially common and partially diverging interests but in any case with common commercial interests. The media presumably is at centre stage because it can supply the other parties involved with a rare commodity, namely (potential) public attention. In sports "the media are able to generate enormous sales in both circulation and advertising."

"Sports sponsorship is acknowledged by the tobacco industry to be valuable advertising. A Tobacco Industry journal in 1994 described the Formula One car as 'The most powerful advertising space in the world'. .... In a cohort study carried out in 22 secondary schools in England in 1994 and 1995 boys whose favourite television sport was motor racing had a 12.8% risk of becoming regular smokers compared to 7.0% of boys who did not follow motor racing."

Not the sale of tickets but transmission rights, sponsoring and merchandising in the meantime make up the largest part of sports association's and sports club's revenues with the IOC (International Olympic Committee) taking the lead. The influence of the media brought many changes in sports including the admittance of new 'trend sports' into the Olympic Games, the alteration of competition distances, changes of rules, animation of spectators, changes of sports facilities, the cult of sports heroes who quickly establish themselves in the advertising and entertaining business because of their media value and last but not least, the naming and renaming of sport stadiums after big companies.

"In sports adjustment into the logic of the media can contribute to the erosion of values such as equal chances or fairness, to excessive demands on athletes through public pressure and multiple exploitation or to deceit (doping, manipulation of results ...). It is in the very interest of the media and sports to counter this danger because media sports can only work as long as sport exists.

Occupation and Commercialisation of Public Space

Every visually perceptible place has potential for advertising. Especially urban areas with their structures but also landscapes in sight of through urban areas with their structures but also landscapes in sight of through fares are more and more turning into media for advertisements. Signs, posters, billboards, flags have become decisive factors in the urban appearance and their numbers are still on the increase. "Outdoor advertising has become unavoidable.

Traditional billboards and transit shelters have cleared the way for more pervasive methods such as wrapped vehicles, sides of buildings, electronic signs, kiosks, taxis, posters, sides of buses, and more. Digital technologies are used on buildings to sport 'urban wall displays'. In urban areas commercial content is placed in our sight and into our consciousness every moment we are in public space. The German Newspaper 'Zeit' called it a new kind of

'dictatorship that one cannot escape'. Over time, this domination of the surroundings has become the "natural" state. Through long-term commercial saturation, it has become implicitly understood by the public that advertising has the right to own, occupy and control every inch of available space. The steady normalization of invasive advertising dulls the public's perception of their surroundings, re-enforcing a general attitude of powerlessness towards creativity and change, thus a cycle develops enabling advertisers to slowly and consistently increase the saturation of advertising with little or no public outcry."

The massive optical orientation towards advertising changes the function of public spaces which are utilised by brands. Urban landmarks are turned into trademarks. The highest pressure is exerted on renown and highly frequented public spaces which are also important for the identity of a city (e.g. Piccadilly Circus, Times Square, Alexanderplatz). Urban spaces are public commodities and in this capacity they are subject to "aesthetical environment protection", mainly through building regulations, heritage protection and landscape protection. "It is in this capacity that these spaces are now being privatised. They are peppered with billboards and signs, they are remodelled into media for advertising."

Socio-cultural Aspects: Sexism, Discrimination and Stereotyping

"Advertising has an "agenda setting function" which is the ability, with huge sums of money, to put consumption as the only item on the agenda. In the battle for a share of the public conscience this amounts to non-treatment (ignorance) of whatever is not commercial and whatever is not advertised for. Advertising should be reflection of society norms and give clear picture of target market. Spheres without commerce and advertising serving the muses and relaxation remain without respect. With increasing force advertising makes itself comfortable in the private sphere so that the voice of commerce becomes the dominant way of expression in society." Advertising critics see advertising as the leading light in our culture. Sut Jhally and James

Twitchell go beyond considering advertising as kind of religion and that advertising even replaces religion as a key institution.

"Corporate advertising (or commercial media) is the largest single psychological project ever undertaken by the human race. Yet for all of that, its impact on us remains unknown and largely ignored.

When I think of the media's influence over years, over decades, I think of those brainwashing experiments conducted by Dr. Ewen Cameron in a Montreal psychiatric hospital in the 1950s. The idea of the CIA-sponsored "depatterning" experiments was to outfit conscious, unconscious or semiconscious subjects with headphones, and flood their brains with thousands of repetitive "driving" messages that would alter their behaviour over time....Advertising aims to do the same thing."

Advertising is especially aimed at young people and children and it increasingly reduces young people to consumers. For Sut Jhally it is not "surprising that something this central and with so much being expended on it should become an important presence in social life. Indeed, commercial interests intent on maximizing the consumption of the immense collection of commodities have colonized more and more of the spaces of our culture.

For instance, almost the entire media system (television and print) has been developed as a delivery system for marketers its prime function is to produce audiences for sale to advertisers. Both the advertisements it carries, as well as the editorial matter that acts as a support for it, celebrate the consumer society.

The movie system, at one time outside the direct influence of the broader marketing system, is now fully integrated into it through the strategies of licensing, tie-ins and product placements. The prime function of many Hollywood films today is to aid in the selling of the immense collection of commodities. As public funds are drained from the non-commercial cultural sector, art galleries, museums and symphonies bid for corporate sponsorship."

In the same way effected is the education system and advertising is increasingly penetrating schools and universities. Cities, such as New York, accept sponsors for public playgrounds.

"Even the pope has been commercialized ... The pope's 4-day visit to Mexico in ...1999 was sponsored by Frito-Lay and PepsiCo. The industry is accused of being one of the engines powering a convoluted economic mass production system which promotes consumption.

As far as social effects are concerned it does not matter whether advertising fuels consumption but which values, patterns of behaviour and assignments of meaning it propagates.

Advertising is accused of hijacking the language and means of pop culture, of protest movements and even of subversive criticism and does not shy away from scandalizing and breaking taboos (e.g. Benneton).

This in turn incites counter action, what Kalle Lasn in 2001 called "Jamming the Jam of the Jammers". Anything goes. "It is a central social-scientific question what people can be made to do by suitable design of conditions and of great practical importance.

For example, from a great number of experimental psychological experiments it can be assumed, that people can be made to do anything they are capable of, when the according social condition can be created."

Advertising often uses stereotype gender specific roles of men and women reinforcing existing clichés and it has been criticized as "inadvertently or even intentionally promoting sexism, racism, and ageism... At very least, advertising often reinforces stereotypes by drawing on recognizable "types" in order to tell stories in a single image or 30 second time frame."

Activities are depicted as typical male or female (stereotyping). In addition people are reduced to their sexuality or equated with commodities and gender specific qualities are exaggerated. Sexualized female bodies, but increasingly also males, serve as eye-catchers.

In advertising it is usually a woman being depicted as:

- Servants of men and children that react to the demands and complaints of their loved ones with a bad conscience and the promise for immediate improvement (wash, food)
- A sexual or emotional play toy for the self-affirmation of men
- A technically totally clueless being (almost always male) that can only manage a childproof operation
- Female expert, but stereotype from the fields of fashion, cosmetics, food or at the most, medicine
- As ultra thin, slim, and very skinny.
- Doing ground-work for others, e.g. , serving coffee while a journalist interviews a politician

A large portion of advertising deals with promotion of products that pertain to the "ideal body image." This is mainly targeted towards women, and, in the past, this type of advertising was aimed nearly exclusively at women.

Women in advertisements are generally portrayed as good-looking women who are in good health. This, however, is not the case of the average woman. Consequently, they give a negative message of body image to the average woman.

Because of the media, girls and women who are overweight, and otherwise "normal" feel almost obligated to take care of themselves and stay fit. They feel under high pressure to maintain an acceptable bodyweight and take care of their health.

Consequences of this are low self-esteem,eating disorders, self mutilations, and beauty operations for those women that just cannot bring themselves eat right or get the motivation to go to the gym.

The EU parliament passed a resolution in 2008 that advertising may not be discriminating and degrading. This shows that politicians are increasingly concerned about the negative impacts of advertising. However, the benefits of promoting overall health and fitness are often overlooked. Men are also negatively portrayed as incompetent and the butt of every joke in advertising.

CHILDREN AND ADOLESCENTS AS TARGET GROUPS

The children's market, where resistance to advertising is weakest, is the "pioneer for ad creep". "Kids are among the most sophisticated observers of ads. They can sing the jingles and identify the logos, and they often have strong feelings about products.

What they generally don't understand, however, are the issues that underlie how advertising works. Mass media are used not only to sell goods but also ideas: how we should behave, what rules are important, who we should respect and what we should value." Youth is increasingly reduced to the role of a consumer.

Not only the makers of toys, sweets, ice cream, breakfast food and sport articles prefer to aim their promotion at children and adolescents. For example, an ad for a breakfast cereal on a channel aimed at adults will have music that is a soft ballad, whereas on a channel aimed at children, the same ad will use a catchy rock jingle of the same song to aim at kids.

Advertising for other products preferably uses media with which they can also reach the next generation of consumers. "Key advertising messages exploit the emerging independence of young people". Cigarettes, for example, "are used as a fashion accessory and appeal to young women.

Other influences on young people include the linking of sporting heroes and smoking through sports sponsorship, the use of cigarettes by popular characters in television programmes and cigarette promotions. Research suggests that young people are aware of the most heavily advertised cigarette brands."

"Product placements show up everywhere, and children aren't exempt. Far from it. The animated film, Foodfight, had 'thousands of products and character icons from the familiar (items) in a grocery store.' Children's books also feature branded items and characters, and millions of them have snack foods as lead characters." Business is interested in children and adolescents because of their buying power and because of their influence on the shopping habits of their parents.

As they are easier to influence they are especially targeted by the advertising business. "The marketing industry is facing increased pressure over claimed links between exposure to food advertising and a range of social problems, especially growing obesity levels."

In 2001, children's programming accounted for over 20% of all US television watching. The global market for children's licensed products was some 132 billion US dollars in 2002.

Advertisers target children because, e.g., in Canada, they "represent three distinct markets:

1. Primary Purchasers ($2.9 billion annually)
2. Future Consumers (Brand-loyal adults)
3. Purchase Influencers ($20 billion annually)

Kids will carry forward brand expectations, whether positive, negative, or indifferent. Kids are already accustomed to being catered to as consumers.

The long term prize: Loyalty of the kid translates into a brand loyal adult customer" The average Canadian child sees 350,000 TV commercials before graduating from high school, spends nearly as much time watching TV as attending classes. In 1980 the Canadian province of Québec banned advertising for children under age 13.

"In upholding the consititutional validity of the Quebec Consumer Protection Act restrictions on advertising to children under age 13 (in the case of a challenge by a toy company) the Court held: '...advertising directed at young children is per se manipulative.Such advertising aims to promote products by convincing those who will always believe.'"

Norway (ads directed at children under age 12), and Sweden (television ads aimed at children under age 12) also have legislated broad bans on advertising to children, during child programmes any kind of advertising is forbidden in Sweden, Denmark, Austria and Flemish Belgium. In Greece there is no advertising for kids products from 7 to 22 h. An attempt to restrict advertising directed at children in the US failed with reference to the First Amendment. In Spain bans are also considered undemocratic.

Opposition and Campaigns Against Advertising

According to critics, the total commercialization of all fields of society, the privatization of public space, the acceleration of consumption and waste of resources including the negative influence on lifestyles and on the environment has not been noticed to the necessary extent. The "hyper-commercialization of the culture is recognized and roundly detested by the citizenry, although the topic scarcely receives a whiff of attention in the media or political culture".

"The greatest damage done by advertising is precisely that it incessantly demonstrates the prostitution of men and women who lend their intellects, their voices, their artistic skills to purposes in which they themselves do not believe, and .... that it helps to shatter and ultimately destroy our most precious non-material possessions: the confidence in the existence of meaningful purposes of human activity and respect for the integrity of man."

"The struggle against advertising is therefore essential if we are to overcome the pervasive alienation from all genuine human needs that currently plays such a corrosive role in our society. But in resisting this type of hyper-commercialism we should not be under any illusions.

Advertising may seem at times to be an almost trivial of omnipresent aspect of our economic system. Yet, as economist A. C. Pigou pointed out, it could only be 'removed altogether' if 'conditions of monopolistic competition' inherent to corporate capitalism were removed. To resist it is to resist the inner logic of capitalism itself, of which it is the pure expression."

"Visual pollution, much of it in the form of advertising, is an issue in all the world's large cities. But what is pollution to some is a vibrant part of a city's fabric to others. New York City without Times Square's huge digital billboards or Tokyo without the Ginza's commercial panorama is unthinkable. Piccadilly Circus would be just a London roundabout without its signage.

Still, other cities, like Moscow, have reached their limit and have begun to crack down on over-the-top outdoor advertising." "Many communities have chosen to regulate billboards to protect and enhance their scenic character.

The following is by no means a complete list of such communities, but it does give a good idea of the geographic diversity of cities, counties and states that prohibit new construction of billboards. Scenic America estimates the nationwide total of cities and communities prohibiting the construction of new billboards to be at least 1500.

A number of States in the US prohibit all billboards:

- *Vermont:* Removed all billboards in 1970s
- *Hawaii:* Removed all billboards in 1920s
- *Maine:* Removed all billboards in 1970s and early 80s
- *Alaska:* State referendum passed in 1998 prohibits billboards
- Almost two years ago the city of Sao Paulo, Brazil, ordered the downsizing or removal of all billboards and most other forms of commercial advertising in the city."

Technical appliances, such as Spam filters, TV-Zappers, Ad-Blockers for TVs and stickers on mail boxes: "No Advertising" and an increasing number of court cases indicate a growing interest of people to restrict or rid themselves of unwelcome advertising.

Consumer protection associations, environment protection groups, globalization opponents, consumption critics, sociologists, media critics, scientists and many others deal with the negative aspects of advertising. "Antipub" in France, "subvertising", culture jamming and adbusting have become established terms in the anti-advertising community.

On the international level globalization critics such as Naomi Klein and Noam Chomsky are also renown media and advertising critics. These groups criticize the complete occupation of public spaces, surfaces, the airwaves, the media, schools etc., and the constant exposure of almost all senses to advertising messages, the invasion of privacy, and that only few consumers are aware that they themselves are bearing the costs for this to the very last penny.

Some of these groups, such as the 'The Billboard Liberation Front Creative Group' in San Francisco or Adbusters in Vancouver, Canada, have manifestos. Grassroots organizations campaign against advertising or certain aspects of it in various forms and strategies and quite often have different roots.

Adbusters, for example contests and challenges the intended meanings of advertising by subverting them and creating unintended meanings instead. Other groups, like 'Illegal Signs Canada' try to stem the flood of billboards by detecting and reporting ones that have been put up without permit.

Examples for various groups and organizations in different countries are 'L'association Résistance à l'Agression Publicitaire' in France, where also media critic Jean Baudrillard is a renown author.

The 'Anti Advertising Agency' works with parody and humour to raise awareness about advertising. and 'Commercial Alert' campaigns for the protection of children, family values, community, environmental integrity and democracy. Media literacy organisations aim at training people, especially children in the workings of the media and advertising in their programmes.

In the US, for example, the 'Media Education Foundation' produces and distributes documentary films and other educational resources. 'MediaWatch', a Canadian non-profit women's organization works to educate consumers about how they can register their concerns with advertisers and regulators.

The Canadian 'Media Awareness Network' offers one of the world's most comprehensive collections of media education and Internet literacy resources. Its member organizations represent the public, non-profit but also private sectors. Although it stresses its independence it accepts financial support from Bell Canada, CTVGlobeMedia, CanWest, TELUS and S-VOX.

To counter the increasing criticism of advertising aiming at children media literacy organizations are also initiated and funded by corporations and the advertising business themselves. In the US 'The Advertising Educational Foundation' was created in 1983 supported by ad agencies, advertisers and media companies.

It is the "advertising industry's provider and distributor of educational content to enrich the understanding of advertising and its role in culture, society and the economy" sponsored for example by American Airlines, Anheuser-Busch, Campbell Soup, Coca-Cola, Colgate-Palmolive, Walt Disney, Ford, General Foods, General Mills, Gillette, Heinz, Johnson and Johnson, Kellogg, Kraft, Nestle, Philip Morris, Quaker Oats, Nabisco, Schering, Sterling, Unilever, Warner Lambert, advertising agencies like Saatchi and Saatchi Compton and media companies like American Broadcasting Companies, CBS, Capital Cities Communications, Cox Enterprises, Forbes, Hearst, Meredith, The New York Times, RCA/NBC, Reader's Digest, Time, Washington Post, just to mention a few.

Canadian businesses established 'Concerned Children's Advertisers' in 1990 "to instill confidence in all relevant publics by actively demonstrating our commitment, concern, responsibility and respect for children". Members are CanWest, Corus, CTV, General Mills, Hasbro, Hershey's, Kellogg's, Loblaw, Kraft, Mattel, McDonald's, Nestle, Pepsi, Walt Disney, Weston as well as almost 50 private broadcast partners and others.

Concerned Children's Advertisers was example for similar organizations in other countries like 'Media smart' in the United Kingdom with offspring in Germany, France, the Netherlands and Sweden. New Zealand has a similar business-funded programme called 'Willie Munchright'.

"While such interventions are claimed to be designed to encourage children to be critical of commercial messages in general, critics of the marketing industry suggest that the motivation is simply to be seen to address a problem created by the industry itself, that is, the negative social impacts to which marketing activity has contributed.

By contributing media literacy education resources, the marketing industry is positioning itself as being part of the solution to these problems, thereby seeking to avoid wide restrictions or outright bans on marketing communication, particularly for food products deemed to have little nutritional value directed at children.

The need to be seen to be taking positive action primarily to avert potential restrictions on advertising is openly acknowledged by some sectors of the industry itself.... Furthermore, Hobbs suggests that such programmes are also in the interest of media organizations that support the interventions to reduce criticism of the potential negative effects of the media themselves."

Taxation as Revenue and Control

Public interest groups suggest that "access to the mental space targeted by advertisers should be taxed, in that at the present moment that space is being freely taken advantage of by advertisers with no compensation paid to the members of the public who are thus being intruded upon.

This kind of tax would be a Pigovian tax in that it would act to reduce what is now increasingly seen as a public nuisance. Efforts to that end are gathering more momentum, with Arkansas and Maine considering bills to implement such a taxation.

Florida enacted such a tax in 1987 but was forced to repeal it after six months, as a result of a concerted effort by national commercial interests, which withdrew planned conventions, causing major losses to the tourism industry, and cancelled advertising, causing a loss of 12 million dollars to the broadcast industry alone".

In the US, for example, advertising is tax deductible and suggestions for possible limits to the advertising tax deduction are met with fierce opposition from the business sector, not to mention suggestions for a special taxation. In other countries, advertising at least is taxed in the same manner services are taxed and in some advertising is subject to special taxation although on a very low level.

In many cases the taxation refers especially to media with advertising (e.g., Austria, Italy, Greece, Netherlands, Turkey, Estonia).

❐

Index